Feather Crown:
The Eighteen Feasts of the Mexica Year

Gordon Brotherston

Publishers

The British Museum
Great Russell Street
London WC1B 3DG

Series Editor

Dr Josephine Turquet

Distributors

The British Museum Press
46 Bloomsbury Street
London WC1B 3QQ

British Museum Research Publication No. 154
Feather Crown
The Eighteen Feasts of the Mexica Year
Gordon Brotherston
ISBN-13 978-0-86159-154-2
ISBN-10 0-86159-154-2
ISSN 0142 4815
© The Trustees of the British Museum 2005
Front cover: Plate 1, Eagle at Tenochtitlan, Tovar Ms *Cuevas de los linajes*, p.4. © The John Carter Brown Library at Brown University

Note the British Museum Occasional Papers series is now entitled
British Museum Research Publications. The OP series ran from 1 to
150, and the RP series, keeping the same ISSN and ISBN preliminary
numbers, begins at number 151.

For a complete catalogue giving information on the full range
of available Occasional Papers and Research Publications see the
website: www.thebritishmuseum.ac.uk/researchpublications
or write to:
Oxbow Books, Park End Place
Oxford OX1 1HN, UK
Tel: (+44) (0) 1865 241249
Fax (+44) (0) 1865 794449
e mail oxbow@oxbowbooks.com
website www.oxbowbooks.com
or
The David Brown Book Co
PO Box 511, Oakville
CT 06779, USA
Tel: (+1) 860 945 9329; Toll free 1 800 791 9354
Fax: (+1) 860 945 9468
e mail david.brown.bk.co@snet.net

Printed and bound in England by 4-print

Contents

Abbreviations

ADV	Adeva: Akademische Druck- und Verlagsanstalt, Graz
BCE	Years 'before the Christian Era' here include the year zero, normally ignored by historians.
BFW	*Book of the Fourth World* (Brotherston 1992)
C1, C10, C11	Correlations 1, 10, 11: the qualifying numbers of Series III year-bearer Signs, as in the example 1516 = 1 Flint = 10 Flint = 11 Flint
F1.1 to F1.9, F2.1 to F2.9	notation used for the Feasts (**Table 1**)
FCE	Fondo de Cultura Económica, Mexico
Flo	Florentine Codex
GMT	the Goodman-Martínez-Thompson correlation of the Christian and Maya calendars
HMAI	*Handbook of Middle American Indians*, see Glass *et al.*
HM	*Histoyre du Mechique*
HMP	*Historia de los mexicanos por sus pinturas*
HTCh	*Historia tolteca-chichimeca*
INAH	Instituto Nacional de Antropología e Historia, Mexico
Key	*A Key to the Mesoamerican Reckoning of Time* (Brotherston 1982)
MNA	Museo Nacional de Antropología, Mexico
PBM	*Painted Books of Mexico* (Brotherston 1995)
Series I–V	Year-bearer Signs (**Table 3**)
Trecena	A sequence of 13 days or years
TTTM	Tepepulco-Tovar-Telleriano-Mexicanus correlation (**Table 1**)

Photographic acknowledgements

Thanks are due to the following for permission to reproduce images:

Boban Calendar Wheel, John Carter Brown Library, Providence. **Pl.8**. Miguel Angel Porrúa, Mexico

Borbonicus Codex (*El Libro del Ciuacoatl*), Codex du Corps Legislatif, Bibliothèque de l'Assemblée Nationale Française, Paris. Y120. **Pls.5, 6**. Fondo de Cultura Económica, Mexico

Kalendario Mexicano, Latino y Castellano, Biblioteca Nacional, Mexico, Ms 1628bis. **Fig.2.3**. Photograph by Bob Schaltwijk

Magliabecchi Codex. Biblioteca Centrale Nazionale, Florence. Ms Magl. XIII-3. **Pl.9**. University of California Press, Berkeley

Matrícula de tributos. Museo Nacional de Antropología, Mexico, 35–52. **Pl.2b**

Mexicanus Codex. Bibliothèque Nationale de France, Paris, Fonds Mexicains 23–24. **Pl.2a**. RJI Philatelics/Album Publishing Company

Primeros memoriales de Sahagún (Tepepulco Ms). Biblioteca del Palacio Real, Madrid. **Pls.3, 7**. Patrimonio Nacional de España; Oklahoma University Press

Tovar Calendar (*Cuevas de los linajes*). **Cover, Pls.1, 4**. The John Carter Brown Library at Brown University, Providence

Veytia Calendar Wheels 4, 5. Museo Nacional de México; Miguel Angel Porrúa, Mexico. **Figs.7.4, 7.5**

For Lúcia

Luis Reyes García
In memoriam

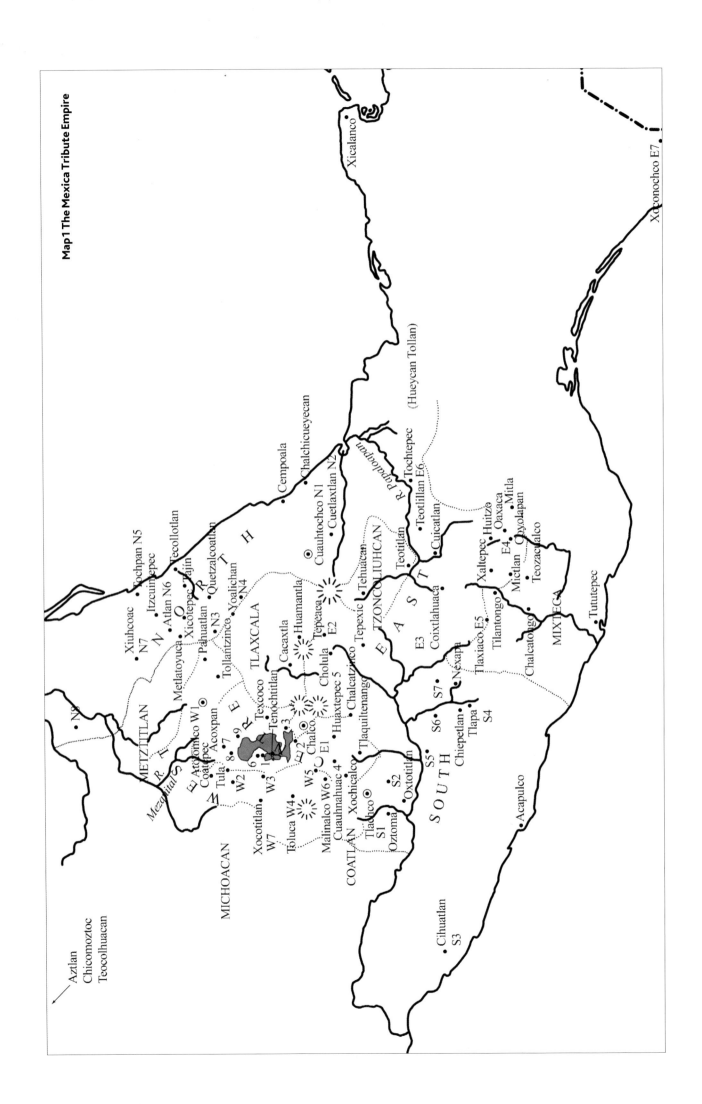

Map 1 The Mexica Tribute Empire

Aztlan
Chicomoztoc
Teocolhuacan

METZTITLAN

MICHOACAN

Xocotitlan W7
Toluca W4
Malinalco W6
Cuauhnahuac 4
Xochicalco
COATLAN
Tlachco S1
Oztoma
Oxtotitlan
S2

Xiuhcoac N7
Tochpan N5
Itzcuinepec
Tecollotlan
Atlan N6 Tajín
Xicotepec Quetzalcoatlan
Pahuatlan N3
Yoalichan
Tollantzinco N4
TLAXCALA
Cacaxtla
Cholula
Chalcatzinco
Huaxtepec 5
Tlaquiltenango

Metlatoyuca
Atotonilco W1
Coatepec
Tula Acoxpan
W2
W3
W5

Texcoco
Tenochtitlan
Chalco
E1
Huamantla
Tepeaca
E2

Cempoala
Chalchicueyecan

Cuauhtochco N1
Cuetlaxtlan N2

(Hueycan Tollan)
Papaloapan R.
Tochtepec E6
Teotitlan Teotlillan E6
Cuicatlan
TZONCOLIUHCAN
Tehuacan
Tepexic
E3
Coixtlahuaca

EAST

Xaltepec Huitzo
Oaxaca Mitla
Mictlan Oyolapan
Teozacualco

Néxapa
S6 S7
Tlaxiaco E5
Chiepetlan Tilantongo
Tlapa S4
Chalcatongo
MIXTECA
Tututepec

SOUTH
S5
Acapulco
Cihuatlan
S3

Xicalanco

Xoconochco E7

Map 2 The Central Highlands

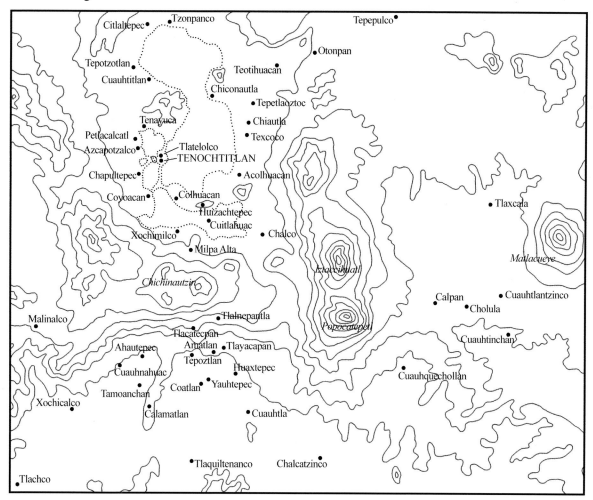

Table 1 The Eighteen Feasts

F1.1	Tozoztli A		F2.1	Pachtli A/Teotleco
F1.2	Tozoztli B		F2.2	Pachtli B/Tepeilhuitl
F1.3	Toxcatl		F2.3	Quecholli
F1.4	Etzalcualiztli		F2.4	Panquetzaliztli
F1.5	Tecuilhuitl A		F2.5	Atemoztli
F1.6	Tecuilhuitl B		F2.6	Tititl
F1.7	Miccailhuitl A/Tlaxochimaco		F2.7	Izcalli
F1.8	Miccailhuitl B/Xocotl huetzi		F2.8	Atlcahualo/Xilomaniztli/Cuautlehua
F1.9	Ochpaniztli		F2.9	Tlacaxipehualiztli/Coailhuitl

	TTTM Gregorian	TTTM Julian			TTTM Gregorian	TTTM Julian
F1.1.1	27/28 March	17/18 March		F2.1.1	23/24 Sept	13/14 Sept
F1.2.1	16/17 April	6/7 April		F2.2.1	13/14 Oct	3/4 Oct
F1.3.1	6/7 May	26/27 April		F2.3.1	2/3 Nov	23/24 Oct
F1.4.1	26/27 May	16/17 May		F2.4.1	22/23 Nov	12/13 Nov
F1.5.1	15/16 June	5/6 June		F2.5.1	12/13 Dec	2/3 Dec
F1.6.1	5/6 July	25/26 July		F2.6.1	1/2 Jan	22/23 Dec
F1.7.1	25/26 July	15/16 July		F2.7.1	21/22 Jan	11/12 Jan
F1.8.1	14/15 August	4/5 August				
F1.9.1	3/4 Sept	24/25 August		F2.8.1	[10/11 Feb	31 Jan/1 Feb
				F2.9.1	2/3 March	20/21 Feb]

TT, the Tovar Tepepulco correlation, is the later of the two dates given; TM, the Telleriano Mexicanus correlation, is the earlier date.

F1.1.1 = first day of Tozoztontli; F2.1.1 = first day of Teotleco/Pachtontli

F2.8.1 and F2.9.1 may fall 5 or 6 six days later because of intercalated Nemotemi

Table 2 The Tonalpoualli

The Twenty Signs

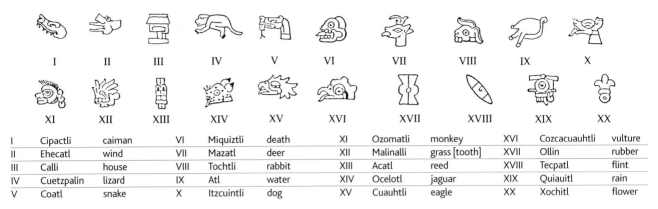

| | I | II | III | IV | V | VI | VII | VIII | IX | X |
| | XI | XII | XIII | XIV | XV | XVI | XVII | XVIII | XIX | XX |

I	Cipactli	caiman	VI	Miquiztli	death	XI	Ozomatli	monkey	XVI	Cozcacuauhtli	vulture
II	Ehecatl	wind	VII	Mazatl	deer	XII	Malinalli	grass [tooth]	XVII	Ollin	rubber
III	Calli	house	VIII	Tochtli	rabbit	XIII	Acatl	reed	XVIII	Tecpatl	flint
IV	Cuetzpalin	lizard	IX	Atl	water	XIV	Ocelotl	jaguar	XIX	Quiauitl	rain
V	Coatl	snake	X	Itzcuintli	dog	XV	Cuauhtli	eagle	XX	Xochitl	flower

The Nine Night Lords (Yoalitecutin)

1	Xiuhtecutli	lord of fire, turquoise, the year
2	Itztli	obsidian
3	Piltzintecutli	precious lord
4	Cinteotl	maize god
5	Mictlantecutli	lord of the underworld
6	Chalchiuhtlicue	jade skirt
7	Tlazoteotl	lust goddess
8	Tepeyolotl	hill heart
9	Tlaloc	falling water

The Thirteen Quecholli and the Thirteen Heroes

1	Huitzilin	hummingbird	Xiuhtecutli	cf Night Lord 1
2	Quetzalhuitzilin	grey hummingbird	Tlaltecutli	lord of earth
3	Huactli	hawk	Chalchiuhtlicue	cf. Night Lord 6
4	Zolin	quail	Tonatiuh	sun
5	Cuauhtli	eagle	Tonaleque/Ciuateteo	workers, 5 male and 5 female
6	Chicuatli	screech owl	Mictlantecutli	- cf Night Lord 5
7	Papalotl	butterfly	Tonacatecutli	lord of our flesh
8	Tlotli	falcon	Tlaloc	- cf Night Lord 9
9	Huexolotl	turkey	Quetzalcoatl	
10	Tecolotl	owl	Tezcatlipoca	
11	Alotl	macaw	Yoaltecutli	lord of the night
12	Quetzal	quetzal	Tlahuizcalpantecutli	lord of house of dawn
13	Toznene	parrot	Ometecutli	lord of duality

Plate 1 Eagle (with 5 tail feathers) at Tenochtitlan, seizing green Parrot (with 5 + 8 feathers), surveyed by Calpan Tochtli and Tenoch. Imperial shield map of the year fashioned in blue, red, yellow and white feathers (upper right). *Cuevas de los linajes…* (in Tovar Ms.) p.4. © The John Carter Brown Library at Brown University

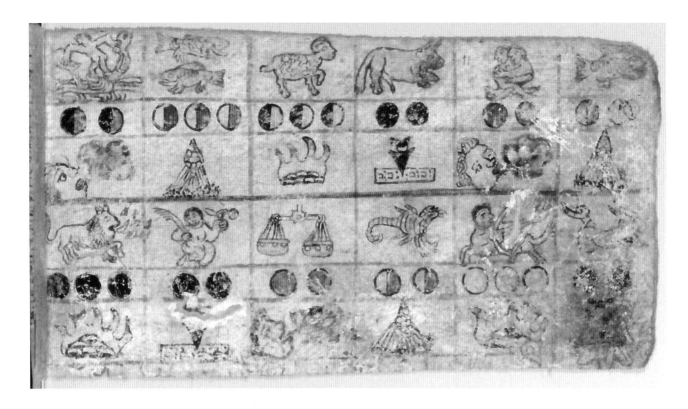

Plate 2a Zodiac: Aquarius/Atemoztli to Cancer/scaley Etzalcualiztli (above) and Leo to Capricorn (below) Mexicanus p.11. © Bibliothèque nationale de France

Plate 2b Oztoma, the caiman cave: Matricula f.1; Mendoza f.18

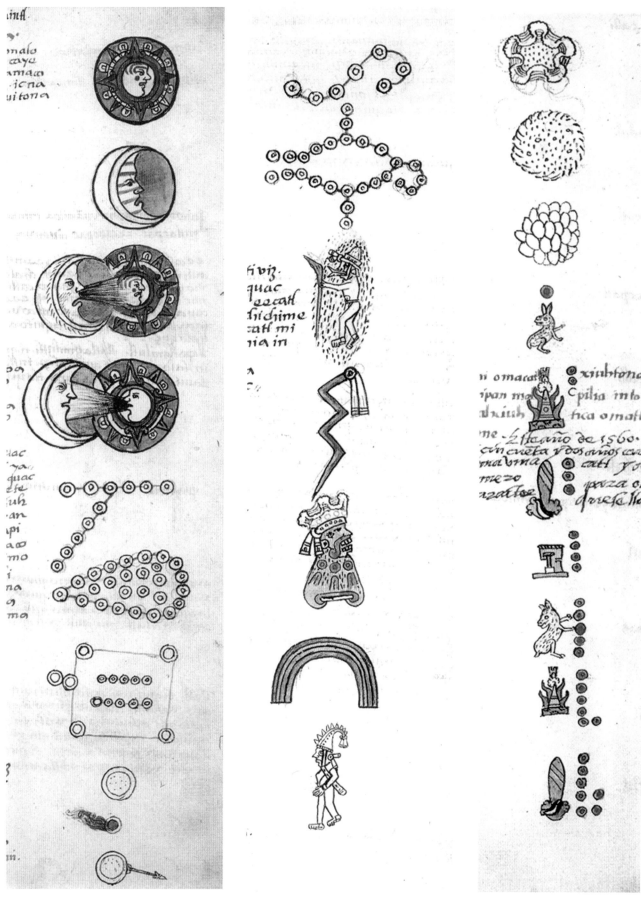

Plate 3a Sun, moon, solar and lunar eclipses; Mamalhuaztli, Miec, Tianquiz; inner planets, comet, meteor. Tepepulco f.282

Plate 3ba Xonecuilli, Colotl. Eecatl, lightning, Tlaloc, rainbow; Itztlacoliuhqui. Tepepulco f.282v

Plate 3c Ice, blizzard, hail. Xiuhmolpilli, beginning with 1 Rabbit and 2 Reed (with Tlacatecpan detail). Tepepulco f.283

Plate 4 Round Dance of the 18: huehuetl drummer plus 6 dancers (right and above); teponaztli drummer plus 10 dancers (left and below). *Cuevas de los linajes* (in Tovar Ms.) p.18. © The John Carter Brown Library at Brown University

Plate 5 Ochpaniztli, with Teteu innan on platform at centre, and Xonecuilli upper left. Borbonicus p.30

Plate 6 Tititl, with Ciuacoatl on platforms below and to left, and 11-step pyramid to right. Borbonicus p.36

Plate 7a Atlcahualo, and supplication for water; Tlacaxipehualiztli, with skinned victim, Mexica knights, and Xipe cap (bottom right); Tozoztli A, with Xochimanaloya fields. Tepepulco f.250

Plate 7b Micailhuitl B, and the tree of Xocotl huetzi; Ochpaniztli, with cotton-clad females and maguey- clad males, and Itztlacoliuhqui (bottom right). Tepepulco f251v

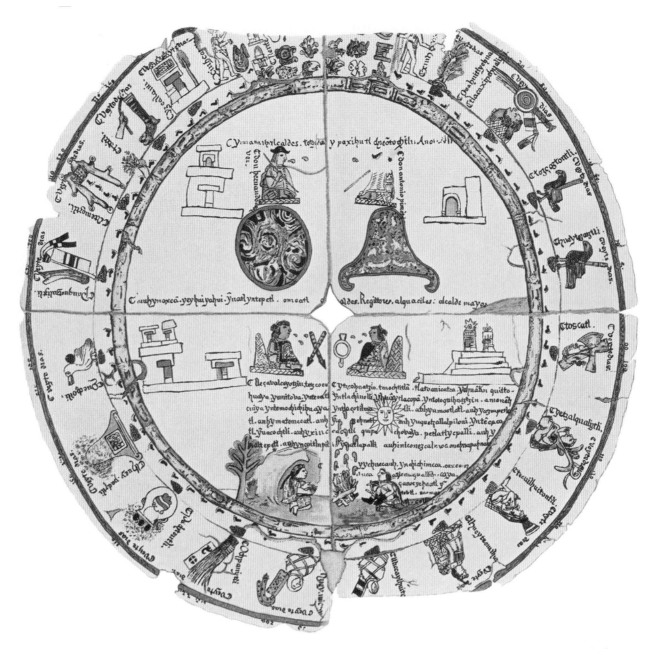

Plate 8 Texcoco history encircled clockwise by the Feasts from Atlcahualo to Izcalli, with Xiuhcoanahual and the Nemotemi to top. Boban Anniversary Wheel

Plate 9 Ciuacoatl, in Tititl, richly attired, with skeletal jaw, 11 (-22) teeth, and protruding tongue. She holds a weaving batten and a round shield, emblems of female and male prowess. Magliabechiano p.45

Feather Crown: the Eighteen Feasts of the Mexica Year

Preface

Many years have turned since the idea of this study germinated. A first statement appeared in an British Museum Occasional Paper (no.38), more than 20 years ago (*A Key to the Mesoamerican Reckoning of Time*). There, the attempt was made to establish the year as a calendar cycle in its own right, made up of 'Feasts' each of 20 days: *ilhuitl* in Nahuatl. Attention was paid to how these Feasts may articulate years of different kinds and measurements (solar, sidereal and civil), and to the different ways they were correlated, in western and eastern Mesoamerica, with the other great calendrical cycle, known in Nahuatl as the Tonalpoualli. In calendrical questions, *A Key...* came to support the wider ranging *Book of the Fourth World* (1992), and *Painted Books of Mexico* (1995), whose propositions are in turn taken as a basis in this study.

The focus here narrows to the Feasts of the Aztec or Mexica who from their capital in the west, Tenochtitlan, exacted tribute from much of Mesoamerica. Stricter in its political purview, this analysis attempts to indicate the mechanisms of the Mexica Feasts, the philosophical and imaginative wealth embedded in them, their origins and roots in worship, and their interface with the imported Christian calendar. It benefits from publications that have appeared meanwhile, notably Munro Edmonson's *Book of the Year* (1988), and Luis Reyes García's masterful commentary on the Codex Borbonicus or *Ciuacoatl* (1992). Conversations with both these scholars have been invaluable and it is painful to remember that neither is now alive to thank. Editions in facsimile have made a decisive difference, especially in cases like the Boban Wheel (1981), Magliabecchiano (1983), Mendoza (1992), the Tepepulco Manuscript (1993; Sahagún's *Primeros memoriales*), Codex Telleriano (1995) and Matrícula de tributos (1995), where previously no reliable reproduction was available. In the line of screenfold books on native paper that continue to celebrate the Feasts still today, Alfonso García Tellez completed the anniversary trio of San Pablito Pahuatlan (1975, 1978, 1981) at just the moment the earlier paper was being written. The understandings of the year fostered in the three Pahuatlan books have likewise been made manifest in the marvellous coloured-seed murals prepared each year for equinoctial celebrations at Tepoztlan (Morelos), whose authors I have learned much from, especially Arturo Demesa. In Mexico and particularly in the state of Morelos, I have also benefitted from the knowledge of those who live at or near sites where the

Feasts are commemorated in inscriptions and artifacts, among them, the Tepozteco temple and pyramid, Tlacatecpan/San Juan Tlacotenco with its small museum, Coatlan (Yauhtepec), Xochicalco, and Chalcatzingo. Similarly, I thank those who have helped me consult the originals of the ancient books or codices that represent the Feasts, saliently the Codex Mexicanus in the Bibliothèque Nationale (Paris), the Mendoza Codex in the Bodleian Library (Oxford), and unpublished annals in the Museo Nacional de Antropología (Mexico). I am obliged to the staff of these institutions for their courtesy.

As always, I owe much to conversations and exchanges with colleagues, particularly at conferences in London, Colchester, Vienna, Nashville, São Paulo, Mexico City and Stanford. For this and for help of other kinds I thank Johannes Neurat, Joanne Harwood, Juergen Stowasser, Elly Wake, Doris Madrigal, Eduardo Natalino, Miguel León-Portilla, Johanna Broda, Alfredo López Austin, and José Rabasa. David Kelley and Anthony Aveni offered incisive comments on the draft. Whatever virtue these pages may have will be due in part to them. I gratefully acknowledge editors of journals and volumes in which earlier versions of these chapters or parts of chapters have appeared or are about to appear: *Estudios de Cultura Nahuatl* (nos.28; 34), the electronic journal *Arara* (nos.2; 6), *Cultural Transgressions. Research Methods in Translation Studies II: Historical and Ideological Issues* (ed. T. Hermans, M. Baker & M. Olohan, Manchester: St Jerome, 2002), *Comparative Cultural Studies and Latin America* (ed. S.A. McCellen & E.E. Fitz, Purdue University Press, 2004), and *Postcoloniality at Large* (ed. M. Moraña, Pittsburg University Press, 2005). Every effort has been made to obtain permission to reproduce copyright materials and those who have kindly granted such permission are listed above.

The maps were drawn by Bayard Colyear, of Stanford University. The university also generously subsidised the publication of the colour plates through the Research Unit of the Division of Literatures, Cultures and Languages. When not otherwise stated, the Figures were drawn by Tony Young. Evelyn Castaneda and Josephine Turquet have been a constant and invaluable help.

Above all, I thank my wife Lúcia for her patience, unstinting support, and conversations that are much to the point.

Gordon Brotherston
Lisbon and San Francisco, April 2004–May 2005

... as they were dancing and singing, they turned into birds of every kind. They flew off and the air filled with feathers, all red and green and yellow and blue. It was beautiful. Now the Water Mother Huiio, the Great Snake, came leaping out of the water and shot into the air. 'I want my crown', she said, looking for birds and feathers for her crown.

Watunna

... that heart fell on to a stone and a nopal cactus grew from it, so grand and beautiful that an eagle dwells in it: it lives up there and feeds on the finest and most splendid birds that there are, stretching out its huge wings and feeling the sun's warmth in the freshness of the morning. Go there early in the day and you will see it amid myriad feathers, green, blue, red, yellow and white. To this place where you will find the nopal with the eagle on it I give the name Tenochtitlan

Origen de los mexicanos

1

The Mexica Embodiment of the Year

Ancient Mexico, like Mesoamerica more generally, is renowned for its extremely complex calendar and, less so, for the understanding and articulation of time it presupposes. Formally, two cycles are fundamental to this calendar: one corresponds to the period of human gestation, the other to the year (**Tables 1 & 2**). Each cycle has its own count of nights and days and is intricately meshed in the 52-year period known as the Round or 'year binding' (**Table 3**), Xiuhmolpilli in Nahuatl (the lingua franca of Mesoamerica when Europe arrived.). Both cycles are amply represented in books (or codices) and other texts that survive from before and after the European invasion, which are written in the native script known as *tlacuilolli* in Nahuatl. The gestation cycle or Tonalpoualli equals the nine moons of human pregnancy and true to its origin typically schedules activities and labour of human life over 260 nights and days (Furst 1986). In its very simplest expression, the Mesoamerican year comprises 18 lots of 20 days; it regulates the civil time of politics and economics and encompasses the rhythms wrought upon the earth by sun and stars. In Nahuatl, the 20-day period is known as *ilhuitl* (plural *ilhuilhuiuh*). This term can also mean special day and its root indicates the idea of becoming manifest (*ilhuia*), as in the count or 'book' (*ilhuihtlapoal amoxtli*) and the broad expanse of the sky (*ilhuica*). Among the Mexica this term found a particular echo with the word for feather (*ihuitl*), of the kind seen sprouting from the vertebrate body in ancient inscriptions of the Olmec (**Fig.1.1**); such feathers also characterized the turquoise or 'year' crown (*xiuhuitzolli*), the rainforest diadem favoured by the Mexica emperors. Here, the 20-day *ilhuitl* is rendered throughout in English as Feast (and occasionally Fast), in preference to the more familiar yet misleading terms 'week' or 'month'.

Confronting the inhabitants of New Spain and anxious to know their ways, missionary friars like Toribio de Benavente

(Motolinia), Bernardino de Sahagún and Diego Durán would ask: when does or did your year begin? Simple enough to Christian minds, this interrogative already sowed the seeds of misunderstanding, and raised questions which had in any case not necessarily been resolved in the imported calendar. The year known to the friars and Europeans in general may have begun liturgically at Easter, but it also had a civil start in January, an academic start at Michaelmas, a fiscal start in April, and so on, concepts which all had equivalents in Mesoamerica, in the years of tribute, hunting and planting, dance, New Fire, and so on. More seriously, the Mesoamericans measured their year by more than one means, with reference to both sun and stars, and to purely metric periods like 365 and 360 days. So which year was being asked about? By the 16th century, west Rome was suffering badly from its failure to measure not just the year of the sun but that of the night sky, which it dismissed from consideration altogether in the Gregorian Reform of the Julian Calendar (1582; introduced into Mexico the following year).

Again, in Mesoamerica, the endings of some types of year mattered more than beginnings, although in all cases years were counted in generally recognized Eras. The most recent Era, that of the Mexica was preceded by that of the Chichimec (In Yeliz Chichimeca), which began half a millennium earlier in the 7th century, and which in turn was encompassed in the larger framework of the Mesoamerican Era itself, that of its 'mother culture' the Olmec, which began in the year identified by the Mexica as 13 Reed, 3113 BCE. For their part, the Christians had inherited their Era from pagan Rome (Ab Urbe Condita) and then based it on the reign of their persecutor Diocletian, and only later opted for years Anno Domini. In the late 16th century, years 'BC' were still being invented, as was the Christian calendrical estimate of the age of the world.

Clear evidence of the antiquity and universality of the year of 18 Feasts throughout Mesoamerica can be found in the sheer structure of the cycle as such. Structural parallels are apparent above all in the pairing of certain Feasts, as the first and second instalments of a double period of 40 days. This pairing is a feature of the Maya hieroglyphic cycle, affecting a majority of the Feasts, and it is discernable already in western Olmec iconography at Oxtotitlan. In Nahuatl and other languages, these parts or halves of double Feasts are referred to as lesser (-*tontli*) or greater (*huey-*): for convenience, they are denoted here by the letters A and B. The Feasts known in Nahuatl as Tozoztli, Tecuilhuitl, Miccailhuitl and Pachtli are most commonly doubled in this way. An exemplary case is Miccailhuitl, the double feast of the dead (*mic-*), whose first and second instalments are otherwise known as Tlaxochimaco and Xocotl huetzi. In the first, a large wooden pole was fetched; in the second, it was set up and fell. In Matlatzinca and Tlaxcalan texts (Serna; Veytia), Atemoztli and Tititl are similarly paired to make up a double Feast. Among the Christians, this doubling

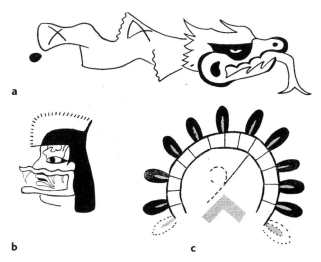

Figure 1.1 Olmec caiman and feather motifs: a) proto Xiuhcoanaual; b) headdress and caiman mask; c) feathers, with ring of possibly 18 segments. Oxtotitlan mural (after Grove 1970: 42, 58, 60)

was equated with the principle of the Octave or sequel (e.g. Durán, 1995, 2:263, with respect to F1.5 and F1.6.

Overall, the doubling principle remained strong enough to reveal that two of the 18 Feasts were preferentially not doubled, and indeed structurally never could be, since they occupy single positions between pairs that precede and come after them in the cycle. Unmistakable in the Otomi and other ancient calendars, these two single Feasts were known among the Mexica as Ochpaniztli and Tlacaxipehualiztli and they coordinated the whole tribute system, effectively marking the equinoctial ends of half years, a nine-Feast 'summer' and a nine-Feast 'winter' (Kubler and Gibson 1950, fig.14). This arrangement aligns with *tlacuilolli* specification of tribute deadlines and with widespread emphasis on Ochpaniztli as the Feast on which the year's two halves hinge. As such the pattern is inscribed in the 'Xiuhcoanaual' on the Sunstone, in the nine-plus-nine units that skirt the primordial Reed; and it survives in the same design in native-paper screenfolds produced today. The first of the three 'great penances' announced in the *Popol vuh* is of twice 'nine score' days (Tedlock 1996:192).

Endorsed by Graulich (1982) and others, this structure suggests a notation for the Feast cycle. Accordingly, the nine Feasts of the first half year, Tozoztli A to Ochpaniztli, are here denoted throughout as F1.1–F1.9, while the nine of the second half, Pachtli A to Tlacaxipehualiztli, are denoted as F2.1–F2.9. More precisely, the first day of the first half year, Tozoztli A 1st, is F1.1.1 while the last, Ochpaniztli 20th 180 days later, is F1.9.20 (**Table 1**). In the creation story told in *Legend of the Suns* (Bierhorst 1992:143), the first Feast to be mentioned as such is the first in this scheme, Tozoztli. In Nahuatl, the very verb from which its name derives, *tozoa*, indicates the first great penance in the *Popol vuh*, while in Telleriano (f.1) Tozoztli 1st is highlighted in the primary Tonalpoualli count within the year.

A main advantage of the notation proposed here is that, in depending on structure, it is not peculiar to the Mexica and holds over time for Mesoamerica as a whole, and is not bound to local notions of year 'beginnings' and intercalated days (the Nemotemi). For more than one Feast evidently served in practice as the 'first' in this sense, over time, and in successive political systems. At the same time, this structure as such points to unsuspected parallels, for example, that between the eponymous *pop* of the *Popol vuh* named by Landa as the start of the Maya year and the opening Feast (F1.5) in certain Mexica and related texts (Rios, *Cuevas*, Tepozteco Inscriptions, Borgia).

First sources

Of the Feast systems that are known, by far the best documented is that of the Mexica. For most purposes interchangeable with the term Aztec, the name Mexica denotes the Nahuatl-speaking people who according to their own records had arrived in the Highland Basin (or Valley of Mexico) by the 14th century, having set off from a homeland far to the northwest two centuries previously. In their capital Tenochtitlan (today Mexico City), they established a line of emperors, beginning with Acamapichtli, who officially acceded to power in the year 1 Flint (1376). At its height, their empire occupied much of modern Mexico, especially in the south (Guerrero today), the north (Veracruz today) and towards the Guatemalan frontier to the east. Tribute was exacted according to deadlines determined by the Feasts of the Mexica Year: this was a far-flung economic

system that had been preceded by several others in the millennial history of Mesoamerica (**Map 1**).

After the death of the ninth Mexica emperor Moctezuma II and the siege of the capital, Cuauhtemoc surrendered to the Tlaxcalans and Cortés in the year 3 House 1521. Nonetheless the line of royal power continued for many decades, as did the use of the Mexica calendar. The conquest of Mexico was in this sense gradual, being effected through a series of impositions, like the installing of the first viceroy Mendoza in 1535, the introduction of Spanish law courts and coinage, and the Gregorian Reform (1583) which made the Christian calendar a fitter instrument of empire. Almost entirely ignored or demeaned in the realm of official culture, education and knowledge, the intelligence that devised the Feast cycle millennia ago lives on today as a paradigm and critical tool, in books of native paper that continue to reflect on the fortune of the Mexica and Mexico.

Details of how the Mexica year functioned are given most authoritatively in texts written by the Mexica themselves, wholly or in part in the native script called *tlacuilolli*, on stone and other hard surfaces but most often on native paper, traditionally fabricated from amate bark or maguey leaves. As a Mesoamerican script as old as the calendar and shared by speakers of many languages, *tlacuilolli* needs some getting used to in itself, since it deploys as one the separate western concepts of picture (layout, format, design), arithmetic (embedded or in autonomous notation) and story-poem. A dozen or so *tlacuilolli* texts inscribed in stone and written on paper, which have survived from before and after Cortés, deal with the Mexica Feasts, in treatments that range from complex single-frame diagrams to full-length chapters in screenfold books. The most significant of these rely entirely on *tlacuilolli* as a script and a script principle, and this approach to the Mexica Feasts defers to a tight cluster of such sources.

Of these, two are fundamental statements inscribed in stone beyond question before any possible contact with the voyagers whose entry into the Caribbean is first reflected in Mexica annals in the year 1 Rabbit 1506. One is the celebrated Sunstone (Piedra de sol), 3.58m in diameter and today the high altar of Mexico City's Museo Nacional de Antropología. This disk is an 'Anniversary Wheel' that celebrates multiple dates, among them the imperial foundation in 1 Flint 1376, and the year it was consecrated 13 Reed 1479 (before the repetition of 1 Flint in 1480, two 52-year Rounds or Xiuhmolpilli later). Deeper in time, 13 Reed evoked in turn the inaugural year of the Era itself. On its rim, the Sunstone acknowledges the Feasts as the outer bound of time, in the metamorphic caiman-snake or dragon known as Xiuhcoanaual (see below pp.14–18).

The other Mexica Feast text inscribed in stone consists of matching sets of 18 and 11 panels in the temple of Ome Tochtli (Two Rabbit) Tepoztecatl, whose cult was incorporated by Tenochtitlan in 10 Rabbit 1502, under the 8th emperor Ahuizotl. Facing the western horizon of the new moon and dedicated to the first drinkers of pulque or alcoholic maguey juice (who became the Pleiades), the temple still stands in Tepoztlan (Morelos) as one of the few in Mexico to have survived destruction at Christian hands. Concentric, the Sunstone is a *summum* of Mexica calendrics that privileges the Feasts to a degree hitherto unsuspected (Chapter 7); *in situ*, Tepoztecatl's temple enables us to reconstruct their choreography, their setting among mountains and stars (Chapter 6). Together these foundational inscriptions in stone invoke the Feasts in distinguishing between the years of the sun and the stars, and of civil society.

Inscribed, the Sunstone and the Tepoztecatl panels belong to a whole corpus of stone texts, all solidly pre-Cortesian, which reveal key antecedents for the Mexica understanding and deployment of the Feasts. For his part, Ome Tochtli had previously appeared in the inscription at Coatlan, Yauhtepec (just south of Tepoztlan. **Map 2**), which also features Cipactonal, master of caiman earth and calendar, who consecrates the annual irrigation system installed there by the Chichimec three or more centuries earlier (see below p.47). As an epic hero, Ome Tochtli had similarly defended this part of Morelos from the tribute demands of Xochicalco, the late Classic centre of calendrical science which imaged itself as the caiman maw that endeavoured to devour him. Going yet further back, to the primordial settlement that Ome Tochtli epitomizes as axe bearer and pulque drinker, this tradition of inscribed texts may be seen to stem from the iconography of the Olmec western frontier (Morelos; northern Guerrero), at sites like Chalcatzingo, Oztoma, and the Oxtotitlan cave with its feathered caiman (**Fig.1.1;** see Grove 1970; 1984).

Among source texts on native paper, pride of place is given to two firmly embedded in the Mexica tradition, the Matrícula de tributos, and the Borbonicus screenfold, whose style and exposition lends them an unrivalled authority on the page. With respect to the Feasts, each commands a palpable genre of texts in its own right.

A supreme ledger of the Mexica economy, the Matrícula's original 19 folios (38 pages; Castillo 1997:22) record the rules of the annual tax system that Tenochtitlan imposed on an ever wider landscape. As a sheaf of unbound amate sheets that could be (and historically was) reshuffled and recast, the text highlights ciphers and constants in the solar year that survived shifts of military fortune. Attentive to hard facts and deadlines, the very mechanism of this tribute system was synonymous with the Mexica Feast cycle and its division into halves and quarters. The notation most appropriate to this mechanism is the one used for convenience here to identify the 18 Feasts throughout, as first and second halves of the year: F1.1–F1.9 (Tozoztli A – Ochpaniztli) and F2.1–F2.9 (Pachtli A – Tlacaxipehualiztli). Now available in facsimile, the Matrícula has been the subject of important commentaries, yet few have dwelt on its calendrical message, indispensable as this is to the full meaning of the text. Conversely, it has been largely excluded from analyses of the Feasts cycle as such, even in the case of scholars who privilege pre-Cortesian evidence or who assume calendrics to be inseparable from political economy.

No doubt since it functioned as a legal-economic document, the Matrícula has in fact been mainly treated as a simple ledger. Its calculations have been compared with what can otherwise be known about Tenochtitlan's tribute empire and have even been deemed 'incorrect' by a certain school of Positivist historians. Less interest has been aroused by how it sets out its claims, the logic and exposition of its argument as such. For, although it consists materially just of loose sheets, sequences and subheadings within the Matrícula are critically important to this argument, as is the format of individual pages. To this extent, the file amply rewards attention paid to it as a literary text. In genre terms, the Matrícula is the first and finest of a whole body

of *tlacuilolli* documents, most of them submitted in later years to the Real Audiencia of New Spain (the viceregal law court), whose legal argument is couched in and depends on the most sophisticated literary exposition (Chapter 3 'Fiscal Acquisition').

The Matrícula's royal pedigree and the terms of its argument mean that as an account of Tenochtitlan's power it may be usefully compared with a Feast text from Texcoco, those two cities having set up the imperial Alliance in 4 Reed 1431. An Anniversary Wheel written on native paper like the Matrícula and known today by the name 'Boban', this Texcoco text dates itself to 7 Rabbit 1538 ('chicome tochtli') and on its rim it appeals to the Feast cycle as validation for its account of former empire, setting within it a story that extends from the Seven Caves of the Chichimec to Charles V's imposition of the viceroyalty in 1535. In principle and format, in framing political history in the circumference of the Feasts, this text from Texcoco belongs with the Sunstone as an 'Anniversary Wheel' (Chapter 7, **Pl. 8**).

At about the time the Boban Wheel was being produced, the Matrícula became the core of the major document on European paper now named the Mendoza Codex, after the first viceroy Antonio de Mendoza (the period is right, the implied authorial role misleads). At the practical level, this Codex helpfully supplies versions of Matrícula pages that are now lost or effaced. The Matrícula and Mendoza (**Pl. 2b**) are meticulously compared in the Berdan/Anawalt edition of the latter (1992) and the independently-prepared Castillo edition of the former (1997). Documenting Tenochtitlan's economy more broadly, Mendoza also matches the regulation of commodity tribute by the Feasts cycle (ff.17–55), which it took from the Matrícula, with chapters on labour and social control (ff.56–71) which thematically belong to the Tonalpoualli, and it prefaces the whole with a quatrefoil map and a chronicle of imperial reigns (ff.2–16). These additions likewise have clear antecedents in pre-Cortesian texts. In the cases of both the Boban Wheel and the Mendoza Codex, the Matrícula cross-references to affirm the primary function of the Feasts in economy and politics and conversely may be illuminated through comparisons with these later invocations of the cycle.

If the Matrícula marks the tax deadlines of the Mexica imperial year, then the Borbonicus screenfold stands as a liturgical counterpart, as celebratory performance. Dedicated to the Feasts, the last of its three chapters makes vivid sense of seasonal and other rhythms of the Mexica year (**Pls 5–6**). As a screenfold, Borbonicus well exemplifies the principle of imbrication and interweaving of motif and meaning between chapters, and of allocating space differentially within a given chapter, notably over the 18 pages of the Feast chapter, which spatially privileges Ochpaniztli. Moreover, though based on calendrical cycles, the three chapters of Borbonicus also invoke specific and unrepeatable moments and events from the past. So that in the Feasts cycle, for example, Panquetzaliztli (F2.4) invokes the New Fire ceremony presided over by Moctezuma II in the year 2 Reed, 1507 AD. Inseparable from the *tlacuilolli* tradition and indispensable to a proper reading of the Boban Wheel, this understanding of time and particularly of the Feasts needless to say defies simplistic Western distinctions between synchronic and diachronic reality.

The Mexican scholars Alfonso Caso and Luis Reyes García each took Borbonicus as a prime authority for their accounts of the Feasts, Caso (1939) to establish correlations with the

Christian and other year calendars, Reyes (1992) to re-immerse the text in the culture and philosophy that produced it. In his page-by-page commentary on the text, Reyes suggested its title should be restored to *Ciuacoatl*, the name of the main character seen in the Feasts chapter (see Chapter 5). While the Feasts are choreographed in this third and final chapter (pp.23–40), the second (pp.21–22), devoted to the Xiuhmolpilli, includes a Mexica reworking of the Coatlan inscription; the first records the Tonalpoualli. As a text divided into chapters that deal with the main cycles of the calendar – Feasts, Tonalpoualli and the intermediary Xiuhmolpilli – Borbonicus belongs to the 'ritual' genre of screenfold books, often referred to as the 'Borgia Group'. The nine classic texts in this chaptered genre have been catalogued by Nowotny (1961; 2005), who like Seler assigns the eponymous Borgia screenfold to Cholula, the 'Rome' of Mesoamerica (PBM 119; see Chapter 2 below; McCafferty 2001). In Borgia, the Feasts form the core of the text, being the subject of the central 18-page chapter (pp.29–46).

Just as the Matrícula and Borbonicus speak to the Mexica Feast system as it functioned before Cortés, so a further text does the same for the impact that Christian calendrics had upon it. This is the Mexicanus Codex, perhaps the most seriously underestimated (and certainly the worst published) of surviving Mexica texts on native paper that deal authoritatively with the Feasts. With its main text completed by 13 Reed 1583, Mexicanus brings us into prolonged contact with the Spanish colonial system. Explicitly loyal to Acamapichtli, it promotes the notion of the 'core history' that resists European attempts to reduce the New World materially and intellectually. Reading Mexicanus, we may lose the aura of an uninterrupted pre-contact source yet we gain a highly informed guide in Nepantla, the invaded land where the Feasts continue to affirm their taxonomy of time. We are given insight into the logic whereby New Fire was re-kindled to mark the start of the new Xiuhmolpilli in 2 Reed 1559, covertly, under the noses of uncomprehending Spaniards, at the nocturnal ceremony designed to honour the recently deceased Charles V (Cervantes de Salazar). Mexicanus has not been published adequately, and the existing commentaries on it by Mengin (1952), Galarza (1966) and Prem (1978, the most incisive) far from exhaust the multiple readings it demands.

Mexicanus is written on native paper and in excellent *tlacuilolli*, yet in engaging with its times as a paginated book it assumes spine rather than screenfold binding. It is easily the single most cogent guide to Mexica understandings of the year to engage with the Christian calendar, of which it offers an astoundingly accurate and thoughtful critique (**Pl. 2a**). Its precise measurements of the Feasts take into account the continuing Julian slippage over the 64 years that elapsed between Cortés's arrival in 1519 and the Gregorian Reform of 1583 (the likely date of composition) and rely on its remarkable Night Sky Grid (pp.13–14; **Table 4**). The structure of the whole is tripartite, like Borbonicus; on the opening page Tezcatlipoca's *tlachialoni* sceptre is thrust high in the Feast of Toxcatl. The very comprehensiveness of its account of the Mexica Feasts, the kinds of year they represent and their interface with Christianity make of this text a yardstick for this study as a whole (Chapter 8).

Anchored by texts inscribed on stone (Sunstone; Tepoztecatl panels) and written on native paper (Matrícula, Boban, Borbonicus, Mexicanus), this preliminary survey of principal Mexica sources can be profitably extended to include works on European paper (and to that extent of diminished pedigree), that interlace their *tlacuilolli* accounts of the Feasts with alphabetic commentaries and explanations. For the most part these works are copies and adaptations of *tlacuilolli* texts designed to explain the calendar to newly-arrived Europeans, and they are referred to here as 'compendia'. Though they need to be scrutinized with care (because of European agency in their production), each of these compendia may be incisively compared with *tlacuilolli* precedents. On this basis, those that deal with the Mexica Feasts fall into several main groups, each identified here by its oldest or major genealogical member: Tepepulco, *Cuevas*, Telleriano, Magliabechiano, Tovar, and Veytia.

Tepepulco

From the mountainous area northeast of Tenochtitlan, this manuscript was produced by the elders of Tepepulco at the behest of the Franciscan friar Sahagún, four decades after the Mexica defeat (1559–61). It is a beautifully written *tlacuilolli* text, to which attaches a Nahuatl commentary in carefully formed alphabetic letters. Also known as the 'Primeros Memoriales', the Tepepulco manuscript is the first in a line of works elicited and increasingly re-structured by Sahagún, among them the Florentine Codex (**Appendix D**), which were then incorporated into his *Historia general de las cosas de esta Nueva España*. Firm in its own taxonomy, the *tlacuilolli* text from Tepepulco falls into four numbered Parts duly acknowledged in Nicholson's excellent edition, whose chapters deal respectively with concepts (-*yotl*) of the ritual year (I), sky and earth (II), government (tlatoayotl; III) and society (tlacameyotl; IV). Part I opens with a choreography of the Feasts (**Pl. 7**) much in the style of Borbonicus or Borgia and supplies details of offerings, attire, Twenty Hymns in Nahuatl, and the plan of the Great Temple (I, ii, iii, v, vii, xiv; ff.250–64; **Appendices B, C**). The four tightly interwoven chapters of Part II (**Pl. 3**) explore how the time made manifest in the Feasts (*ilhuitlapoal amoxtli*) relates to the sun, moon and stars (i), the seasons (ii) and the counts of years (Xiuhpoualli; iii) and days (Tonalpoualli; iv; **Pls 4–6**). The account of the night sky (II,i) is structured on the constellations seen in the Borgia Feasts, notably the oval cluster of the Many (Pleiades), the Market womb of our galaxy (Scorpio/Sagittarius), and the S-shaped Septentrion Xonecuilli; the account of the seasons (II,ii) echoes the Coatlan Inscription (see Chapter 4 below). The crisp and highly informative *tlacuilolli* images in this manuscript were distorted in early reproductions but are now revealed in a facsimile (Sahagún 1993) which for the first time renders the text available for detailed study.

Cuevas de los siete linajes

Extant today only in copies on European paper, this finely written *tlacuilolli* work takes its name from the Spanish gloss on the first of its 32 pages. Generally, its identity as a text has been subsumed under the names of friar historians who drew heavily on it, notably the Dominican Diego Durán, and the Jesuits Juan Tovar and José Acosta. The page numbers cited here correspond to the 32 colour plates in Lafaye's 1972 edition of Tovar's *Relación del origen de los yndios* (1583–87; HMAI 1131), the manuscript of which is in the the John Carter Brown Library.

Analogous in its chaptering to Mendoza, Borbonicus, and Mexicanus, *Cuevas...* deals with the calendrical foundation of

Tenochtitlan (pp.1–18, where Tenoch is advised by 'Tochtli Calpan', Calpan lying on Cholula's western border with the Mexica, **Pl. 1**); gods and cults regulated by the Tonalpoualli (pp.19–29); and the year (pp.30–32). The Feasts play a key role throughout, with a specifically Mexica interplay between feather and Feast (*ihuitl, ilhuitl*), and on the Quecholli, the name both of a Feast (F2.3) and of the 13 fliers of the Tonalpoualli. Beginning with the Seven Caves of the Chichimec at Chicomoztoc (whence the titular gloss *Cuevas...*), the foundation chapter culminates in a brilliant feather-adorned choreography of the Feasts (p.18. **Pl. 4**). As such, the final chapter (pp.30–2; amplified in Durán) permutates the Feasts as Quecholli (**Table 3c**), distinguishes alternative Feast names in terms of class and ethnicity, and recalls Borgia in locating them in upper and lower registers of sky and earth.

The structuring and argument of *Cuevas...* antedate and owe nothing whatsoever to missionary design and in all respects adhere to *tlacuilolli* norms, notably in their subtle imbrication of theme within and between chapters (in Lafaye's edition, plates III and IX have demonstrably been transposed). Its textual authority is brought out through comparison with the alphabetic transcriptions of it, chiefly Durán's *Historia de las Indias de Nueva España* (1579–81. HMAI 1036) and Tovar's *Relación*, the very division of these works into parts or tratados being determined by the structure of *Cuevas*. Durán went yet further, amplifying *Cuevas* with copies of other *tlacuilolli* originals, when illustrating the three Tratados of his history. While as illustrations of alphabetic Spanish, these copies largely cease to function as *tlacuilolli* script, much can be learned from them, notably the set that represents the year in the third Tratado. Indeed, when composing the corresponding paragraphs in this Tratado Durán expressly acknowledges the 18 Feast images to be a *tlacuilolli* source that is legible in its own right (Durán 1995, 2:245–93, láminas 39–56).

Telleriano Remensis

Written in finer *tlacuilolli* than its twin the Codex Vaticanus A or Rios, Telleriano belongs with it to what has been called the 'Huitzilopochtli Group' (after a supposed common prototype); they also share a connection with the friar Pedro de los Rios. Rios however preserves pages of Telleriano that are now lost, notably in the Feasts chapter. Telleriano is missing initial folios that correspond to the Feasts from Quauitleoa to Etzalcualiztli (F2.8–F1.4) though it does include the Nemotemi, the extra 'useless' days in the year added to the 360 of the 18 Feasts (Tena 2000). As well as making good the now depleted Telleriano Feast cycle, Rios prefaces it with an account of their origins (ff.IV–IoV). Glossed in Italian and scrutinized by scholars in the Vatican (where the manuscript still is, hence the title 'Vaticanus A'), this account follows Borgia in explaining the cosmic significance and time depth of the Feasts and here is entitled 'Genesis' (see below p.46). In the annals section common to both Telleriano and Rios, the latter also retains the critical years 1 Reed to 3 House 1519–21, the corresponding pages having been torn out of the former. There, Tenochtitlan's last days of autonomy are highlighted in 'Encounter with Europe', a Feast sequence likewise deserving of attention in its own right (see below pp.8–10). While aligned with Tenochtitlan as the term 'Huitzilopochtli Group' suggests, Telleriano and Rios cast back to doctrines of Cholula. Telleriano especially was subjected to

many alphabetic glosses by often crude European hands, which however sometimes yield good information precisely because their authors recorded yet failed to understand what they were being told; this text as a whole is now more legible thanks to the well-produced facsimile edited by Quiñones Keber (1995).

Magliabechiano

The Magliabechiano Codex is chief among a cluster of texts, named after figures as diverse as Ixtlilxochitl of Texcoco and the historian Antonio de Herrera (Boone; Riese; Doesburg). These Magliabechiano texts share a Feast chapter, which gives prominence to Tezcatlipoca's sceptre *tlachialoni* (in Toxcatl) and to the Milky Way goddess Ilamatecutli (in Tititl). Several also feature sets of towns lying along the Tepoztlan ridge, on the southern rim of the highland Basin, which were famous for their companies of nocturnal pulque drinkers, shown to number 11, and hence reveal a link with the Feast inscriptions in the temple of Tepoztlan itself. Lacking the precision seen in Tepepulco, the *tlacuilo* (scribe) of Magliabechiano nonetheless writes better than his successors in the group as a whole. The accompanying alphabetic commentaries, in Spanish, respond only coarsely to the *tlacuilolli* text.

Tovar

Not to be confused with *Cuevas de los linajes*, the Tovar Feasts calendar (HMAI 364) shares with it its location in the John Carter Brown Library and a most complex history, recounted in detail by Kubler and Gibson in their edition (1950); the first of its 11 folios even reproduces the Xiuhmolpilli seen on p. 30 of *Cuevas*. Bound with the *Cantares mexicanos* manuscript, the Tovar Feasts cycle relates closely to that in the *Kalendario mexicano, latino y castellano* (c. 1585; HMAI 205), having a similar iconography, along with a common correlation with the Julian calendar, its months, zodiac signs, and dominical or Sunday letters. These coincidences have been attributed to a missing common source, the *tlacuilolli* pages of what has been called the Crónica X. However that may be, there is a strong link between Tovar and the opening chapter of Mexicanus, the latter, on native paper, being clearly the more authoritative.

Veytia

In the broader sense, texts whose format is that of a 'Calendar Wheel' abound in Mesoamerica (PBM 112); several pertaining to the year were gathered in the 17th century by Jacinto de la Serna, and in the 18th, by Mariano Veytia, patron and disciple of Lorenzo Boturini. These latter comprise a set of seven (Porrúa 1994), of which numbers 4 and 5 show the Feasts in a circle concentric with that of the Tonalpoualli cycles, while in No.2 they mesh with a larger Xiuhmolpilli wheel below. These Veytia Wheels appear 'Europeanized' yet numbers 4 and 5 ingeniously appeal to Feast emblems when reflecting on the 'second coming' of European aggressors, in the form of a manically determined Inquisition, in 1 Reed 1571 (i.e. 52 years or one Xiuhmolpilli after Cortés). In so doing they demand to be included fully in the category of 'Anniversary Wheels', of which the Sunstone and the Boban Wheel are classic examples, and whose philosophy of time endures today in native-paper screenfolds from Pahuatlan (see Chapter 7).

Still within what might be called this classic corpus of *tlacuilolli* texts relevant to the Mexica Feasts, we may further mention the clearly defined genre known in Nahuatl as Xiuhtlapoualli, year counts or annals. The only surviving Mexica example of annals on native paper and in screenfold format, the 'Tira de la peregrinación' (in fact, it is not a 'tira' but a 21- page book), is most often identified by the name of the 18th- century Italian collector Boturini. These annals tell the Mexica foundation story synthesized on the Sunstone, Mexicanus (pp.16– 17), the Mendoza quatrefoil map (f.2) and *Cuevas* (pp.1–4), and narrated at length in other Mexica annals, like those also in Mexicanus (pp.18–88), Azcatitlan, Aubin, and the Telleriano/Rios compendium (whence 'Encounter with Europe'). As an example of the Xiuhtlapoualli genre in screenfold format, Boturini has precedents in annals, mostly on skin, that focus on the fortune of earlier centres of political power, like Tlapa, Xicotepec, Itzcuintepec, Cuicatlan, Quiotepec, Tilantongo and other Mixtec towns, and above all Tepexic, a long-standing ally of Coixtlahuaca. Especially significant is the common interest in the New Fire year 2 Reed evident in both the Mexica annals and the 52-page Tepexic year count in the Vienna Codex, which formally covers a period commensurate with the Era datings typical of the Olmec and Maya inscriptions. These origins are brought closer to home in the *Historia tolteca-chichimeca* (HTCh), famous for its masterful depiction of Chicomoztoc Seven Caves, and for the rich calendrical detail it gives in recording the annals of Cuauhtinchan.

There exists a yet further category of native texts relevant to the Mexica Feasts: those transcribed into the alphabet and written mostly in Nahuatl (as the *Historia tolteca chichimeca* partly is) or Spanish. In other words, they take further the process of transcription by native hands begun in compendia like the Tepepulco Ms., and for our purposes the most significant among them are narratives that serve to confirm or explain the *tlacuilolli* corpus. Those furthest from *tlacuilolli* originals have typically caused most problems for scholarly attempts at interpretation and correlation of the Feasts.

Several *tlacuilolli* annals have been transcribed into alphabetic script, signally the annals of Cuauhtitlan, which consistently cross-reference with those of Cuauhtinchan, and include the Mexica story in a year count that starts at the 7th-century Chichimec base-date and run continuously up to 13 Rabbit 1518, the eve of European invasion (17 Xiuhmolpilli later. Bierhorst 1992). Turning on year names of especial resonance, these annals also cast back deep into cosmogony, complementing insights and information given in 'Genesis' and in Nahuatl narratives like the *Legend of the Suns* (Bierhorst 1992); and they explicitly adhere to *tlacuilolli* models in setting their histories of the highland Basin in the larger cosmic framework of the Era and the world ages ('Suns'), for which the Feasts provide a key reference, as on the Sunstone (**Appendix A**). These narratives belong with analogous texts transcribed from *tlacuilolli* yet mediated by Spaniards, like *Historia de los mexicanos por sus pinturas* (HMP) and *Histoire du Mechique* (HM; Garibay 1965; Tena 2002), as well as later works signed by native historians like Tezozomoc, Ixtlilxochitl and Chimalpahin.

While these annals and histories can be seen to derive directly from *tlacuilolli* antecedents, the process of transcription is evidently more complex in the case of a complementary group of alphabetic spoken and 'performed' texts relevant to the Feasts, saliently the *Icuic* or Twenty Hymns in Tepepulco (I, vii; their numbering defers to that of the Feasts); and the *Cantares*

mexicanos bound with Tovar, which as it were attach sound to the choreography. Fundamental to the very taxonomy of the Feasts is *Coloquios*, the Mexica refutation and rejection of the Christian mission in 1524 (**Appendix E**). It is here that we learn of the three social callings, of priest, planter and hunter-warrior, and their respective origins in the Mesoamerican cosmos: present in the classic inscriptions, exactly this tripartite model is presumed in *tlacuilolli* settings of the Feasts in the Sunstone, Mendoza, Tepepulco, *Cuevas*, Rios (especially 'Genesis'), and Mexicanus (pp.9–15).

Together, like the *Popol vuh* of the Quiche Maya, all these *tlacuilolli* sources and their alphabetic derivatives, though diverse materially and in date and purpose, cohere in aiding our attempts to understand the Mexica Feasts, laying out paradigms and lines of thought, and establishing norms and criteria for correlation.

Correlation and interface with Europe

A great deal has been written about the difficulties of correlating the calendars of Mesoamerica and Christendom, and most of it lies well beyond the scope and purpose of this enquiry into the Mexica Feasts. When we concentrate on these last and respect the indications of *tlacuilolli* scribes, a clear preliminary message emerges. It is that the division of the year into halves, explicit in the notation F1.1–F1.9, F2.1–F2.9, indeed has astronomical significance, since the hinge between the halves coincides with the autumn equinox, 22nd–23rd September. This date in the Julian calendar (where it falls 10 days earlier, i.e. 12th/13th) is equated with the culmination of Ochpaniztli (F1.9.20) quite unambiguously and without exception in all the *tlacuilolli* accounts of the Mexica Feasts which include an internally consistent correlation with the Christian calendar, that is, Mexicanus, and the compendia Tepepulco, Telleriano and Tovar (**Table 1**). Telleriano and Rios say that on 22nd September (12th Julian) Ochpaniztli ends, in Spanish 'entra', an exact though unfortunately often misunderstood translation of the Nahuatl *calaquia*, to go in, to enter a house or enclosure. Mexicanus specifies the same day by connecting the glyph for the culmination of Ochpaniztli, Teteu innan's broom, with 12th September (dominical letter **c**, Lunar Letter **m**; see Chapter 8). For its part Tovar appeals to the same dominical letter cycle when establishing the 20th day of Ochpaniztli, duly identified by the broom glyph, as the 13th September and **d**, in which it coincides perfectly with the Tepepulco representation of Ochpaniztli and Teteu innan and the note 'In ilhuitl quiçaya ipan in augusto meztli ic cempoalli unmacuilli' (This Feast began on 25th of the month August), that is, it ended on 13th September Julian.

We may speak then of the Tepepulco - Tovar (TT) and the Telleriano/Rios - Mexicanus (TM) correlations, and through them find the Mexica year tied to the solar phenomenon of the equinoxes. Indeed the difference of at most a Christian day between the two accommodates Julian ambiguity about the exact dates of these equinoxes, so that in practice they might well be considered to be one, the TTTM correlation. Astronomically, TTTM also aligns with the zenith passage of the sun, which in that part of Mexico occurs in mid-Toxcatl and mid-May. As a formula good for the year of the Gregorian Reform, TTTM is conveniently expressed as: F1.1.1 = 27th March
In applying the formula, allowance needs always to be made for

Figure 1.2 Tepeilhuitl, Quecholli, and the month of November. Mexicanus p.7 (after Mengin 1952)

a least a day, because of such factors as (and combinations thereof): the equinox cannot be precisely dated to the day; dates in the Julian year continued to slip back after first contact; both Mexica and Christian days have been thought to begin at different hours of day and night.

Only one other correlation attaches to the *tlacuilolli* account of the Mexica Feasts, which exceeds these limits, that given in Magliabechiano and other texts in its group, and it is internally inconsistent. This very inconsistency could however be due to European confusion about exactly when or whether the Nemotemi or five useless days were inserted into the three different kinds of Mexica year, particularly with respect to the Feast Izcalli and St Gilbert's Day, 4th February, which if put right may yield the TTTM correlation. While plagued by such misunderstanding even the correlations forged by missionaries, to help them in their task of conversion, may respect TTTM, Durán being a signal case (see next chapter below).

In its account of the months October and November, Mexicanus further refines the TTTM correlation. There, the ending of the Pachtli B (2.2.20) is noted, consistently, as 22nd October. However, this same Feast is given another ending under its alternative name, Tepeilhuitl, and this falls just 10 days later, on All Souls Day, November 1st (**Fig.1.2**). This sort of double entry is unique in the Mexicanus Feast chapter; and historically it corresponds to what actually happened during those months in 1583, when the Gregorian Reform of the Julian Calendar (1582) was officially introduced in the viceroyalty of New Spain. This year of Reform proves to be a main focus in Mexicanus and as 13 Reed in the Annals chapter it stands as the last of the years fully reported in *tlacuilolli* (see Chapter 8, 'Mexicanus'). In Mexico in 1583, in order to adjust the Christian year to the seasons and the movement of the earth around the sun, 10 month-dates had to be omitted in October, meaning that the ending of Pachtli B/Tepeilhuitl (F2.2) moved nominally from 22nd October (Julian) to Halloween and All Souls, 1st November (Gregorian).

Even more refined in Mexicanus, is the recognition of the fact that after the moment of encounter with Europe in 1519, the Julian calendar did not cease to slip back in the year, until the general Reform of 1582–83, and that at exactly 64 years this period of continued slippage produced a further lapse of a 12-hour day. This much is indicated in the vertical lines on the page that mark Feast endings, where the main bold line has a fainter one a day to the right of it, so that Ochpaniztli, for example, is shown to end currently on 22nd and residually on 23rd. In this way, Mexicanus contrives to account not just for Christian ambiguity about exactly when the Autumn equinox falls, but for the continuing 1519–83 slippage which apart from anything else readily explains the difference of a day between the TT and TM correlations. As terms of the calendrically significant 64-year period, the years 1519 and 1583 are highlighted in the chapter by the appearance of two unique and anomalously recent heads (p.7, p.6), which respectively attach to those in its gallery of saints. Hence, Cortés hovers above St Martin (12th November) as he arrives in Tenochtitlan in 1 Reed 1519; viceroy Suarez is tied to St Francis, on whose day (4th October) he arrived (Prem 1978:271) and who died, the annals tell us, in 1583.

In *tlacuilolli* narratives of the actual invasion, the TTTM correlation serves well to date events otherwise recorded in European chronicles, and above all in bringing out the significance of those events in the Feast cycle. Even if it does not resolve every conundrum, especially with respect to Tonalpoualli days, it is apt and coherent overall. Cross-referencing Mexica and Christian accounts is eased by Hugh Thomas' thoroughly documented *The Conquest of Mexico* (1992); (cf. also Doesburg and Carrera González 1996:115–26).

According to Aubin (f.40v), Moctezuma first felt foreboding of European approach in 3 Flint 1508, right at the start of the 52-year Xiuhmolpilli which he had presided over the year before (2 Reed 1507); this foreboding is dated to an omen seen in the same year in Book 12 of the Florentine Codex (Flo XII, 6), a decade before Moctezuma's spies boarded a Spanish ship in

Figure 1.3 (this page and oppostie) 'Encounter with Europe'. 1 Reed to 3 House, 1519 to 1521: Feasts Quecholli (F2.3) to Tecuilhuitl B (F1.6). Rios ff.87–88

Xicalanco. The 1507 New Fire proved to be the last autonomously celebrated by the Mexica; Moctezuma's performance at the grandly choreographed event hinted at approaching doom through the shifting aspect of the Xiuhcoanaual mantle he wore (Borbonicus pp.23, 35; see p.15 below). His unease was caused by the 'coming down' of the Tlacauillome, the dove-men whose white boat-like bodies and upright wings visually reflect the European sails that by then were becoming a less extraordinary sight in the Caribbean. Moctezuma had Cortés tracked as he approached from the east, along the northern coast of his northern tribute province Cuauhtochco, and greeted him when he landed at Chalchicueyecan (Veracruz) at Easter 1519. Precisely on the morning of this, the greatest Christian feast (Thomas 1992:176), he arranged for sumptuous presents to be delivered to him, in itself no mean a calendrical achievement.

The gifts are shown in 'Encounter with Europe': exemplifying Europe's double metal standards, the horse-borne recipient holds a golden trefoil cross surmounted by a pennant in one hand and, in the other, a sword of blue steel. Moctezuma's next contact came six months later, after the September equinox, Cortés having spent the intervening half year outside the empire, in Totonac and Tlaxcalan territory. For, destined for Tenochtitlan, Cortés was escorted into the empire by the Tlaxcalans during Teotleco (the 'arrival of the gods'; F2.1), and left outside Cholula. Having spent the previous night in a ditch, he was admitted to that city exactly on the culminating day of Teotleco (F2.1.20, 12th October; Thomas 1992:257), and thereupon proceeded to slaughter his hosts at worship. In depicting the scene, Tlaxcala Lienzo specifies Quetzalcoatl as the god being worshiped, for Cholulans chief

among those who 'arrived' in this Feast.

From here on the story is correlated with the Feasts, one by one, in a literal subtext on the annal pages of 'Encounter with Europe', during the Spaniards' stay in Tenochtitlan in 1 Reed and 2 Flint 1519–20 (13 Feasts) and subsequent siege of the city in 3 House 1521 (5 Feasts). As in Chichimec history (Cuauhtitlan Annals), these footnote Feast emblems intensify the time in which the corresponding events occur (**Fig.1.3**).

Directed as ever by Malintzin and the Tlaxcalans, Cortés reached Tenochtitlan in Quecholli (F2.3). Mexicanus notes his presence on St Martin's day (November 12th, F2.3.12) though loosely, since Cortés made less of an impact being invited into the city than he did taking Moctezuma hostage a few days later, having armed men hustle the emperor off to the temple quarters that had graciously been allotted to him (Flo XII, 17). Quecholli was the Feast of the Chichimec *par excellence*, the one when these predecessors of the Mexica would recall ancestral teachings, notably when likewise under threat (CtA ; see p. 17 below). As in Tepepulco and Borbonicus, the Chichimec hunter of Quecholli seen in 'Encounter' has arrows and wears a traverse nose adornment, his prey being the migrant birds from the north that landed on the highland lakes at this season (the homonymous Quecholli or 13 'fliers' of the calendar: see **Table 2**). This hunter is however separated from his arrows, which in any case lack the noticeably sharp tips of those in Tepepulco, for example, or of those used in battle against the Tlaxcalans the previous year 13 Rabbit. In November 1519, many Mexica strongly disagreed with Moctezuma's decision to allow the migrant bird Cortés into Tenochtitlan in Quecholli without a fight, despite his by then proven record as a butcher.

Figure 1.3 (this page and oppostie) 'Encounter with Europe'. 1 Reed to 3 House, 1519 to 1521: Feasts Toxcatl (F1.3) to Micailhuitl A (F1.7). Rios ff.87–88

As is the norm, in 'Encounter' a banner (*pantli*) marks Panquetzaliztli (F2.4), one of the tribute-quarter Feasts. These characteristically also invoke the quarters of the sidereal year through the S-shaped polar constellation Xonecuilli, indicating its advance over the shorter solar year and, with that, ideas of regulation and justice. The banner pennant here is however abnormally long, and on its tip Xonecuilli has been shattered. Above, black-capped Cortés is seen ensconced in his temple quarters, exerting the power acquired by detaining Moctezuma as his hostage, and again dispensing Spanish 'justice' in the Xonecuilli palace at Coyoacan. Indeed, Panquetzaliztli's banner goes on and on, even into solstitial Atemoztli (F2.5, 'water falling'), the winter watershed, to the point of impinging on the aqueducts (similarly modified in the Veytia Wheels) that were due in that Feast to be readied for irrigation and planting. The planting season began in Tititl (F2.6), when Ciuacoatl stuck her tongue out (cf. **Pls 6,9**), here perhaps with more than usual defiance. The sunken cheeks of Izcalli (F2.7), nominally the Feast of growth and stretching, recall solar year adjustments of former empires, like the aging Xiuhcoanaual in Tepepulco, while in the annals here the actual New Year 2 Flint, boxed in Mexica fashion, aligns with Atlcahualo (F2.8), whose now firmly rooted plant as normal denotes lesser need for irrigation (see Chapter 4, pp.41–7 below).

Thereupon Tlacaxipehualiztli (F2.9) arrives, its last day announcing the March equinox and therewith the end of the fiscal or tribute year (F2.9.20. Mendoza f.47; see p.34 below). This Feast's emblem, Xipe's peaked-hat, was institutionalized in the 'A'-type year marker used in Cholula and the east (**Table 3d**), and the egg-like dot placed under it here in fact marks the anniversary of the encounter in Chalchicueyecan the previous

Easter. Despite the emperor's predicament, those in the metropolitan district of the temple where Cortés and he were living did not fail to deliver tribute on time, notably the military outfits that were paid yearly and which took the Spaniards' fancy. The *tlacuilolli* record of this tribute is notably conventionalized (Flo XII, 18; Mendoza f.20), like that of the daily supplies of water and food demanded earlier by Malintzin with less than acceptable courtesy (whence the satire of her person in Flo, much elaborated in the longest of the *Cantares mexicanos;* Bierhorst 1985:58).

Hard to parse overall yet clearly suggestive in given emphases and variations, the Feast emblems that accentuate the narrative in these texts ('Encounter', Flo XII, Tlaxcala Lienzo) indicate not only the powerful fact of Spanish presence in Tenochtitlan from Quecholli to Tlacaxipehualiztli (F2.3–F2.9) but the tension between host and guest, and the practical consequences it had in the day to day life in the city.

The Feast Tozoztli A (F1.1), the first in the scheme of equinoctial semesters, has the Parrot as its emblem in 'Encounter', complemented in Tozoztli B (F1.2) by Cinteotl's tunic and the customary clump of early rooted maize. As in several other sources, the Parrot's Nahuatl name, *toznene,* phonetically initiates the four-year cycle of priestly penance (*tozoa*) begun at that time, along with the fiscal year (F1.1.1, 27th March). The Parrot's Quecholli Number, which tops the set of Thirteen Quecholli, serves to count the Feasts of the penance, as we shall see when considering the Eagle of Tenochtitlan as well as Christian readings of pagan penance (Chapter 2 below). The Parrot depicted here, however, has lost lustre and significance in sound and number, its tiny body and wings looking more like those of a European chicken.

By contrast, the image of the warrior who appears in and as Toxcatl (F1.3) had its feathers applied with the usual immense care (Flo XII, 19) and is noticeably more imposing, for it was then, in mid-May 1520, that the standard of resistance – Tezcatlipoca's *tlachialoni* – was finally raised. The uprising came in response to Alvarado's butchery of the dancers at the Toxcatl Feast, epitomized in the macabre detail of the drummer's severed hand (Flo XII, 20; **Appendix D**), and led to Moctezuma's disgrace and to the Spaniards being imprisoned ('caltzauhcticatca'; Aubin f.43v) throughout Etzalcualiztli (F1.4). The full pot of maize and beans that denotes plentiful harvest at this Feast meant particularly 'good food' for those once again in control of Tenochtitlan, who went on nobly to release the Spaniards in the lordly Feast Tecuilhuitl, and to trounce them when they tried ignobly to sneak out of the city (the so-called Noche Triste). The enormity of the Toxcatl massacre reminded the Mexica of Cholula (Aubin f.43), and the uprising it provoked is acknowledged even by the Tlaxcalans in their Lienzo (f.14), in this Feast's Tezcatlipoca warrior glyph. Loyalist Mexicanus starts off (p.1) by celebrating the pride of the insurgent Mexica through Tezcatlipoca's all-seeing device, the *tlachialoni*.

Once they had got rid of their guests and with Moctezuma also gone, the Mexica burned the bodies and strewn limbs that lay everywhere, an activity appropriate to the Feast of the Dead Micailhuitl (F1.7–F1.8), no less than was the broom, Ochpaniztli's emblem (F1.9), with which they cleaned and refurbished the city, fashioning its feather crowns anew. The tally of the dead cremated rose thanks to the smallpox the Spaniards also left behind, along with loads of filth, which tested the strength of even the broom of Ochpaniztli whose archetypal owner was Teteu innan, Mother of the Gods (Flo XII, 27).

Toxcatl and the three subsequent Feasts during which resistance to the invaders grew, to the point of their being thrown out, are repeated in 'Encounter' in the following year, 3 House 1521. Over the summer these Feasts mark the siege of Tenochtitlan, and its fall in August, at the end of Micailhuitl A, 100 days in all (F1.3–F1.7; f.87v)). In the annals above, Cortés sets the siege hoisting the snake banner that phonetically prompts his name ('coa-tl', 'Cortés'), in a bloody sequel to the 1519 Easter landing on the previous page (f.87).

This time round in 1521, the Feast emblems are boxed in, like the city itself, and the imperial successor Cuauhtemoctzin (installed in the Nemotemi of F2.8; Aubin f.45) makes his last stand in Tlatelolco, the Eagle's last perch. Toxcatl's warrior is adorned with far fewer feathers (F1.3), and Etzalcualiztli's pot is emptied by the famine famously narrated in the Tlatelolco Annals (F1.4). The loss of Xochimilco and Coyoacan to the south drove Cuauhtemoc to find water closer by, as his *Ordenanza* shows (Reyes 2000:36), and is registered in the Tlaxcala Lienzo in a quincunx map of the siege (p.42), identical with the Feast emblem of Tecuilhuitl (F1.5–F1.6). This is the map format which on the Sunstone had served to celebrate the Mexica triumph over Coixtlahuaca. Regarding Cortés as their ally (rather than themselves as his), the Tlaxcalans may then be said to have appealed through Tecuilhuitl's quincunx to the cosmogony they shared with the Mexica, thereby acknowledging the world-shattering significance of the siege and impending fall of Tenochtitlan. From within, the Mexica recorded the squeeze on the quincunx, the imperial shield, and the stone cactus of the city itself (**Pl. 1**; Flo XII, 29).

All this found its sombre end in Micailhuitl A, the Feast of the Dead whose emblem is a corpse or mummy shrouded in black. It was clear to Cortés that Cuauhtemoc, in the last redoubt of Tlatelolco, repeatedly postponed what seemed to all inevitable surrender (Thomas 1993:522– 24). The Mexica continued to perform amazing acts of bravery, and as the Feast of the Dead Micailhuitl approached (F1.7), they boosted morale by skewering enemy skulls on the *tzonpantli* (4 + 4 human, 4 horse), thereby mocking Christian piety and calendrical fondness for the duodecimal (Flo XII, 35). The Quetzal among the Quecholli, 12 characteristically numbers the Lords of the underworld Mictlan and their relentless teeth). Were the Mexica emulating the warlike males who strove to reach Teteu innan in the performance of Ochpaniztli (F1.9; see p.65 below)? Though some claim the Mexica surrendered half way through Micailhuitl B (F1.8.10), on St Hippolytus' Day (13th August Julian), the black-shrouded emblem in 'Encounter with Europe' makes this end coincide rather with the end of Micailhuitl A (F1.7.20; 13th August Gregorian). Memory of the fateful interstice between Micailhuitl's black Feasts (F1.7– F1.8), which resonates with the start of the Mesoamerican Era itself, is preserved today in *tlacuilolli*, in the equinoctial model of the year on the title page on the Pahuatlan screenfold of August 1978.

Closely following these *tlacuilolli* narratives of invasion can leave little doubt that for the Mexica the Feasts charged time with multiple meaning, the more so insofar as they resonated in patterns within the year. Some indication of these patterns was given by the Mexica priests when responding to The Twelve Franciscans who by 6 Flint 1524 were ensconced with their scriptures ('Encounter' f.88), much as Cortés had been in 1519, though in plainer (and it turned out) longer-term wattle quarters. 'Opening the treasury fisk (*petlacal*) a little', the priests of Tenochtitlan trace their beliefs to three origins which correspond to kinds of year in their calendar. Corroborated in *tlacuilolli*, this model is meticulously compared with the Christian calendrics in Mexicanus at the end of the Julian Era in Mexico, in 13 Reed 1583 (see **Appendix E** and pp.82–91 below).

It might be objected: if the TTTM correlation of Mexica Feasts with Christian months may be so readily deduced and fits well with narratives of the invasion, why has it not been more generally known and accepted? There are many possible responses to this question, starting with Christian repression and book burning and the confusion that the Julian calendar itself generated, for both invader and invaded, before the 1582–83 Reform. Certainly, as the most authoritative sources now available, the few surviving *tlacuilolli* accounts of the Mexica Feasts have not always enjoyed the prestige they deserve, while conversely great historiographical faith has often been placed in reports offered by intellectually ill-equipped Europeans. This is especially unfortunate since, because of the calendar and literary tradition they belong to, these very *tlacuilolli* texts dwell most informatively on the idea of correlation itself, asking what does the matching entail? what kinds of time are involved on either side of the equation? They enquire not just who entered whose history in 1519, but which calendar, Mexica or Christian, should be the yardstick, which was the better equipped to measure the other. Most effectively, in representing their own time (and even that of the Christians) they avoid the anachronic and universalist tendencies in western thought. That is, as *tlacuilolli* statements they will convey given historical moments according to the conventions, and in the imaginary, of those moments.

Eagle at Tenochtitlan

With the basic correlation with the Julian calendar in place, understanding the nature and role of the Mexica Feasts is helped by observing how they emerged and impinged on life historically before Cortés, as always, according to the native account. Overall, the texts of the Mexica tend to distinguish stages in their rise to power, which are at once historical and calendrical, and in which their 18 Feasts are accorded a categorical role. Indeed, in these sources the whole experience strives towards attaining the feather crowns worn by the emperors, famously by Moctezuma, so that celebrating the Feasts (*ilhuitl*) of the imperial calendar comes to emulate the upward surge of the Thirteen fliers or Quecholli (**Table 2**), from whose wings (*azteca*) sprout *ihuitl* feathers (**Appendix C**).

The texts in question include Mexicanus, Mendoza, Vaticanus and Telleriano, *Cuevas de los linajes*, the Boturini screenfold, Azcatitlan, Aubin and other annals. With differences of emphasis, these accounts integrate the story of the Mexica Feasts into that of how the capital Tenochtitlan was found and founded. The first phase of the story takes the Mexica from their remote homeland beyond Mesoamerica, across the northwestern frontier to Tula Coatepec; the second concerns how once there, they gained footholds in the densely populated highland Basin, before crowning their dynast Acamapichtli at Tenochtitlan in 1376. Succinct models of this experience are provided in Mexicanus (pp.16–7), the Mendoza title-page map (f.2), and the opening passage in *Cuevas* (pp.1–4), which for these purposes may be read in *tlacuilolli* fashion as a semiotic square: the eponymous Tenoch and his adviser Calpan appear critically to sum up each phase, at Tula and then Tenochtitlan.

As Aztecs, former inhabitants of Aztlan (island of herons or wings), the Mexica begin by generalizing their geographical origin as the mountainous Colhuacan (Teoculuacan) that guards the seven ancestral caves (Chicomoztoc, 'Cuevas de los linajes') of their Chichimec predecessors. Located by Europeans in Nuevo Mexico, that is Mexico's greater northwest (including the southwest of the US), this land lay and lies beyond the tropics and Mesoamerica. In the climate of these extra tropical latitudes, dark and cold define winter, to the extent that north denotes the underworld that Mesoamerican texts normally locate to the south.

At this beginning, the Mexica measure the year and human gestation not yet by the Feasts and the Tonalpoualli characteristic of Mesoamerica, but by moons. These moons are visible numerically in the white clad ancestors whose seats are the Seven Caves, 12 in the upper 4 caves to the west, who intimate halves and quarters of the year, and 9 in the lower 3 caves to the east, whose average matches the trimesters of pregnancy (*Cuevas* p.1. **Fig.1.4**). The gender of the ancestors, 10 male and 11 female, along with the 'facing-page' pectorals of the latter (i.e. 22 'pages'), obeys norms of both body and the stars, which are roughly ratified in the counts of the boulders that frame the cave orifices, in the decimal 4x10 above and the 3 x 11 below. Such number norms have ample resonance in the corpus of Mexica and Chichimec texts registering the emergence from Chicomoztoc, whose master example is the *Historia tolteca chichimeca*. These confirm the decimal significance of the Chichimec 'Dog' as Sign X (as in Mexicanus; see pp.88–9 below), and of the 40-unit Cuauhquecholli that is applicable to days and years alike and literally crosses (and hence multiplies) the diagonal necks of the pair of Eagles in the Quecholli set (5 and 8; HTCh ff.39–40). Eleven (and its double) have long been consecrated as a stellar cipher throughout the American continent.

Tlacuilolli detail of this order on the opening page of the *Cuevas de los linajes* (p.1) prompted Tovar to insist that however rude the image (*traça*) may appear at first sight, these ancestral origins implied 'mucho orden y policía de república' (Relación f.2a), which translates here into the remarkable sophistication seen in Mexica and Chichimec account overall. For example, to west and east, the upper 12 and lower 9 ancestors multiply to

Figure 1.4 Seven Caves. *Cuevas de los siete linajes* p.1

Figure 1.5 Tula, contemplated by Tochtli Calpan and Tenoch. *Cuevas* ...p.2

produce just the 108 said to have been the first to emerge who are listed one by one in the *Historia* (HTCh ff.16, 21–22). The 108 are likewise counted in this text by Tezcatlipoca who, luring the ancestors out of the caves, characterised himself as the powers cross-generated by the first two primes (i.e. 2^2 x 3^3), the second approximating the sidereal moon cycle denoted by the 'smoke mirror' of his name ('machnome machney' HTCh f.17v; cf. *Cuevas* p.22); still today, the 108 are commemorated in the region in the 27 quadrilles of Chichimec dances. Indeed, notably refined in its seemingly rude setting, Chicomoztoc arithmetic generally underlies calendrics native to the area. Directly germane to the Mexica Feasts is the model of the lunar-solar equinoxes that define the winter halves or northern 'nights' of the year, and the annals known as Winter Counts that gather and sum years in the lifetime hoops of 70, of the kind seen around Chicomoztoc's Seven Cave mouths (**Fig.1.4**).

From this land claimed as ancestral, the Mexica are guided on their long trek southeast by the hummingbird Huitzilopochtli, the feathered migrant from the south (-opochtli) and first of the Quecholli, who knows the way well and who can recall the prior Xiuhmolpilli of the Chichimec drive in that direction. The trek slows as the Mexica enter Mesoamerica and comes to a significant pause just north of the Basin at Tula (Hidalgo), and nearby Coatepec, the 'snake hill' re-cast at Tenochtitlan as the Great Pyramid. The last Toltec stronghold in the central highlands, Tula had been sacked in 1 Flint 1064; the 'mortandad' at this date is duly detected in the *Cuevas* Xiuhmolpilli wheel (p.30) by Duran, at 8x52 in the Chichimec Era (1995, 2:226). Coatepec is the site of the first Mexica kindling of New Fire, in 2 Reed 1195, and hence of systemic involvement with Mesoamerican calendrics proper. The place of bulrushes, Tula in its normally arid landscape is dreamt and depicted as the island of the fish-keepers in Boturini (p.7) and *Cuevas* (p.2), surrounded by diverted river water that supports lush vegetation (**Fig.1.5**).

As overseers, Tenoch and his adviser Calpan heed local Mesoamerican calendrical usage in scheduling the moment to kindle New Fire at Coatepec and the work of transformation at Tula. The years prior to New Fire (2 House 1169 to 2 Reed 1195) are carried by Series III bearers (House, Rabbit, Reed, Flint; the

first two are ratified in Tochtli Calpan's name glyph) and are placed in standard Mexica year-marker boxes; in Boturini (p.6) they ascend along boustrophedon rows. In the ensuing score of years that leads to the departure from Tula in 9 Reed 1215, the years run down and up boustrophedon columns, as they do in principle for the rest of the text. The switch to vertical alignment begins just prior to New Fire in 1 Rabbit 1194, and of itself it might suggest the concern with the lengths and heights of the year as such, which is also legible in markings on Coatepec's snake (that annually sloughs its skin) and in Tula's bulrushes (that annually renew their fivefold clumps).

At their first New Fire, at Coatepec in 2 Reed 1195, the Mexica saw or foresaw this epochal moment extend over three nights, a detail shown in the annals (Azcatitlan; Mexicanus) which some have dismissed as 'mythical' but which has precise calendrical meaning. For three nights is how much their New Fire ceremony had advanced in the year by the time it was first kindled in their own space at the pyramid named Coatepec in Tenochtitlan, in 2 Reed 1403, after the migration, four Xiuhmolpilli and three lifetimes later: the reason is that the exact moment of these kindlings was determined not by the sun but by the stars, that is, not by the solar year but by its slightly longer sidereal counterpart.

In *Cuevas*, the scheduling of New Fire above in the stars is read socially, since it governs work below, the *coatequitl* of snake-hill Coatepec, through the bands imprinted on the toponymic snake's annually sloughed skin. From head to tail these ophidian bands diminish in width from the initial 11 of the stars to the complementary 7 that make up the 18 of the Feasts, and conclude in the 9.3 which in nights complete the sidereal moon's 27.3 (**Fig.1.5**). As in the year calendar that is the norm in classic Mesoamerican texts (Olmec, Maya, Toltec), the 18 thus governed from above demand to be read not as seasonal Feasts but as mere 20-day work periods, that mesh mechanically with the 365-day metric year and the Tonalpoualli alike. Indifferent to seasonal adjustment as the classic inscriptions show, this metric year served upper class interest, in its craving for stellar ancestry above and need for unrelenting control of work periods below.

The latter concept is visible in *Cuevas*, in the work that was needed to transform the landscape at Tula: artificially diverted, the shell-tipped irrigating streams are forced to conform to the workhand's 10 digits, rather than flow as the natural nine of Water (Sign IX) and the equinoctial span of nine Feasts. At this point in the story, Mexicanus (p.16), Azcatitlan and other accounts invoke the Jade-*pantli* formula of Chalco, whereby the metric year, being shorter than the solar year, wins 20 days from the seasons every 80 years, effectively making 10 Feasts out of nine (HTCh ff.39–40). As such, Boturini attaches the Jade to fields of Chalco in 5 Flint 1276, 80 years after the first New Fire and as many before the third and the end of the text (6 Reed 1355). Impressed by its debt to classical norms at this stage, many scholars have wished to restrict the cycle of the Mexica Feasts to the metric year, denying that it ever allowed for seasonal or leap- year adjustment.

As water and hill, Tula Coatepec represents the Altepetl, the archetypal settlement in Nahuatl. Yet on inspection in *Cuevas*, it is more like a floating island, lacking roots, whirled by the night sky and the metric time of theory and work. It proved all too dependent on an artificial water supply that could be cut off at any moment (Calpan's warning on this very point visibly shocks Tenoch), and geopolitically it was not yet the place for the Mexica to be 'señor de las cuatro partes del mundo' (Tovar f.6b). So Huitzilopochtli goads them on, to fulfill their destiny and land firmly on their true island in the Basin. He does this in his solar role, one who, (re)born at the solstice, brings the stars down: this feat is celebrated in his Hymn (**Appendix C**), and it was reinforced in the night vigils of the midwinter Feast Atemoztli, where the child (*niño*) emerges from the sky as the Pleiades sink westwards into the earth (Durán 1996, 2:285). In calendrical terms, Huitzilopochtli's insistence that the Mexica move on from Tula Coatepec may be read as conducive to their recovering the solar year as a defining factor of the Mesoamerican Feast cycle.

To reach the rim of the Basin, the Mexica go upstream opposing Tula's north-flowing rivers (shown as such in Azcatitlan), and crossing the watershed to the lake of the skull rack Tzonpanco, today Zumpango; and then eventually on to Chapultepec, grasshopper hill on the western shore of lake Texcoco, on the boundary between Tepanec Azcapotzalco and Colhua Colhuacan. To defend themselves from foes to either hand at Chapultepec, they construct stone platforms and guard them night and day (Durán 1996, 1:78–79), preparing for their third New Fire in 2 Reed 1351. In Boturini (p.19), they defend themselves for 19 years, from 9 Flint to 1 Rabbit (1332–50), while in *Cuevas* (p.3), the platforms are featured as 19 pairs of even black and white horizontal bands. Jointly and in calendrical terms, these statements revert to the equinoxes (equal night and day) while invoking the 19-year lunar-solar metonic cycle. In practice the kindling of 1351 leads to the Mexica being expelled from Chapultepec, the capture and death of their captain Huitzilihuitl, and the final short leg of the pilgrimage, northeast to Tenochtitlan. Intrepid defender of his people at Chapultepec and the first to be accorded the honour of sitting on a throne, 'hummingbird feather' Huitzilihuitl is however secondary to Huitzilopochtli: among the Quecholli he is in fact the second grey Hummingbird, who lacks the iridescence and precision of the first. The three feathers or Feasts of his name glyph, less than a crown, suggest only a rough and ruffled match with the moons of his watch on grasshopper hill.

Climax and culmination of the whole quest, the stone cactus (*te-noch-*) of Tenochtitlan is revealed (as every Mexican knows) by the Eagle perched upon it, the magnificent predator who stretches his wings under the sun and nods to greet the Mexica arrivals (**Pl.1**). Tenoch and Calpan reappear (the latter with his name glyph reconfigured fully to incorporate Rabbit), in order to confirm that the fourth and last leg of the journey is over. Recorded in foot and toe prints (5x5), the onward movement ends as that of moisture rising through the hard stone to feed the green cactus root, a numerical indication of leap-year flexibility. This stone cactus stands as the pillar and support that locates Tenochtitlan in its own right, in its own space south of Tlatelolco guarded by stone cactus boundary markers, and constituted by its own four quarters, of which the perching Eagle favours the southeastern 'stone support' Teipan, the dynastic house of Acamapichtli and the barrio of Mexico City christened San Pablo (Mexicanus pp.9,16c,d; see Chapter 8).

At the founding of Tenochtitlan, the Eagle's preferred diet is said to be the upper set of the Quecholli, Macaw, Quetzal and Parrot (11, 12, 13; cf. **Table 3c**); their brilliant feathers fly in a flurry as he feeds, only to be fashioned into the multicolour featherwork shield that anticipates Mendoza in mapping the solar core and quarters of Tenochtitlan's future empire, and the lunar arithmetic of its dependent tribute districts (*Cuevas* p.4; **Pl. 1**). Perched on the cactus the Eagle is actually about to devour the green Parrot, in a *tlacuilolli* figure which confirms the tail and wing feathers of each as its Quecholli Number, 5 and 13. As *ihuitl* hinging on the Spring equinox, the feathers of the Parrot (*toznene*) amount to the Feasts of penance (*tozoa*) that earned the Mexica their far-reaching right to tribute and schedule it to culminate at the spring equinox (see Chapter 3 below). Epiphanous, the Quecholli pair augurs nothing less than the year of Mexica Feasts (i.e. 5+13 = 18).

The body of the empire gestated through the nine 'night-cloaked' emperors who from Acamapichtli to Moctezuma II increased its size and power. As the *tlacuilolli* accounts show, recovering Chapultepec, and taking Tlatelolco, Tzonpanco and Chalco confirmed the Mexica as owners of island and Basin, while subjecting Coixtlahuaca opened for them the Mesoamerican tribute highway between west and east. When Cortés interrupted in 1 Reed 1519, colour drains from the year (Mendoza) and the queen mothers are ferried away (Azcatitlan); yet the blood line runs on through the plunging Eagle Cuauhtemoc (Mexicanus p.18) and recollection of the Feast of iridescent feathers outshines the ugliest Toxcatl massacre (*Cuevas* p.18; **Pl. 4**).

The augury of empire was powered ideologically by the Hummingbird Huitzilopochtli honoured in the Twenty Hymns (**Appendix C**), who all sources agree is distinctively Mexica. He leads the cast of gods in Tepepulco, and in *Cuevas*, where he poses at the moment of transition, the journey behind him and plenty awaiting his beak ahead. The ladder of his ascent so far serves now as a horizontal support, a pair of small and large flags (*pantli*) aligned with its rungs to indicate the shift from decimal to vigesimal. The feathers that adorn him lavishly conjure memory and logic: the seven that crown the back of his head recall its and Chicomoztoc's seven orifices; the 17 on his body affirm the wisdom of his teeth. Of the Thirteen Quecholli, 7 is the metamorphic heart of it all, the butterfly whose equal wings extend numerically to either tip (1 and 13, Hummingbird and Parrot); at the swirling dance of Toxcatl, 7 counts the Feasts from F1.9 to F2.6 (see **Pl. 4** and p.50 below). The next prime after the Quecholli 13, 17 numbers the blooms they feed on at midsummer (Borbonicus; see p.45 below), seen streaming down multicoloured in murals at Teotihuacan and in the Xochitlauhtli ipilcayan at Cholula (HTCh f.7v). In the year, the 17 feather Feasts (also the factor in the *Popol vuh*'s other great penance of '340' days) are supplemented in *Cuevas* by just the 5 x 5 days footprinted on Tenochtitlan's stone cactus at the foundation (p.4) and produced numerically here (p.18) by Huitzilopochtli's diagonal sceptre: a Snake (Sign V) with 5 year rattles (hence 17 x 20 + 5 x 5 = 365; see pp.95–6 below).

The solar nature of Huitzilopochtli's year is overwhelmingly affirmed in the twin temples he and Tlaloc share to south and north atop the city's main pyramid, each heralding its solstice (Tepepulco I,vii f.269; *Cuevas* p.20). Huitzilopochtli goes on to calculate trade beyond the tropics on Tzonpanco's skull-rack abacus, and the push east that returned blood up the stairway to the sky (*Cuevas* pp.20–21). Further, thrusting as arriviste Mexica into the Mesoamerican value and calendar system exactly as in Borbonicus, he comes to compare with the great Toltec-Chichimec Heroes Tezcatlipoca and Quetzalcoatl, who as allies and antagonists between them govern the rites of penance, funeral, and gladiatorial combat (*Cuevas* pp. 22–27). Completing Huitzilopochtli's 11-page team in *Cuevas*, he, Tezcatlipoca and Quetzalcoatl are then matched in gender by mother and maid (mistresses of the Feasts in Laud) as they are in space by Camaxtli, also Chichimec but now hostile over the border in Tlaxcala (pp. 28–29).

As *tlacuilolli* statements, the Eagle-Parrot augury for Tenochtitlan and the Hummingbird Huitzilopochtli's realisation of it deserve meditation far more prolonged than is possible here. Graphically, they foresee access to the glittering wealth of the east (Parrot's tropical lowlands) that Moctezuma gained upon taking Coixtlahuaca, the height the Mexica attained as Eagle knights, despite their lowly origins, and their transformation into masters of city, empire and emporium. Numerically, they offer nothing less than the key to the philosophy that framed Tenochtitlan's imperial economy and the *tlacuilolli* expression of it. Bold as it may appear, this notion is meticulously confirmed in the three tabular pages that sum up *Cuevas*, in the Xiuhmolpilli Wheel and the Feasts (pp.30–32). As Durán was able to learn, the Wheel (p.30) in *Cuevas* invokes Quecholli numbers to date the rise of the Mexica, to calculate its economics, and to augur its fate (see **Table 3c**). The matching Feasts cycle in *Cuevas* (pp.31–32) starts at midsummer (F1.5.10, 24 June) like that in Borgia and 'Genesis' and similarly depicts ancient and high rites in the sky; it ends in Etzalcualiztli (F1.4), the deadline for agricultural tribute below and the time when peasants honoured their tools, and their patron Tlaloc, Huitzilopochtli's companion atop Tenochtitlan's pyramid.

The tale the Mexica told of themselves and their origins increasingly promotes a 'feathered' reading of the Feasts, peculiar to them, which highlights the winged Quecholli. The hummingbird Huitzilopochtli (1) is seconded by captain Huitzilihuitl (2); the Eagle (5) reveals the site of Tenochtitlan gripping the fine-feathered Parrot (13); and, namesake of the captain, the second emperor is identified by Huitzilopochtli's iridescent feather (1). The multilayered diadem of this Huitzilihuitl's name glyph (approved by his *tlacuilo* wife?) rises arithmetically from a base of 18 feathers, as he presides over the first imperial New Fire in 2 Reed 1403, at the pyramid Coatepec (Azcatitlan pp.28–29).

The convention of 13 numbered Quecholli fliers certainly did not originate with the Mexica, and already in Olmec thought their feathers sprout from the primordial snake-caiman, as we have seen. Yet in imagining and imaging their year through them, the Mexica interfused feather and Feast, *ihuitl* and *ilhuitl*. Indeed, the guises and behaviours characteristic of the Thirteen Quecholli greatly enlivened the very geography and arithmetic of Tenochtitlan's tribute system, just as they choreographed brilliant dance and song at court where, arrayed with feathers, nobles represented the Feasts cycle in all its complexity (**Pl. 4**).

Like any foundational fiction, the Mexica version of their origins may be (and by some has been) doubted as material history. Yet it has the virtue of respecting the principle (rarely regarded in western historiography) of representing events in calendrical terms proper to the time-space and the imaginary in which they occur. As a result, it has much to teach about the particularity of the feather crown sought by the Mexica in the larger story of the Mesoamerican calendar.

Xiuhcoanaual: the protean year with a caiman head

The philosophy and distinctive features of the Mexica Feasts owe much, as we have just seen, to notions of flight and transformation articulated in the Quecholli and the *ihuitl* feather, most pertinent to the long migration from beyond Mesoamerica's northwestern frontier. As they appear in Mexica texts, the Feasts embody a complementary philosophy no less significant, synonymous in Nahuatl with the protean Xiuhcoanaual. In *tlacuilolli*, this creature-concept resides in the very terrestrial vertebrate bodies of the Caiman and the Snake, I and V of the Twenty Signs that came to define Mesoamerica: the pair is celebrated in the earliest known iconography of the tropics (including Amazonia) millennia before any origin claimed by the Mexica. At Round 30 of the Era (about 1600 BCE), the Tepexic Annals (p.10 [43]) show the arrival of a warrior whose head and back are protected by a Xiuhcoanaual exactly of the kind seen in stelae in eastern Maya cities, in Nicaragua, and yet further east towards the Amazon watershed. Two millennia later, on lintels 24–26 at Yaxchilan dated to 725 AD, Xiuhcoanaual again shields a warrior, as a Vision Serpent conjured in the night by penance and bloodletting (Miller and Martin 2004: 106–7). At the start of 'Genesis', it endorses the prime mover of things, at the height of midsummer (pp.45–6 below).

In the *tlacuilolli* corpus generally as in 'Genesis', the year of 18 Feasts is introduced by and actually embodied in this life-form, notably in four key Mexica texts: the Sunstone, the screenfold Borbonicus, the compendium Tepepulco, and Mexicanus. In each of them, the Xiuhcoanaual defines a pair of figures that makes a calendrical statement about the year, initiating a dialectic. Examining them reveals a strong internal logic which then may be cross referenced between all four, which helps decode this polysemic concept.

As a compendium, Tepepulco (I, iii) also provides an alphabetic transcription into Nahuatl of the *tlacuilolli* Xiuh-coanaual. This is how we can be sure of the three verbal components of the term in that language. The meanings of the first component Xiuh-itl are comet, turquoise, grass, and (not least) year, to which we should add the identification of

Xiuhtecutli, first of the Night Lords (-tecutli), with kindling of fire and life. The second component coa-tl is if anything yet more polysemic, meaning the life form which in *tlacuilolli* may represent primordial flow in the elongated body, the snake that annually sloughs its skin, the penis within foreskin; anatomically, coa-tl's spine typifies the vertebrate which acquired the head, forearms and legs of the caiman that may sprout *ihuitl* feathers as in the Olmec inscriptions, and the word comes to denote twin, cooperation, community, social counterpart (a notion alive today in the Mexican term *cuate*, friend or mate). The protean acquisition of saurian characteristics and even feathers is indicated in the final component of the name, naual or nahual, the animal self in which the human resides and it intimates corresponding orders of transformation and metempsychosis.

In the choreographies of the Feasts recorded in Borbonicus (pp.23–40) and in Tepepulco (Part I), Xiuhcoanaual is seen as a creature and artefact worn by the participants, especially the Year Lord Xiuhtecutli (see Chapters 5 and 6). On the Sunstone, Xiuhcoanauals literally embrace the whole text as guises for Xiuhtecutli and his companion (see Chapter 7); and the most powerful Xiuhcoanauals known in *tlacuilolli* are seen in the Coixtlahuaca Map that served as the model for this circular stone inscription. At the other extreme, Xiuhcoanaual scarcely survives, boxed in and much diminished, in the Mexicanus table that deals with the beginnings of Lent on Septuagesima Sunday and Ash Wednesday. Where explicit, the Feasts which particularly attach to Xiuhcoanaual vary according to function, Tititl (F2.6) being to agriculture what Izcalli (F2.7) is to year naming and correlation with other calendrical cycles. Paired in each text, these *tlacuilolli* representations of Xiuhcoanaual demand to be read with the closest attention to such factors as relative size, position and shape, colour, countable units on the body, and concepts significant in the history of the Mesoamerican calendar.

In the Borbonicus chapter (our richest source), Xiuhcoanaual appears in Izcalli (F2.7; p.23). At the left-hand margin of the page, it is in fact the very first image to be seen (**Fig.1.6a**). It is the back shield in the array ('mochichiuaya') of Xiuhtecutli the Year Lord, a human figure who stands facing right (the screenfold reads from left to right). At the end, in a

repetition of Izcalli (p.37), Xiuhcoanaual reappears as the very last image in the Feasts sequence, being still the back shield of Xiuhtecutli, who now faces left, having Ciuacoatl as his partner on both occasions. Hence, Xiuhcoanaual effectively encloses and marks the terms of the Feast sequence at start and end. Visually, this back shield comprises a caiman whose upper jaw curls right back, a snake body with six saurian scales but no legs, and a pointed tail which bears a round knot and tie. A red artery flows down to the tail and up to the last bend in the elongated upper jaw. One of the meanings of Izcalli is the 'stretching' that fosters vertebrate growth.

Of the two Xiuhcoanauals worn by Xiuhtecutli in the Borbonicus account of the Feast Izcalli, the second is shown to be smaller. The three scales on the upper body crumple and the pointed red tail at the end of the lower three is lost. The Spanish glosses link this attrition to the impending entry of the Spaniards into the city, which was once shown on these very pages during the Xiuhmolpilli begun by Moctezuma in Panquetzaliztli 2 Reed 1507. As 'dios de los agüeros', Ciuacoatl tells how 'habían de venir los españoles a ellos y los habían de sujetar', and as 'dios de los mayzes [maizes, just possibly meses, i.e. Feasts] o hechiceros' Xiuhtecutli confirms this prediction, as if with the authority of his protean mantle Xiuhcoanaual. For Moctezuma, this doom was legible in a comet (xiuh-) and the attendant annual phenomenon of meteors, which might suggest a further reading for this Xiuhcoanaual's six-scaled brownish body and knotted tail (a comet is typically visible as body with head and tail, 'an almost straight spine with knots in it, consisting of gas driven out at high speed by the solar wind; and up to six brownish curves...; and time-striations across all of them'; Ottewell 2001: 42). At all events, it is hard not to connect the second diminished Xiuhcoanaual in this Feasts chapter with the native account of 'Encounter with Europe' (pp.8–10 above). Textually, this entails acknowledging the position and semantics of Xiuhcoanaual on the page, in order to insert current politics into the greater time of both moving bodies in the sky and vertebrate species on earth.

In the Borbonicus screenfold, the Xiuhcoanauals of the Feasts (pp.23–) have antecedents in the previous chapter (pp.21–22), which features the paired figures of Oxomoco/Cipactonal and Quetzalcoatl/Tezcatlipoca. In the

a   b   c

Figure 1.6 Xiuhcoanaual as backshield or hood: **a)** for Xiuhtecutli. Borbonicus p.23; **b)** for Huitzilopochtli. Tepepulco f.261; **c)** for Ixcozauhqui (who holds up a black and gold *tlachialoni*). Tepepulco f.262

story of genesis and invention, these pairs intervene at critical transitions, in what might be thought of as deepening time levels or strata. Connecting them vertically as it were, proto-forms of Xiuhcoanaual characterize the second figure in each pair.

Complementing each other across facing pages in Borbonicus, Oxomoco and Cipactonal, Quetzalcoatl and Tezcatlipoca, are framed by consecutive halves of a Series III Xiuhmolpilli that begin in 1 Rabbit (VIII) and 1 Flint (XVIII). Of paper, Cipactonal's back shield snakes down to record the enigmatic number sequence which is repeated on the Sunstone Xiuhcoanaual (7.9.9.6.5), beneath (though not attached to) the name glyph Cipactonal, the caiman head that is the first of the Twenty Signs (see p.72 below). In the sequel pair, Xiuhcoanaual guards Tezcatlipoca as a back shield. It has an elongated upper jaw reminiscent of Xonecuilli and is adorned with the set of seven stars likewise seen on its Sunstone counterpart. This confirms the wearer's stellar role as the Great Bear ('porque dicen que la Ursa maior se abaja al agua, porque es Tezcatlipoca y está allá memoria de él'; HMP, Garibay 1996:30). Testifying to the multiple world age layers inherent in the Era, these proto Xiuhcoanauals culminate in the fuller life form that serves as the Year Lord's back shield in the Feast chapter that follows in Borbonicus.

Since the Xiuhcoanauals in the Borbonicus Feast chapter and the one before it embody current politics in nothing less than creation itself, they can hardly be analysed here in any detail. Most immediately relevant to the Mexica Feasts as such is the version of the founder pairs to whom they attach at the Chichimec horizon and whose interventions begin with that horizon and the emergence from Seven Caves Chicomoztoc. At that moment in history (equivalent to 1 Flint 648), the Chichimec calendar base was established – In Yeliz Chichimeca – when: 'The year count (Xiuhtlapoualli), the Tonalpoualli, and the count of the 20-day Feasts (Cecempoualli) were made the responsibility of those known as Oxomoco and Cipactonal' (Cuautitlan Annals f.1).

Other *tlacuilolli* texts confirm the success of the pair in this role, complemented by Quetzalcoatl and Tezcatlipoca. In the Cuauhtinchan Map 2, having been lured by Tezcaltipoca from Seven Caves, the Chichimecs first kindle New Fire, in a long log that is the Xiuhcoanaual's snake body, punctuated by drill holes that emit smoke (**Fig.1.7b**). Further developed by the Mexica in their own way, in the Xiuhcoanauals on the Sunstone (see pp.70–3 below), this trope here marks a common vertical coordinate for the year of the stars and the slightly shorter year of the sun, in smoke that rises directly to the sky, at the start of the tribute year (Tozoztli F1.1.1; Bierhorst 1992:142). Reporting on the role of Tezcatlipoca as the driller of this fire, *Legend of the Suns* likewise mentions Oxomoco and Cipactonal's role in divining the source of maize for the Chichimec (Bierhorst 1992:147). Hence, in the Coatlan Inscription, the pair can be seen doing just that when establishing the year of agriculture and the planting seasons. They do so in a configuration that closely matches that of the corresponding Borbonicus page, and where moreover the 9+9 teeth exposed in Xiuhcoanaual's caiman maw are paired horizontally so as to specify the Feasts of the planting seasons that turn on Tititl (F2.6; see pp.47–8 below).

In the extensive account of the year given in Tepepulco Part I, *tlacuilolli* versions of Xiuhcoanaual appear in two chapters, dedicated to the choreography of the Feasts (I, ii) and the arrays, that is, the dress and adornment, of the participants (I,v). In the former, it serves as a back shield in Izcalli as it does in Borbonicus, only here this Feast is the last in a cycle beginning in Cuahuitl (F2.8), rather than Izcalli (F2.7), and it is worn by Ixcozauhqui. In the explanatory chapter, Xiuhcoanaual is confirmed as belonging to the array of Ixcozauhqui, whose Hymn (*Icuic* no.6) mentions the metamorphic nature of his house ('naualcalli') and his array or disguise, yet it also seen in that of Huitzilopochtli, first in the list of participants. In the Xiuhcoanauals seen Izcalli and in the paired listing of arrays, the caiman head dwarfs the body (**Fig.1.6b,c**).

In the first Xiuhcoanaual in the Tepepulco list of arrays (Huitzilopochtli's), the caiman head is divided at the eye between a turquoise face and a red crown, these being the two colours of the box-frame markers which in the Telleriano annals and elsewhere distinguish year names in the Chichimec and Mexica tradition (turquoise, like year, being xiuh-). In Mendoza, rows of such year frames are identified with the flow of water through the canals of Tenochtitlan, while the red may be generally read as blood or Xiuhtecutli's fire. Compared with the first, the other Xiuhcoanaual head (Ixcozauhqui's), looks more ancient and hangs residually like an academic hood. It has a pale face, colourless eye, missing teeth and a wizened snout, while its black underside suggests bile or ash. The pointed tail in this apparently older Xiuhcoanaual also identifies the year but does so rather by means of the A marker used in classic times, which in this same Feasts cycle is shown in the parapet typical of architecture in Teotihuacan, Cholula and other ancient cities (**Table 3d**; see Chapter 6 below). In short, Huitzilopochtli's Xiuhcoanaual, with its water and fire (these being the colour concepts of energy and war) might then be seen to stand to military vigour as Ixcozauhqui's does to decadence. This model contrast is especially pertinent to beginnings in the Feast cycle and to conventions of year naming: contrasts between current and archaic usage with regard to Izcalli are likewise suggested by the Xiuhcoanaual head beside the Nemotemi in the Boban Wheel (**Pl. 8**), and by the Lent dates in Mexicanus (p.15), and further afield by counterparts in the 'Borgia Group' (Borgia p.39; Fejérváry p.5; Cospi p. 21; Laud p.44).

The turquoise box, used to frame year names in a great range of texts in western Mesoamerica, dominates in annals of the Mexica and, before them, of the Chichimec. Found in classic cities, the triangular marker is adapted in the solar ray A marker typical of later Cholulan texts like Borgia, and spreads to Tepexic, east along the Tehuacan-Papaloapan valley to Coixtlahuaca and Cuicatlan, and south into the Mixteca. A critical difference between texts using one or other of these two markers is that while moments in the year may be dated by Tonalpoualli days in either (though more often in the latter, the triangle), only with the former (the turquoise box) are the Feasts typically used for this purpose. We saw Feasts functioning in this way in 'Encounter with Europe', and they have a textual precedent in Chichimec annals, which highlight Feasts within the year to similar ends. Colhua presence in Cuauhtitlan for 15 Feasts in 1348–49 and their subsequent ejection prefigure what happened with the Spaniards in Tenochtitlan in 1519–20, the root of resistance in this former case being the teachings of Itzpapalotl which 'they always remembered during Quecholli' (Bierhorst 1992:70). Moreover, such Feast dates in the year may

help to make a point as exceptions to seasonal norms: hence, in *Legend of the Suns*, the end of highland Tula in 1 Flint 1064 is heralded in Tecuilhuitl by a freak midsummer snowfall (F1.5–F1.6; Bierhorst 1992:156).

Tracing Mexica understandings of the Feasts back to the Chichimec enriches and much complicates the analysis being attempted here. The corpus of texts that includes the Cuauhtitlan Annals and consistently respects the Chichimec horizon in Mesoamerica, acknowledging the 7th-century calendar base (In Yeliz Chichimeca, 1 Flint 648), also splinters on the question of the Feasts. Nonetheless, it is worth noting that the material source of the turquoise year box lay in the general direction from which the Chichimec and later the Mexica claimed to have emerged (Seven Caves, far to the northwest), and that, after remote occurrences in the area of the western Olmec (Guerrero), this mineral spread through Mesoamerica

much as they did. The turquoise face of the Xiuhcoanaual worn in Tepepulco by the war leader Huitzilopochtli is readily visible as one of many artefacts made by the Mexica of that mineral which allude to the year.

For their part, the Xiuhcoanauals incised on the Sunstone have long bodies that encircle the whole text, caiman heads and nascent forearms. Rather than topping an array, they plunge down each rim to left and right, like the comets which warned Moctezuma of his doom, having similarly impinged on the life of the Mixtec hero Eight Deer half a millennium previously (Nuttall pp.74, 81). Upended, these Xiuhcoanauals serve not only as back shields for figures in human form but enclose and protect all but their faces, in this case, those of the Year Lord Xiuhtecutli (again), to the left, and Tonatiuh to the right. The largest and most magnificent of surviving representations, this pair of Xiuhcoanauals is also the most numerate, counting out the Feast total of 18 on the body scales (9+9, 12+6) as well as on the head and tail (7+11).

Like the Feast chapter in Borbonicus, the Sunstone names years significant in Mexica experience (see Chapter 7). The three years 1 Flint seen at the central face correspond to the migration begun in 1168, the imperial drive begun under Acamapichtli in 1376 (exactly 7+7 Xiuhmolpilli from the Chichimeca calendar base), and the taking of Coixtlahuaca that led to the composition of this text in 1480. In taking this place (the gateway to the east) and making their Sunstone, the Mexica re-positioned the Xiuhcoanauals seen in the Coixtlahuaca Map, where they rise to power in the west as giant saurians that take economic and political control: the upper Xiuhcoanaual rears up on huge hind legs, acquires dorsal feathers, and gets to grip the peak of the northwestern bastion Tepexic (where the Chichimec heraldically inset their Seven Caves). Like that of the Xiuhcoanaual at Chicomoztoc, its caiman maw projects a tongue of flame (**Fig.1.7a, b**). It is from this height that the Xiuhcoanauals on the Mexica Sunstone make their imperial swoop (cf. **Fig. 7.2**).

As the eve of these 1 Flint occasions, the year 13 Reed is held uppermost on the Sunstone, between the pointed Xiuhcoanaual tails. In this position, however, 13 Reed commands far greater time depth, since it simultaneously names (in C1) the year in which the Mesoamerican Era itself begins in Olmec and Maya texts (3113 BCE) and in which its Mexica name, Four Ollin, marked the spring equinox, 22nd March. How this Era Four Ollin embodies yet greater depth is shown at the centre, in the names of the four world ages or Suns that inhere in it, within the ring of the Twenty Signs. As the outer bound of all this metamorphic energy, the Xiuhcoanaual vertebrates on the rim of the Sunstone fuse Snake and Caiman (Sign V and Sign I, end terms in the Series of year-bearer Signs), in a numerate dragon body that proclaims an all-embracing philosophy of the year: see **Appendix A** and **Tables 2,3**.

After announcing such imperial and intellectual might on the Sunstone, the Xiuhcoanaual had shrunk almost beyond recognition by the following 13 Reed, 1583, the year that introduced the Gregorian Calendar Reform into New Spain. The '10 lost days' prescribed by this Reform were most exactly measured in the Mexicanus Codex (pp.1–8), as we have seen above, a text which goes on to reflect (pp.9–15), ever in *tlacuilolli*, on its larger consequences for the three origins and services articulated in *Coloquios*. This philosophical reflection in Mexicanus assesses Christian doctrines of origin, especially those once explicit in Septuagesima and Lent and now eradicated altogether from Roman thought. In the process, the four last of the Julian years that officially ran their course in the Pope's New World, 1579–82, are identified with a figure best legible as a Xiuhcoanaual, albeit no less severely diminished than the understandings of time imposed by the Reform (see Chapter 8 below). In the circumstances in which the authors of

Mexicanus found themselves by the time of the Gregorian Reform, there could hardly be a sharper contrast between their knowledge and intellect, on the one hand, and on the other the opprobrium emblemized in this much reduced Xiuhcoanaual (see p.89 below).

Summary are they are, these descriptions of Xiuhcoanaual as it is featured in Mexica and allied texts are designed to point up the wealth of meaning accumulated in its image and Nahuatl name, all with emphasis on the first syllable that denotes the year of the Feasts. Inseparable from this meaning is an understanding of time that can fuse current politics with the aeons of creation, and measure their spans with extreme precision.

Information about the year cycle of 18 Feasts which the Mexica incorporated into their calendar abounds in texts written in *tlacuilolli*, and these deserve to be treated as the best authority initially available to us. Although they differ in date, genre and other respects, on this subject the *tlacuilolli* accounts cross-reference usefully, highlighting basic paradigms and concepts, like the pairing of Feasts, and the hinge position of the equinoctial Feasts Ochpaniztli and Tlacaxipehualiztli. They offer to contribute authoritatively to the vexed question of correlation with the Julian calendar introduced after Cortés, and in the larger story of the Mexica within Mesoamerica they affirm decisive emphases on the equinoxes and the solar year. In this, they reveal key links between the Feasts, on the one hand, and the Number and Signs sets of the Tonpoualli, on the other. As fifth of the Thirteen Quecholli, the Eagle expertly reveals Tenochtitlan to the Mexica as future capital and regulator of time and the feathered Feasts of their year; and it projects their capture of the 'hotlands' to the east in its seizure of the Parrot, the 13th Quecholli (i.e. 5+13 = 18). For its part, in earthing the Twenty Signs, the Xiuhcoanaual dragon frames the immense contemplation of time and the year that is inscribed on the Sunstone.

Thanks to this initial analysis of primary sources, we may now concentrate more on the kinds of year operative in the Mexica calendar which have been detected and described since first contact with Europe. In this we are guided by the advice given by the Mexica when responding to the Christian threat, both at the very start in the *Coloquios* of 1524 and towards the end of the 16th century in Mexicanus. For the years which the Mexica defined in these texts correspond precisely to those of the priest, farmer and hunter-warrior, being differentiated by function, starting point, celestial correlative, choreography and subgroupings or phrases of the 18. Such a plurality of years need hardly come as a surprise in the Mesoamerican system to which the Mexica calendar belongs, whose complexity is unrivalled anywhere on the planet, certainly by anything to be found in the late medieval Europe that first entered America. With that in mind, we turn to accounts of the Feasts elicited by the Christian inquisition and western scholarship.

2
Missionaries and Scholars

In Mesoamerican time-reckoning (notably in Michoacan), the year of 18 Feasts was long and deeply enough ingrained as a concept to have existed in its own right as a calendrical cycle, independent in principle and in practice of the Tonalpoualli. This fact was fully recognized by those Europeans who first described the calendar used by the Mexica, yet compared to the Tonalpoualli, the year of the Feasts remains very much the poor cousin as far as western scholarship goes. This is so despite the huge scope and power ascribed to the imaginary of the year in a great range of texts, and despite the fact that the Feasts continue to affect the rhythms of life in Mesoamerica today, mediated through the calendar of Christian saints and even in their original form.

A reason why the Feasts have been neglected in scholarship might be found in the daunting variety of names given to them individually over time and by region, and even sometimes within what otherwise appears to be the same system. Furthermore, practices differed with respect to the Series of year-bearer Signs (**Table 3a,b**) and to when, how or even whether extra days were added to the 360 produced by the 18 Feasts, in order to approximate the 365-day year. While in early calendars, time-periods were named terminally, they were later named initially, and so on. These variations are reflected in the different *tlacuilolli* year markers (**Table 3d**) and in context may be readily understood to result from differences in climate, economic priority, and political administration, within the larger Mesoamerican frame.

Western curiosity about the Mexica Feasts began in the 16th century with the invasion itself, in Christian attempts to interpret or subvert their pagan meaning, and in the viceregal law courts that acted for the Crown in accepting evidence in native script. The third arm of colonial power, the conquistador-encomendero faction, remained less intrigued, although Cortés's devotee and biographer López de Gómara set the friars' findings into what became (thanks in turn to Montaigne) an encyclopedic frame. Since that time, western scholars have striven to understand the Feasts, their nature and functions, the first concerted efforts in that direction having been made by Christian missionaries. Helpful in the absence of other testimony, these early reports were nonetheless hampered from the start by their authors' professional need to extirpate the very knowledge they gathered, by alerting fellow missionaries to tell-tale remnants of pagan practice. They also suffer from the deficiencies, practical and theoretical, of the Julian calendar that was imported and imposed on Mexico after Cortés. Historiographically, this is a problem that has not always been overcome even today.

Orders from Rome, origins at home
The clearer Christian insights into the Feasts tend to be collective and cross-reference intelligibly between missionary friars and the Orders to which they belonged: the Franciscans who arrived as The Twelve in 1524, the Dominicans in 1526, the Augustinians in 1533, and the Jesuits in 1 Reed 1571. In the 'second coming' 52 years after Cortés, these last came to help the Inquisition with its enquiries (see Chapter 7). The findings of each Order help affirm the TTTM correlation, though far from disinterestedly, or consistently, and for the most part quite indirectly, through fragmentary comments on the kinds of year taken as premises in the *Coloquios* (which were recorded by Sahagún). The Augustinian Alonso de la Veracruz, depicted in Aubin (f.59v) with his college in San Pablo Teipan, took as a paradigm (as José Rabasa has noted) the imperial Mexica system that is expounded in Mexicanus (where the college is cited; p.9); readily demonstrated are the characterizations of the year common to the Franciscans Motolinia and Olmos (two of The Twelve) and Sahagún, the Dominicans Diego Durán and Pedro de los Rios, and the Jesuit Tovar.

Entering Tenochtitlan five years after Cortés, The Twelve, soon reinforced and joined by the Dominicans, began Rome's 'spiritual conquest', that is, the campaign of inquisition and extirpation: annals that record this campaign in *tlacuilolli* are seen in Telleriano and Rios (in the continuation of 'Encounter with Europe'), Aubin, and Mexicanus. The first archbishop Zumárraga burns books from the ruined temple and the Sunstone is buried at the corner of what would be the cathedral next to it. Forays are soon made to Cholula, the Mesoamerican Rome, which was continuing to draw pilgrims from far to the east; and, hot on the heels of the troops (the last *tlacuilolli* image in Durán history), to the still active Tlacatecpan temple at Tepoztlan where the idol Ome Tochtli, centrepiece of the Feast inscriptions, is hurled from the cliff (though refuses to shatter). The spectacular bonfire at Texcoco witnessed by Sahagún (fresh from Spain) ends the life of books and their owner Don Carlos Ome Tochtli, prompting the dynastic claim framed by the Feasts in the Wheel of 7 Rabbit (1538) (**Pl. 8**). Having asked local elders to comment on the Tepepulco manuscript, Sahagún made further enquiries at Tlatelolco, beside the very pyramid which the siege had closed in on, and whose inscriptions correlate the Twenty Signs and Year Bearers in just the plan seen on the Izcalli page of the Borgia Feast chapter (p.40). All this led to the much-cited friars' reports on the Feasts, not least the monumental 12 volumes of Sahagún's *Historia general*, which re-configure (and traduce) their *tlacuilolli* sources.

Guided by the *Coloquios*, which The Twelve participated in and which Sahagún recorded, the friars enquired into the three origins and cults framed in that text (**Appendix E**). Reflected in the very architecture of Palenque and other classic cities no less than in the Mexica model of migration (INW 197–200), these origin cults focused on the vigil of ancient night, Tlaloc's crops, and the imperial acquisitions of the hunter-warrior.

Table 3 The 52-year Xiuhmolpilli

a. The five Series of four year-bearer Signs

I	VI	XI	XVI
II	VII	XII	XVII
III	VIII	XIII	XVIII
IV	IX	XIV	XIX
V	X	XV	XX

b. The 52 Series III Year Bearers

1 III	2 VIII	3 XIII	4 XVIII	5 III	6 VIII	7 XIII	8 XVIII	9 III	10 VIII	11 XIII	12 XVIII	13 III
1 VIII	2 XIII	3 XVIII	4 III	5 VIII	6 XIII	7 XVIII	8 III	9 VIII	10 XIII	11 XVIII	12 III	13 VIII
1 XIII	2 XVIII	3 III	4 VIII	5 XIII	6 XVIII	7 III	8 VIII	9 XIII	10 XVIII	11 III	12 VIII	13 XIII
1 XVIII	2 III	3 VIII	4 XIII	5 XVIII	6 III	7 VIII	8 XIII	9 XVIII	10 III	11 VIII	12 XIII	13 XVIII

c. Series III with Quecholli co-efficients, Cuevas... Wheel, p. 30

As the cumulative count of the Quecholli numbers (i.e. up to and including 13), the norm in each of the four rows equals the days in the quarter year (91). In row 1 VIII (Rabbit), the tropical set Macaw, Quetzal, and Parrot is replaced by Eagle, Owl and Butterfly (5, 6, 7), the difference being equal to the Feasts in the year (18).

Sign	Co-efficient													Absent					replaced by 2nd		3rd	new	
XIII	**1**	5	9	12	4	7	13	3	6	11	2	6	10		8				6				=91 less 2
XVIII	2	7	10	**1**	5	7	14	3	7	11	2	6	10	4	8	9	12	13	2	10	7	14	=91 less 6
III	3	7	10	2	7	10	**1**	5	14	8	4	9	7	6		11	12	13	10		7	14	=91 less 4
VIII	4	5	9	3	6	7	2	8	6	**1**	5	7	10			11	12	13	5	6	7		=91 less 18

d. Year markers

a   b   c   d   e

a) Monte Alban;   b) Tepepulco Ms, Metlatoyuca Lienzo;
c) Fejérváry, Tepechpan Annals;   d) Tepetlaoztoc;
e) Tochpan, Tlapa, and norm for Otomi, Chichimec, Mexica;
f) Baranda Roll, Tulancingo Lienzo;   g) Xochicalco;
h) Borgia, Tepexic, Cuicatlan, Oaxaca, and norm for Mixtec;
i) Chiepetlan Lienzo

f   g   h   i

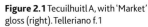

Figure 2.1 Tecuilhuitl A, with 'Market' gloss (right). Telleriano f.1

In the night vigil, the friars detected practices that they themselves prized: penance, fasting, burning incense, chastity, along with the blood-letting that was the tenet of their medicine; they accepted that the Mexica discipline was more stringent than theirs but only to realize, yet again, how cunning the devil could be. Piecing together the details they give reveals much of the all-encompassing 'whole service' of the night hours that tops the list in *Coloquios*, and of the key role played in it by the Feasts or fasts, in determining when to offer copal incense to the stars and to let blood (*tozoa*) (**Appendix E**).

One of The Twelve, Motolinia (I, ix) was assured of Moctezuma's deep faith in this service, and he learned much of its detail when destroying Cholula – the ancient precedents to the east (blood drops on the pages of the open book, propitious to revealing the Xiuhcoanaual at Yaxchilan; Miller and Martin 2004: 106–8), the extreme rigour, and the schedule that synchronized heartbeats with the coursing of the stars above. Collating what Motolinia has to say with what fellow Franciscan Sahagún learned in Tepepulco makes clear how this first service arithmetically correlated the coursings of blood and stars, through four-thorn maguey spines ('cañas', 'varas') that punctured the novice's veins at midnight during each Feast over four years. Motolinia reports that after these four years, each of 18 midnights, the novice proved his endurance by showing 17,280 blood-soaked thorns ('montabanse si no me engaño a diez y siete mil y doscientas ochenta'; 2001: 106). The Nahuatl commentary made for Sahagún in Tepepulco establishes how four-directional offerings of incense divided the tropical night into six periods or watches of about two hours and that the constellations decided how and when these maguey thorns were to be applied ('uitztli mocui'), at a stellar 'midnight' ('ticatla') that could fall discernibly later than the midnight that is midway between the sun's dusk and dawn (Nepantla. **Appendix B**). Exact, these details enable us to reconstruct and begin to interpret the 'whole service', when careful note is first taken of the corresponding *tlacuilolli* texts (the Tepepulco Ms, *Cuevas*, Mendoza, the Sunstone, and 'Genesis' – pondered and annotated like Telleriano by Friar Rios and the Dominicans. **Fig. 2.1**). In affirming the 18 Feasts as the prime Mexica measure of the year and time in every sense, this comparison highlights the complementarity of the solar and the sidereal year; and within the latter, of the zodiac and the circumpolar septentrion Xonecuilli; and within the zodiac, the 'rivals' Pleiades and Market (Miec, Tianquiz) that mark the intersections with the Milky Way. The night activities reported in Mendoza (f.63) confirm the four-directional offerings of incense, and likewise attach to the zodiac (the east-west flow of Citlaltonac's 11+11 stars) and the Milky Way (the sky's fringe or skirt of Citlalicue's, 8+9 stars.).

This first service is nobly performed for the lifelords (Teteu ipalnemoa), for whom the penitents cried out heart and belly, asking 'for light and life for their vassals and their domain' (*Popol vuh*. Tedlock 1996:192). The nocturnal training it involved, like the galactic umbilicus reported probably by Olmos in *Histoire du Mechique* (Tena 2002:146), makes the outermost innermost and vice versa, and presupposes awareness of the year as protean Xiuhcoanaual. Its utmost beginnings are to be found in the galactic hub, Ilamatecutli's Market shown overhead at midsummer in Tecuilhuitl (F1.5), the first Feast in Borgia (p.29), *Cuevas* (p.31), the temple at Tepoztlan, and 'Genesis'

(f.1), where Xiuhcoanaual caps the first cause. The penitent's role model is the pair Tezcatlipoca and Quetzalcoatl, the epic heroes who plunge into the mouth and belly of the earth in order to attain Citlaltonac and Citlalicue's constellations and bring this world and Era into being. They do this opposing each other at the equinoxes, Tezcatlipoca in Teotleco (F2.1.1), and Quetzalcoatl in Tozoztli (F1.1.1), on the first day of the year ('le premier jour de l'an'), in a time scale that extends to multiples of '102,000 ans' (Garibay 1995:105; Tena 2002: 146). Supervised by Citlaltonac and Citlalicue, this initial day of Tozoztli, right after the flood, is the first specified in *Legend of the Suns* (Bierhorst 1992:143) (**Table 4**); in 'Genesis', Quetzalcoatl's blood-letting culminates at the Spring equinox in Tlacaxipehualiztli (F2.9.20), and prepares for the start of the current Era. A hand inserted to help Rios read Telleriano when in Rome literally assigns Quetzalcoatl's blood-letting to the Tonalpoualli day-name Nine Wind (9 II), which most widely celebrates this lordly patron in Mesoamerica, tellingly in the first of the three temples of origin at Palenque (David Kelley indicated this to me). In short, then, the friars' enquiries into the first service revealed the Feasts as definitive not just in rites similar to theirs but in measurements of the year superior to their astronomy and in world-age cosmogony corrosive of their Genesis.

When it comes to the second origin and service in *Coloquios*, Tlaloc's, the European friars adapted as they could to the tropical year of the Mexica and Mesoamerica. As with the night watch, they supplied much valuable detail, ever suspecting the work of the devil in what they understood only dimly, if at all. Making explicit their belief in Tlaloc, the advisers to Sahagún in Tepepulco spelt out (in *tlacuilolli* and Nahuatl) the annual planting seasons, with their pattern of irrigation and monsoon (water and rain, Signs IX and XIX), the seeds won from the star-clustered Market of Ilamatecutli and distributed by Ciuacoatl in Tititl (F2.6), the winds that set in with the year in Tozoztli (F1.1.1) having shaped Tlaloc's crown over millennia, and the pride in fieldwork, roundly condemned in the biblical Cain, yet exulted in here, in the 'good food' of maize and beans in Etzalcualiztli (F1.4) that was supplied as tribute to Tenochtitlan. For his part, as a great Nahuatlato who lived close to the land himself, Durán was alerted to the solar drive common to hummingbird migration and rising sap; he described tamales by season and the altars on which tools were revered and the maize and bean feasts were prepared in peasant homes in Etzalcualiztli (F1.4), as the summer solstice approached. He noted too how the aqueducts were cleaned out under Toci's aegis when all planting had ended at the fall equinox in Ochpaniztli (F1.9: 'por este tiempo limpiaban las acequias y los rios y las fuentes'. 1995, 2:275). At the end of the six non-planting Feasts, like Sahagún (Flo II, 26) he appealed to the *tlacuilolli* image of Atemoztli (F2.5) to establish its mid-moment as both the solstitial rebirth of the sun and the vigil focused on the Pleiades as they set ever later into the waiting earth. Yet also like Sahagún, he despised these beliefs and called them low ('baxo'); he even scorned Etzalcualiztli's literal Feast as 'torpe y sucia comida' (1995, 2:262; cf. Flo VIII, prologue).

In his turn, fellow Dominican Rios, through the Italian commentary on 'Genesis', was able to confirm that the epic of agriculture had emerged from the innocent sloth of naked gatherers, was set in motion by Tezcatlipoca in Teotleco (F2.1.1), lasted 12,800 years, and culminated in the current 5,200-year

Era and the maize agriculture instituted by Quetzalcoatl in Tlacaxipehualiztli (F2.9.20). In this text (duly correlated with *Legend of the Suns*, HM, and HMP), the food plants – aquatic, arboreal, cereal – that precede maize reflect the metamorphoses and diets of the vertebrates who precede humans able gracefully to clothe themselves in cotton, and invoke the yet deeper time of the world ages named at the heart of the Sunstone (**Appendix A**). Running from equinox to equinox, the food epic in 'Genesis' and the world-age experience accumulated in it appeal to the Great Year as the unit of measure, the epic being one half as the Era is one fifth, thereby articulating time in spans heretically in excess of Biblical teaching.

Introducing the third origin and service in *Coloquios*, the Mexica priests place its when and where in the Mesoamerican Era. More or less sarcastically, they ask their Christian counterparts what they know about empire, power and glory in Cemanahuac (that is, Mesoamerica or, as Tovar put it, the land between the south and north oceans), about the urban enterprise that runs from Tollan, the first named city, to Teotihuacan, the last before the four antecedents acknowledged in the Mexica migration, and in fact better located in the Christian Era by Motolinia and the friars than by many modern scholars: Chichimec, (highland) Toltec, Colhua and Tepanec. The laws of this service ('tlamanitiliz') belong to the hunter-warrior, like his acquisitions ('tlamaliztli'), and are as various as the political systems imposed on Mesoamerica over the millennia acknowledged by Sahagún (Flo VIII, Prologue). That of the Mexica, assailed by Cortés and the Orders from Rome, is epitomized in their tribute year, in the brilliant enactments of the Feasts at the court in Tenochitlan, in the culmination in Cholula of 'Genesis', and in the cults incorporated into the system by Moctezuma I when he took Coixtlahuaca, Tepexic and the east: the Naolin of the Sunstone as the March equinox, Quetzalcoatl Nine Wind as initiator of the first Feast (F1.1.1), and the New Fire year Two Reed as arbiter between stars and sun.

As he contemplated the ruins of the main pyramid and Quetzalcoatl's round temple in Tenochtitlan, Durán focused on the Tonalpoualli dates of the Sunstone buried nearby (Naolin, 4 XVII) and the name Nine Wind (9 II), supplying Julian equivalents. In his version of TTTM, these propose Naolin as the March equinox, and Nine Wind (five days later and pointed to by the hand in Telleriano) as the first day of the Mexica year (F1.1.1), correlating them with the Era's primordial Tonalpoualli (viz. 13 x 20 days from F1.1.1 to F2.4.20, Tozoztli 1 to Panquetzaliztli 20, 27 March to 12 December). According to the preferred correlation of the Christian and Olmec (Mesoamerican) calendars, the Era's inaugural year is 3113 BCE, 13 Reed on the Sunstone, and in it Naolin 4 XVII is the March equinox, 11 trecenas before 4 XX (4 Ahau in Maya), at the interstice of Micailhuitl (**Table 4**).

What the friars learned about the three origins and services in *Coloquios* further corroborates TTTM overall and may help reconcile to it Julian dates they invented (notably Sahagún and Durán) for missionary purposes of their own. Like the shaman priest above them, farmer and hunter are shown living out their respective callings, whose beginnings and Eras are sensed in ancient rhythms of sun and stars and are precisely calculated to heartbeat and hour, night and day, Feast and year, Xiuhmolpilli and larger spans. This lends abundant time depth to the midnight penance, the planting seasons, and validation of

temporal power. No less than the Xiuhcoanaual rim is to the Sunstone, the Feast cycle is indispensable to this articulation of time through multiple levels and concentricities – innermost in the pulse and outermost in the galaxy. As such, the triple-origin model shapes the present study of the Mexica Feasts, in clarifying the time depths proper to creation and relived in penance and the dance; to the weather and seasons of the planter; and to the urban story of conquest and tribute. Its profound import as antecedent to the Christian year imposed by the Christians is explored in detail in Mexicanus (chapter 8 below).

Understandings of the Mexica year elicited, reported or provoked by the Christian mission, have in practice served as the foundation for western enquiry. Our chances of reading them aright are enhanced by ever acknowledging their non-Christian source and authority, cruelly assaulted at the moment of 'encounter' and taxonomically traduced, yet by no means extinct. (For the example of the Pahuatlan screenfolds noted by Reyes, see Chapter 7 below).

Towards restitution in Mexico

The programme to restitute Mexico's past that was born with the 1910–20 Revolution had a direct impact on understandings of the Mexica year. The work of two scholars in particular – who had little to do with each other – well exemplifies the new look at ancient texts which it encouraged: Alfonso Caso, a founder of Latin America's first national archaeology; and Angel María Garibay, the Franciscan friar who followed Sahagún to work in Tepepulco, yet in the cause of the Revolution. Their contribution may fairly be considered the platform for any interpretation of the Feasts that is at all sympathetic to the restitutive intelligence born of the 1910–20 upheaval. It is a Mexican furthering *in situ* of the Mesoamerican scholarship developed, mainly in late 19th-century Germany, by Eduard Seler and his fellow Amerikanisten, which by no means neglects the Mexica year (witness the Borbonicus Ochpaniztli page incorporated into Diego Rivera's murals, or the Sunstone which became the high altar of the Museo Nacional de Antropología in Chapultepec).

For Caso, archaeology was inseparable from anthropology and, in complete contrast to the scientism that subsequently came to dominate these disciplines, both had always to respect and take into account the records of the peoples and cultures subjected to scrutiny. Hence, alternating excavation with careful readings of *tlacuilolli* books Caso was able to reconstruct the earlier history of Oaxaca, through the fortunes, under Zapotec, Mixtec and Toltec, of such former cities as central Monte Alban and northern Coixtlahuaca, as well as other regions of what is now Mexico. He unearthed the lunar roots of the Tonalpoualli's Nine Night Lords and Thirteen Quecholli, in times prior even to the elaboration of the Twenty Signs. In all this, Caso privileged the calendar as a precise manifestation of knowledge and social organization; and as a result for more than three decades he embarked on a series of detailed analyses, of which the first was 'La correlación de los años azteca y cristiano' (1939), based largely on Borbonicus. Fundamental, this statement deserves duly to be acknowledged as the first to affirm the TTTM correlation of Mexica and Christian years, i.e. Ochpaniztli culminates in the September equinox (F1.9.20 = 22nd/23rd September), even if Caso went on to tie the Mexica too tightly to Classic non-solar norms.

While forging this link with the Christian calendar, Caso yet more critically established patterns of correlation within the native system itself, between kinds and datings of years used calendrically over time in the various regions of Mesoamerica. A celebrated case is his equation of Mexica and Mixtec years, 11 Flint = 10 Flint = 1516, what here are called Correlations 11 and 10 (C11 and C10), of Series III years. His pioneering work on the Coixtlahuaca Valley and its textual corpus opened the way to a third Series III Correlation, C1, known also in Cholula. This is the correlation used by the Mexica in identifying 13 Reed 3113 BCE as the first year of the Era, and is consistent with the 'GMT' correlation of the Olmec-Maya 'Long Count' in which Caso was in turn involved ('the only acceptable solution to the correlation question'; Edmonson 1988:ix)

Garibay's main contribution was shaped by his knowledge of Amerikanistik, on the one hand, and on the other, professional involvement in Christian ritual, thorough immersion in Nahuatl, and deep familiarity with Mexican custom and landscape. Thus qualified, he revealed how significant the Feast cycle is for any adequate reading of the Twenty Hymns (*Icuic*), repeatedly invoked in this study, which the elders of Tepepulco had passed on to Sahagún when exemplifying the rituals of the year. Not least, like Caso's, Garibay's scholarship has served as a local resource for whole schools of interpreters, among them Miguel León-Portilla, Pedro Castillo, Johanna Broda, Luis Reyes García, and Rafael Tena, whose insights into the Mexica Feasts have largely been unmatched elsewhere. Grounded in actual experience of Mexico, it affirmed the relevance of local knowledge, not least in the fraught matter of whether or not the Mexica Feasts at all took account of the solar year. Those against the idea (e.g. Prem, Graulich) have effectively privileged systems that made no such adjustment, like the *tun* calendar that served the urban Maya élite. Those for it (Castillo; Broda; Tena) have asked about the workability, without such adjustment, of economies as clearly dependent on seasonal agriculture as the Mexica.

In his commentary on Borbonicus, Reyes repeatedly notes how the understanding of the year articulated by the Mexica Feasts lives still, in performance and custom of the kind usually examined by anthropologists. It informs artefacts which might otherwise be dismissed as tourist curios, like jaguar masks from Guerrero, seed murals in Tepoztlan, and amate (native paper) screenfolds edited in the Nahua-Otomi redoubt of Pahuatlan, whose years of issue, in 1975, 1978 and 1981, he took care to record precisely (see p. 71 below). His deep knowledge of belief systems operative in Mexico today ensured that he respected the intelligence embedded in *tlacuilolli*, as few others have done. As he helps us see, the 1978 Pahuatlan screenfold dates itself at six lifetimes after the last Mexica New Fire, a 420-year period imaged as leaves of the pre-Christian tree (6x7) multiplied by the 10 human digits and literally rooted in the 18 Feasts (**Fig. 2.2**). As a Nahuatlato and Mexican scholar, Reyes has gone further, in explicitly defining his approach and position today, with respect to the missionary friars. He takes issue with Diego Durán, for instance, noting how the Dominican suspected in ever more paranoid fashion that the pagan Feasts were still being celebrated in Mexico as if deliberately to undermine the faith imported by friars such as himself, fears horribly confirmed when a Mexica priestess told him: 'We too had Christmas and Easter like you and at the same times of year as you, and Corpus

Figure 2.2 Dios del arbol, with Feast feet. Pahuatlan screenfold 1978, p.27

Christi, and other feasts' (Durán quoted in Reyes 1991: 196). Reyes respects, rather, the age-old philosophy embedded in those Feasts and its adaptive powers:

> The impotent censure of the friar, who tried in vain to change an entire society and way of life, indirectly documents for us the indigenous reaction. The 16th century was a case not just of baptisms and the imposing of a new faith, but also of indigenous spiritual leaders and intellectuals consciously translating the values of the oppressor into their own tradition, so as to save their ancestral philosophy (1991:90).

Handlist, Katalog, Book of the Year

Enquiries into the Mexica Feasts in the Amerikanistik tradition yet conducted largely by scholars outside Mexico offer key insights of their own, thanks partly to western institutions that have become the new homes of Mexica manuscripts. This is certainly the case with studies published over the last half century by George Kubler and Charles Gibson, Karl Nowotny and Munro Edmonson. When it appeared in 1951, Kubler and Gibson's *The Tovar Calendar: An illustrated Mexican manuscript of ca. 1585* set up something of a landmark. For in editing and contextualizing the Tovar compendium (acquired in 1947 by the John Carter Brown Library), these US scholars furnished a hugely useful Handlist of extant *tlacuilolli* and alphabetic texts that deal with the Mexica Feasts. Art historian and historian, George Kubler and Charles Gibson were both colonialists who combined their expertise in the Tovar project. Named after (though certainly not the work of) the Jesuit Juan de Tovar and closely akin to the *Kalendario*, this *tlacuilolli* text correlates the Mexica Feasts with the zodiac signs and dominical letters of the Christian calendar, as we noted above (**Figs 2.3, 2.4**). The 'commentary and handlist' of comparable manuscripts included in their edition much enriched the 'Survey' and 'Census' of Native Middle American Pictorial Manuscripts published by John Glass and Donald Robertston (another art historian) in the *Handbook of Middle American Indians* (HMAI). For its part, Kubler's concern with format and iconography has clarified the manner in which the Feasts may be represented and has affected later studies in the discipline of art history (Couch 1985; Baird 1993).

Figure 2.3 Panquetzaliztli and Atemoztli. *Kalendario* ff.97v–98

Solidly within the tradition of colonialist historiography, the Kubler-Gibson survey excels in revealing the network of friars who first commented on Mexica Feast texts (Motolinia, Sahagún, Durán, Rios, Acosta, Tovar himself). It is immensely valuable for the way it examines the provenance and style of compendia which like Tovar deal with the Mexica year, and for the way it interrelates them, as post-Cortesian manuscripts written on European paper in *tlacuilolli* and the alphabet. It duly notes milestone transmissions of the Feasts in print, like the publication of Veytia Wheel no. 2 in the mestizo Valadés's *Rhetorica christiana* (Perugia 1579) which possibly inspired Giordano Bruno's 1584 admiring reference to the New World's calculations of 10,000 years and more, and Gemelli Careri's publication of Wheel no.4 (*Giro del Mondo*, Naples 1699–1700, vol.6) and its inclusion in the engraved self portrait that adorns *Idea de una nueva historia general de la América septentrional* (1746) by Lorenzo Boturini, disciple of Giambattista Vico. In line with López de Gómara's *La conquista de México* (1552), which incorporated Motolinia's account of the Feasts and the reading of the Sunstone drawn on in turn by Montaigne, these transmissions extended the friars' network to include many who came to question Biblical philosophy and estimates of the age of the world, among them creoles like Sigüenza y Góngora, Veytia, and León y Gama, and European intellectuals and *philosophes,* the neo-Pythagoreans, Marlowe and the Elizabethan School of Night, Bruno the apostate Dominican, codex-collector Laud and his admirer Ussher, Purchas, Boturini, and Humboldt (first of the Amerikanisten). Along these paths, the Feasts came to

impinge on the history of (western) ideas far more than has been generally acknowledged, as León-Portilla has indicated in telling detail (2003:168–78).

Besides its historiographical contribution in contextualizing the 16th-century Mexica compendia, the Kubler-Gibson survey illuminates the way that the Feasts may be represented formally. It suggests that, in these terms, 'illustrations' of the Feasts fall into five categories: simultaneous, showing more than one ritual at once, like Tepepulco and Borbonicus; analytical, showing successive stages of the same Feast, like the Florentine Codex Book II; emblematic, involving medieval style impersonators, like Tovar; theomorphic, like the patron deities seen in Vaticanus and Magliabechiano; and ideographic, or phonetic identifications of the kind found in Mexicanus and the calendar Wheels. (1951:39–41). In this scheme, examples of the ideograms are the tree-moss of Pachtli, or the parrot of Tozoztli, which denotes that Feast as a phoneme, parrot being *toz-nene* and hence evocative of the *tozoa* in Tozoztli, to do penance in the 'first service'. The more substantial 'theomorphic' versions will present a series of presiding figures, in full regalia, sometimes with supplementary figures or emblems. More elaborately again, ceremonies may be depicted separately or simultaneously in full page scenes, replete with choreography and architecture, of the kind epitomized in Borbonicus, the one surviving ritual screenfold in the Mexica tradition. While acknowledging these five categories, the present study places yet greater emphasis on sheer format and layout, finds more common ground than cultural difference in the emblematic and

Figure 2.4 Pagination of Borbonicus Feasts. Nowotny 1961:243

p. 23 a	XVIII.	izcalli	A 1 VIII
p. 23 b	I.	atlcaualo	
p. 24 a	II.	tlacaxipeualiztli	
p. 24 b	III.	tozoztli	
p. 25	IV.	ueitozoztli	
p. 26 a	V.	toxcatl	
p. 26 b	VI.	etzalqualiztli	
p. 27 a	VII.	tecuilhuitl	
p. 27 b	VIII.	ueitecuilhuitl	
p. 28 a	IX.	tlaxochimaco	
p. 28 b	X.	xocotlhuetzi	
p. 29–31	XI.	ochpaniztli	
	(XII.	teotleco)	
p. 32	XIII.	tepeilhuitl	
p. 33	XIV.	quecholli	
p. 34	XV.	panquetzaliztli	A 2 XIII
p. 35	XVI.	atemoztli	
p. 36	XVII.	tititl	
p. 37, 38	XVIII.	izcalli	A 3 XVIII
			A4III–A2XIII

the ideographic, avoids the theomorphic as too essentialist, and attempts to reconcile the simultaneous and the analytical in Mexica (rather than western) terms.

Concise, the ideograms/emblems expose most readily the lack of standardization among the images and names used to identify individual Feasts, which in part reflects differences in regional industries, climates and schedules. In part, it simply reflects the fact that different ceremonial highpoints from any one twenty-day Feast could be chosen to represent it, notably the climactic final day(s). This last notion is made clear in the multiple images of the Feasts recorded in Borbonicus, the Florentine Codex, the upper and lower levels specified in *Cuevas* and Durán, and in the alphabetic glosses added to several other texts. Successive days and moments within a Feast may even be represented numerically or proportionally by footprints. In the Tepepulco account of Toxcatl, Tezcatlipoca's *tlachialoni* is located by these means in mid-Feast, while his crooked stick is placed at the end.

The ideogram/emblem sequences, necessarily those found in the Anniversary Wheels, tend to identify the Feasts serially one to one (between the spokes as it were). This is also generally true of the emblematic/theomorphic full-figure sequences, despite the extra information and page space allotted to certain of them. With the simultaneous scene sequences however, things are different. In the 18-page chapter in Borbonicus (pp.23–40), only 15 pages are actually dedicated to the Feasts, and the first Feast recurs cyclically at the end (Izcalli; pp.23, 37). Moreover, the regularity of the serial page arrangement is modified by the fact that after the first 11 Feasts, enormous attention is paid to the Mother of Gods Teteu innan in Ochpaniztli, whose scene intrudes on to scenes before and after (pp.29–30) and announces a far more spacious arrangement of scenes, one per page or more, compared with the two per page or less before. An analogous treatment of Teteu innan is found in the Tepepulco Ms where, as Baird has keenly shown, this presiding figure appears before and after, as well as in, her own scene, since her presence was felt to be threaded into the preceding and subsequent Feasts, in what Baird believes may once have been a vertical screenfold format (Baird 1993:116). With respect to Panquetzaliztli (F2.4), the accompanying Nahuatl text reports that this Feast was marked by a dance that lasted no less than 80 days, or the four Feasts of the tribute

quarter-year (F2.1– F2.4). The Florentine Codex records several cases of overlapping Feasts, like the mock fights of Panquetzaliztli which ran on into Atemoztli, or the nocturnal wild-flower gathering that began two nights before the official start of flowery Tlaxochimaco.

Hence, Kubler and Gibson's formal analysis of how the Feasts are actually depicted on the page has helped reaffirm the notion that within this variety and variation, they nonetheless always belong to a cycle of no more and no less than 18 in all known sources; and they always follow comparable sequences. It has also helped privilege image-concepts that typify many of the Mexica Feasts and pairs of Feasts, like Tezcatlipoca's *tlachialoni* sceptre (Toxcatl), Tlaloc's pozole stew pot (Etzalcualiztli), mummy bundle (Miccailhuitl), Teteu innan's broom and spindle (Ochpaniztli), footprint trail (Teotleco), hunting gear (Quecholli), flag or banner (Panquetzaliztli), falling water (Atemoztli), weaving batten (Tititl), and Xipe's knotted conical hat (Tlacaxipehualiztli). The Nahuatl names of these emblems tend to be legible etymologically, and the consistency they display in all major cases makes of them a template for the cycle as a whole, even outside the Mexica corpus.

Much of value is likewise to be found in the Feast by Feast analysis which Kubler and Gibson offer of Tovar. For example, their observation that the Atemoztli-like form given to the zodiac sign Aquarius is 'neither entirely Indian nor European' prepares us for how the same Feast and sign are deployed to complex ends in the closely related *Kalendario* (**Fig. 2.3**), as well as in Mexicanus (p.11; **Pl. 2a**) and Veytia Wheel 5; again, in discussing Tititl (p.34) they make highly suggestive comparisons between Tovar and the Vienna screenfold (Tepexic Annals) and usefully note this Feast's resonance in cosmic as well as political time (p.34). Not least, they drew up a table which effectively reveals how, in *tlacuilolli* sources, initial Feasts of the Mexica ritual year progress from Atemoztli to Tlacaxipehualiztli (F2.5 to F2.9), a range which in non-Mexica sources begins earlier in Panquetzaliztli and ends later in Toxcatl (F2.4 to F1.3; see their Table D, p.47).

True to their disciplines and purpose, Kubler and Gibson privileged colonial historiography and western aesthetics in their account of the Feasts. As a result they tended to rely more on (western) alphabetic report than on *tlaculolli* texts. As an Anniversary Wheel, for example, Boban receives less recognition than it deserves as a native-paper text whose historical perspective is entirely indigenous; though drawn on by friars Durán, Tovar and others, the *Cuevas* manuscript is not recognized or named in its own right. Again, little was made of the economic dimension of the Feasts, exemplarily in the pre-Cortesian Matrícula de tributos; or of the strikingly sophisticated treatment of the Feasts in Mexicanus and its masterful correlation of them with the Christian calendar. The authoritativeness of these texts – Boban, Matrícula, Mexicanus – is not acknowledged *per se* even though unlike Tovar and the compendia they are not just written in *tlacuilolli* but made materially of native paper.

In practice, Kubler and Gibson's Spanish colonial bias even led them to doubt that in principle any *tlacuilolli* representation of the Feasts antedates Cortés – as if native scribes had somehow been in need of newly-arrived European intelligence in order visually and literarily to organize their year. Of the Veytia

Wheels, Glass and Robertson's Census (HMAI 14:230) rather discouragingly observes that 'there is no compelling reason to attribute any of the seven to Indian authorship'. Brown (1978) went on openly to proclaim this negative view. Partly thanks to Kubler and Gibson's colonizing tendencies, many other subsequent pronouncements on the Feasts have continued to pay less attention to codices written in *tlacuilolli* than to alphabetic transcriptions or other derivatives of them, including stray observations made by invading Spaniards in the 16th century. A main aim of this enquiry is to restore the notion of native authorship and authority with respect to the 18 Feasts, and with that to vindicate the cycle as fundamental to Mexica and Mesoamerican literature generally. The Tepepulco Ms, for example, may fairly be identified as Sahagún's *Primeros memoriales* yet it hardly represents 'first notes' for its authors.

The whole question of precedent and continuity in this sense was helpfully recast in Karl Nowotny's *Tlacuilolli. Die mexikanischen Bilderhandschriften. Stil und Inhalt mit einem Katalog der Codex-Borgia-Gruppe* (1961), which comprehensively describes texts in that script tradition formally devoted to the dual components of the Mesoamerican calendar, the Tonalpoualli and year, texts which he and his Amerikanisten precursors called 'ritual'. Subtitled a 'Katalog', Nowotny's work establishes a classic corpus of nine such ritual texts, widely identified with the 'Codex Borgia Group', after its most conspicuous member. All nine members of the group are of native manufacture (deerskin, amate paper) and are paginated as screenfold books, except for the single-page Coixtlahuaca quincunx map (see p.8 above). On arithmetical grounds, appealing to the two main ritual cycles of the year and the Tonalpoualli, Nowotny exhaustively identified and cross-referenced the theme chapters which comprise these texts, in various combinations, revealing the true chaptering of American experience which characterizes this genre. Hence, in the *Katalog* the three chapters of Borbonicus, the one Mexica member of the ritual group of nine, are compared with chapters in the other texts that likewise deal with the Tonalpoualli, the 52-year Xiuhmolpilli, and the Feasts of the year. He made further comparisons with landscapes and events seen in certain of the screenfold annals and later histories, saliently the Upper Papaloapan quincunx defined in the Tepexic Annals (Vienna Codex), and the northern Chichimec rites and artefacts depicted in both Borgia and the *Historia tolteca chichimeca* (he even linked *tlacuilolli* time-maps to Anasazi dry paintings). He also took in the compendia, which he called 'Theken', and other post-Cortesian texts like Mexicanus. The publishing in facsimile of most of the nine classics (only two continue to languish in poor reproduction) has critically enhanced this kind of analysis, as have certain of the accompanying commentaries, not least Nowotny's on Borgia (1975), and Reyes García's on Borbonicus (1992).

Nowotny's focus on the classic corpus of the nine ritual texts typified by Borgia meant that he had relatively little to say about Mexica texts, besides Borbonicus, that is. In general he had a low estimate of the compendia (Tepepulco, Telleriano, Magliabechiano); he largely ignored Tovar along with *Cuevas* and in his brief commentary on Mexicanus he chose to highlight not so much its furthering of the pre-Cortesian tradition as what for him was evidence of western 'acculturation'. At the same time, it is his *Katalog* which best establishes the textual norms

against which cultural change may be measured in the first place.

Thorough as it is, Nowotny's arithmetical catalogue pays more attention to the Tonalpoualli than to the Feasts cycle. This bias is partly prompted by the classic codices themselves since, of the 357 pages that the nine ritual texts collectively consist of, no less than four fifths (about 284 pages) are devoted to the Tonalpoualli, permutating its 260 nights as 9 x 29 less 1 and as $2(7^2 + 9^2)$, and matching its 260 days with the Thirteen Numbers and Twenty Signs, arraying them in halves, quarters, fifths, and in the 20-day and 13-day periods known in Spanish, the 'Veintena' and the 'Trecena'. Occupying 73 pages of the 357 total, the remaining six chapters in the nine classic codices, Nowotny freely recognized, cannot be accounted for arithmetically by the Tonalpoualli. One of these six non-Tonalpoualli chapters is the 18-page chapter in Borbonicus, which is quite satisfactorily accounted for in Nowotny's own terms by being assigned to the year of 18 Feasts (**Fig. 2.4**). The other five chapters, however, are not so readily accounted for, those found in Borgia (pp.29–46), Fejérváry (pp.5–22), Laud (pp.21–22; pp.39–44), and Cospi (pp.21–38). Because of their opener and less regular format, and because for him none appeared to have an overarching numerical definition, Nowotny left these five non-Tonalpoualli chapters to the end (1961:244–75). Wishing to connect them more with folk custom reported in the fieldwork of Schultze Jena than with the calendrics and astronomy of Seler's ancient 'high culture', he off-loaded them into the all-purpose categories 'Tempelkult' (Borgia) and 'Rituale mit Bündeln abgezählter Gegenstände' (Cospi, Fejérváry, Laud). Here, they are referred to as Nowotny's five 'Enigmatic Chapters'.

None of the classic screenfolds in which these five Enigmatic Chapters are found can by any means be thought Mexica, and they likely stem from Cholula, the 'Rome' of Mesoamerica (Borgia; Cospi) and other centres that consciously conserved Olmec thought (and arithmetic), like Teotlillan on the eastern tribute road (Laud), and Xiuhtecutlan, overlooking the Gulf Coast (Fejérváry). Yet, being classic in the larger literary tradition of Mesoamerica, they impinge on the Mexica Feast cycle. The 18-page chapter in Borgia has been insistently invoked as a precedent in discussions of the Feasts, not least by Nowotny himself, when cataloguing the temples used over the liturgical year at Cholula (see also Milbrath 1989; Baird 1993; Brotherston 2003). Structurally, the Borgia chapter predicates later representations of the Feasts that rehearse the Cholula doctrine, notably 'Genesis' in Rios. A subsidiary aim of this enquiry into the Mexica Feasts is to show that all five of Nowotny's Enigmatic Chapters in fact relate (like Borbonicus's third chapter) to the Feasts of the year, so that in the entire body of nine classic ritual texts every single page may be arithmetically ascribed, on Nowotny's own terms, to one or other of the two component cycles of the Mesoamerican calendar: the Tonalpoualli, and the Feasts of the year. Of the classic accounts of the Feasts ransomed here, easily the most multilayered and multifaceted (hence previous difficulties with identifying it fully) is the 18-page chapter which lies at the heart of Borgia (pp.29–46); from any point of view, this chapter demands to be ranked with the most compelling and brilliant *tlacuilolli* literature extant.

By attending to the 18-page core chapter in Borgia (pp.29–46), Nowotny further prepared the way for recognizing its pertinence to the Feast cycle through a concern with layout on the page reminiscent of Kubler and Gibson. He pointed out the ancient pair of celestial and terrestrial figures, star-skirted above and caiman-scaled below, which wax and wane between strip (*streifenformig*) and page frame, effectively defining the sky-earth model of the Feasts seen in *Cuevas* and 'Genesis'. In this way, the Borgia chapter can be seen to define the yearly archetypes of night sky and planting seasons elaborated in Tepepulco (II, i, ii. See p.41 below).

In formally surveying and describing texts in the classic corpus, Nowotny's *Tlacuilolli* is unrivalled and indispensable (though unhelpfully often overlooked by those who know no German. An English translation is promised, at last, for 2005). Cataloguing the constituent chapters of the ritual texts, it shows how they not only deal with the Tonalpoualli and the Feasts but actually derive from these cycles their measure and principles of reading, as in poetry or music. In genre terms, this is their diagnostic and it distinguishes them as 'great books' (*teoamoxtli*) or 'dream books' (*temicamatl*) from the more narrative annals (Xiuhtlapoualli), these corresponding to the main genre division made in Motolinia's 'Epistola proemial'. Turning the pages of a screenfold book, the reader may move from right or left, up or down, or may move one way in order to return the other in another register, all of which puts great premium on the principle which directs the reading in the first place (in his words: 'ein im Stoff selbst liegendes Ordnungsprinzip'). In surviving screenfolds, this principle can only ever be one of two kinds: the ritual number cycles of the Tonalpoualli and the Feasts of the year; or year-dates in the annals. The year-dates signpost the linear or boustrophedon path of the migrations, municipal histories and biographies that make up the annals genre. The number cycles, not least the 18 of the Feasts, define the chapters of books in the ritual genre and give measure to the themes they develop.

In the study of the Feast cycle, the publication in 1988 of Munro Edmonson's *The Book of the Year. Middle American Calendrical Systems* decisively broadened the theoretical base. For this work considers the 18-Feast cycle within the framework of the Mesoamerican calendar as a whole, its start date and span, and its universal day count. It is concerned with nothing less than 'the unitary calendrical system of Middle America' (p.ix), that is, (Cem)anahuac, the 'land between the seas' (p.1). The examples it adduces range from the earliest known inscriptions of the Olmec calendar 'inaugurated on the summer solstice of 739 bc' (p.x), which establish the Era base in the year 3113 bce, to alphabetic texts in Nahuatl, Maya and other languages which register the impact of Christendom that has continued for centuries after Cortés. Edmonson's terms of mathematical and astronomical reference assume native competence from early in the Era; they entirely encompass and largely endorse the correlations of Caso and Thompson (GMT), where necessary supplement (or correct) those assumed in Kubler and Gibson's survey and Nowotny's catalogue, and broadly support TTTM.

Drawing as ever on the Amerikanisten, Edmonson established main lines of meaning in the Feasts, detecting calendrical coherences that underlie the greatest diversity in name, concept and practice in Mesoamerica (1984: Table pp.216–17). He then integrated the Feasts, as 20-day periods, into the mechanisms by which 365-day years are named in the Mesoamerican calendar, terminally or initially, by their 'New

Year' days, in the five-fold Series (I–V) of four year-bearers (**Table 3a**). Outlining reforms made over millennia in order to keep track of the solar year, Edmonson shows how the year-bearer Series were incremental over time, so that in general – and allowing for initial and terminal naming – the lower the Series number, the older the local system, and how these reforms affected the correlation of New Year days with the Feasts cycle, albeit within the window of no more than a quarter year revealed by Kubler and Gibson (an 'astonishing' example of 'deeply rooted historical conservatism' pp.16–17). He likewise alerts us to

> the fact that the calculation of the solar (tropical) year by the astronomers of Kaminaljuyu of 433 BCE was identical to the fourth decimal place with the corresponding calculations of modern astronomy. The era of 29 calendar rounds (1,508 years) completes 1,507 tropical years of 365.2422 days each (p.277).

In this, Edmonson has gone further than anyone in clarifying the most diverse evidence of correlations made between given systems, that is, without any necessary reliance whatsoever on the Christian calendar imported in the 16th century. While many such correlations exist between year Series, notably between II and III, the commonest kind of correlation in surviving texts is that made between the numerical qualifiers of Signs within Series III, where, to recall the preponderant examples of C11, C10 and C1, year 11 Flint (Sign XVIII) of the Mexica in Tenochtitlan equals 10 Flint of the Mixtec in Tilantongo (as Caso showed) equals 1 Flint of the 'Toltec' Popoloca in Coixtlahuaca and Tepexic (extended to Cholula by Edmonson, p.224). Edmonson's scheme is particularly suggestive in offering to correlate both year Series and numerical qualifiers with the Feast cycle, so that, to take one of his firmer examples, Etzalcualiztli (F1.4), in midsummer, is the Feast in which the year of Series III C1 culminates.

Contemplating Edmonson's achievement, it is hard not to share his sentiment:

> The day of the New Year stands as a monument to the astronomical date of its birth – a monument on the road of the sun. In the cyclic time of Middle America, it is, by the same token, a nearly-perfect prediction. In its elegance, precision, and antiquity, the year count is testimonial to a conquest of time that stands alone in the annals of world civilization (p.277).

Like other experts in Mesoamerican calendrics, Edmonson was concerned with system as such, that is, registering data in good astronomy and good mathematics, and making valid correlations. In practice, this must always leave little space for considering context, how such data are represented in specific texts, and the arguments or demonstrations into which they are formally integrated. Hence though *Book of the Year* provides invaluable coordinates for understanding the Feasts of the Mexica and Mesoamerica, it scarcely offers (and could scarcely be expected to offer) full readings of those Feasts as they are represented in the *tlacuilolli* texts. In fact, these texts can be shown to appeal to concepts of the year that escape notice in *Book of the Year*, indispensable as it is in its own terms.

In its very comprehensiveness and insistence on mathematical and astronomical precision, *Book of the Year* cannot but raise major technical questions about the year which it itself does not address, among them, the existence of more than one day count (cf. Doesburg's comments on the Ixtlilxochitl Codex 1996), the continuing slip of the Julian year over 64 years

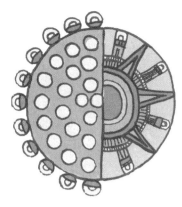

Figure 2.5 Sun, 19 moons, 11 stars. Borbonicus p.11

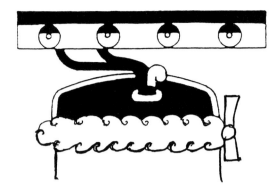

Figure 2.6 Forward movement (r – l) of stars in year 2 Reed, above 18 seasonal clouds tied with year knot. Tepexic Annals p.10

from 1519 to 1583 noted in Mexicanus, the different measures of the year inherent in Xiuhcoanaual, and the three origins and kinds of year spelt out by the Mexica priests in 1524. In Edmonson's study we learn about civil or metric years of varying length, years of 365, 360 and even 400 days, all of them matched in their way with the Feasts cycle. We also learn about the relationship of these metric years to the year of the sun, measured as we saw to an accuracy of the fourth decimal place, at 365.2422 days. This is the year of seasons and harvests, of sunrises and sunsets shifting along the eastern and western horizons between equinox and solstice, and (in the tropics) of a corresponding shift of the midday sun north and south of the zenith. Yet in Mexica and Mesoamerican calendrics and custom the solar year is not the only type of year determined by the sky: as we saw, the timing of penance and of the New Fire ceremony was determined not just by the sun but by the stars at midnight. The year in question here is not the solar year but the slightly longer sidereal year, each having its own relationship with the moon (**Fig. 2.5**). The difference between the two – the precession of the equinoxes – amounts per year to 0.014 days (the 20 minutes or so of nocturnal penance), a day every 70.5 years, three days or so every four Xiuhmolpilli as at Coatepec (1195–1403), 6 days every 423 years (1168–1590 in Mexicanus; 1559–1981 in Pahuatlan), 22 days every 1551 years and 66 days every 4653 years (the page- tables in Mexicanus pp.12–13). In this Mexica reckoning, from a given starting point it takes 25,750 years for the sun and the stars to get back in step, the Great or Platonic Year, of which our Quinto Sol is a fifth.

In other words, *Book of the Year* has the self-imposed technical limitation of identifying the year of its title only with the sun (the tropical or synodical year of 365.242 days), a point made explicit in the Mexican translation *El libro del año solar*. It leaves quite to one side the sun's astronomical counterpart in human experience, the stars of the night sky (the sidereal year of 365.256 days). Since the Gregorian Reform, the difference between these two years has been ignored in the Christian calendar (and belief) that has spread itself so far and wide. But it certainly was not and indeed could not have been ignored in the Mesoamerican calendar, where the Feasts of the year were tied to the sun and harvests on the one hand, and on the other to the stars that determined the first service of penance and blood-letting and the exact moment when New Fire was kindled and a new Xiuhmolpilli was initiated. Over the millennia that stretch from Olmec to Mexica, the slippage between the solar and sidereal years grew to much more than a Feast, a fact registered

in several native sources though very rarely mentioned in western commentaries on them. Closely read, texts relating to the Feasts repeatedly reveal a concern with this slippage, between the precession of the equinoctial sun and the corresponding advance of the constellations (**Fig. 2.6**); and they do so characteristically invoking the night-sky cipher 11 and its double 22. Clear examples will be seen in the Tepepulco constellations, of which fire-drilling Mamalhuaztli comprises 11 stars (**Pl. 3a**) like its prototype in Borgia, and in Mexicanus, which deconstructs the 12-fold Christian zodiac in just these terms (pp.92–3 below).

For their part, representations of the Feasts in the Enigmatic Chapters take the night-sky cipher 11 as the basis of sophisticated astronomical calculations, while contriving to depict the advance of the constellations on the page, from right to left. Legible thanks to Tepepulco and other compendia, the key indigenous constellations in this process are those that mark the two intersections of the ecliptic – the zodiac path of sun, moon and planets – with the Milky Way, specifically the 'Many' (Pleiades) and the 'Market', the brightly-adorned Star Skirt of Ilamatecutli (the galactic hub), who 'rival' each other (Telleriano f.1. **Fig. 2.1**). Along with the circumpolar Xonecuilli, these constellations may be seen advancing dramatically through the Mexica Feasts, in tandem with the New Fire ceremony, as well as other activities governed by the night sky. These last include the pulque drinking of the 11, also celebrated in the temple at Tepoztlan over seasons similarly measured by the Feasts and the constellations. In all, far from being marginal or illusory, precession in this way proves to sustain the whole principle of the Feasts that weave between night and day. The difference between the years that night and day respectively embody finds a graphic match in the double-ring *tlachialoni* sceptres, calibrated in black-and-white or black-and-gold sectors, held respectively by Tezcatlipoca the god of knowing and intelligence in Toxcatl, and by Ixcozauhqui, god of calendrical adjustment in Izcalli and wearer of the Xiuhcoanaual array.

Reading the text

Concentrating on the work of the Mexica themselves, the approach taken in this study is above all textual. That is, the analyses and arguments proposed in every case derive from specific pages in specific texts, and they respect the norms and principles these adhere to as primary sources, rather than dismember them so as to fit the bits into imported western schemes. The argument is grounded on close readings of the *tlacuilolli* text itself, its physical shape, confection, pagination, chaptering, layout, colour, style, format, and not from pre-conceived alien patterns. Such was the approach which led to the better insights in Nowotny's *Tlacuilolli*. In having this categorical role, the texts in question all belong fully to the native-script tradition, and embody the historiography of *tlacuilolli*, which privileges native intelligence, rather than that of the alphabet, most often blind or blinkered to anything not written in it. With respect to the Mexica Feasts, many problems of western historiography have in this sense been self-generated, caused by undue weight being placed on European rather than native report.

The importance attached here to the chosen texts is linked to the reasons and circumstances of their production, to definitions of authorship and authority: they are considered as statements in their own right, rather than data that are extractable with impunity or provided by 'informants' in the service of an invading power. After all, native understanding of time and its cycles can for obvious historical reasons be expected to be inimical to that imposed and inherited still (to a surprising degree) by the Christian West. In the Mexica domain and indeed throughout Mesoamerica, books were perceived as threatening by Europe from the first moment of contact. They were burned in Texcoco by Cortés's troops, and again in 8 Reed 1539 along with their owner Don Carlos Ome Tochtli, in Tenochtitlan by the first archbishop Zumárraga (a Franciscan), and again in 3 Flint 1560, a conflagration (*yn tlatlacamatl*) that followed upon the founding of the first European university in America.

Having their own argument and integrity, the Mexica texts examined here were written to be read rather than simply decoded, that is, they are susceptible to readings that are in the best sense literary. The books of Mesoamerica have been extensively discussed by scholars loyal to such disciplines as ethnography, art history, semiotics, archaeology and linguistics. May literature have its turn, with its concern for the very idea of the book and script, along with such key concepts as genre, pagination, chaptering, exposition, theme, style, perspective and point of view, levels of reading, reflexivity, and wit.

The two chapters that open this study have been devoted to Mexica imagining of the yearly Feasts and to western efforts at understanding them. The concern has been with script and source texts, structure, year beginnings and lengths, correlations within Mesoamerica and with the year introduced by the Christians, the particular history of the Mexica and the iconography and norms they favoured, the paradigm of triple origins and functions, and the contrary pull of stars and sun. These concepts underlie and anticipate the arguments developed in the following six chapters, which likewise fall into pairs wholly concentrated on the Feasts and devoted to: principal functions of the solar year; choreography; and technically dense statements of correlation. Respecting the Mexica priests' mentions of the fisc (*petlacalli*) and the warrior-hunter's booty (*tlamaliztli*), 'Fiscal Acquisition' (Chapter 3) examines Tenochtitlan's tribute system in Cemanahuac (Mesoamerica), the annual landscape of its metropolis and quarters, imperial interest in Olmec precedent and the arithmetical marriage of earth and sky. 'Planting Seasons' (Chapter 4) concerns the supper and breakfast (*in tococha in toneuhca*) produced by the farmer, ever mindful of Huitzilopochtli's ancient compadre Tlaloc: it traces the highland geography of weather and winds and their corresponding agricultural almanac, delving into older fields of reverence and ingenuity. While this pair of chapters deals with the solar year of tribute and planting, two of the three paradigmatic origins, the following pair focuses on elaborate performances of the Feasts, whirled by sun and stars and manifold in drumbeat and phase. The stage, personae and action in 'Like waves breaking': the Great Dance (Chapter 5) are transposed to social and cultural venues elsewhere in 'Prior Hosts' (Chapter 6). Set down on the page in concentric circles and multi-dimensional tables, this order of complexity is then examined in the final pair of chapters. 'Anniversary Wheels'(Chapter 7) begins with the world ages inscribed on the Sunstone and extends to prognosis long subsequent to the fall of Tenochtitlan, acknowledging the levels of reading – historical, geopolitical, augural – shown to Durán in the *Cuevas* wheel (p.30; Durán 2002, 2:226–29). 'Mexicanus' (Chapter 8) ponders the subtlest responses to Christendom, made in the name of Acamapichtli, and rooted in the three origins of the year and time.

3
Fiscal Acquisition

As the tax schedule stated in the Matrícula de tributos, the Feasts cycle was indispensable to the running of Tenochitltan's economic empire. In the analysis that follows, it is not a question of claiming that somehow the entire Mexica economy is exhaustively reflected in this text. There is doubtless an emphasis on luxury tribute, for example, commodity items desired and required by the aristocracy (and by Cortés, when Moctezuma's guest); and overall, the Aztec arrangement, as Zantwijk called it, was ceaselessly adjusted to changing circumstances. Rather, it is a matter of respecting the text for what it says and of detecting in it the paradigms that enabled the system to function as it did. As well as making such paradigms explicit in the cycle of 18 Feasts, consulting the Matrícula and other tribute documents reminds us how the notion of paying hard commodity items is continuous with that of making ritual offerings. Following Tepepulco (I, i), the Florentine Codex (Book 2) equates 'debt-paying' (*nextlaoaliztli*) with Feast (*ilhuitl*).

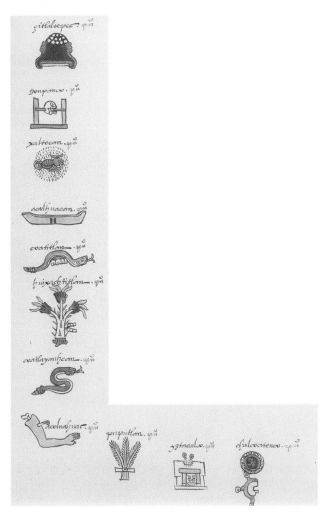

Figure 3.1 Citlaltepec (star mountain) as first of the upper 11 strongholds. Mendoza f.17v

As a sheaf or file of amate sheets, the Matrícula regulated Mexica tribute economy in practice. As a text it exemplifies the principles and ciphers, above all the Feasts cycle, in which that economy had its ideological base. In both functions it is elegant and extremely succinct, never giving more information than is necessary or presupposed. Hence, discovering the norms that made this succinctness possible, principally with respect to the Feasts, is a prerequisite for a full reading of the text. From the start it will be clear that as defined by debt and payment deadlines, the reality faced by tributaries to Tenochtitlan was a lingua franca, had a coherence, and promoted an urge to comply in time (Hassig 1988), no less powerful in its colonized day and landscape than that imposed currently on the last corner of the globe by such institutions as the IMF. To this extent, then, awareness of the Mexica Feasts and the timing of them in this function overrode all calendrical variation within the empire

Matrícula opens with a look at the logistics that secured the system, in the form of 11 resource centres in the metropolitan area in theHighland Basin (now seen only in Mendoza; **Fig. 3.1**), plus a second 11 garrisons that guarded the surrounding provinces. These sets of strongholds, inner/upper and outer/lower, have great prefigurative power and might be referred to as 'hendecarchies' for want of a better term. There follows a page devoted to the unique case of tribute due to the temple Huitznahuac, in the heart of the capital, and payable by Tlatelolco. As the text reminds us, this practice stemmed historically from rivalry between Tenochtitlan and Tlatelolco, begun under the rulers Acamapichtli and Cuauhtlatoa and resolved when Axayacatzin humiliated Moquihuix and made Tlatelolco into a tributary. Huitznahuac has its own Hymn (*Icuic* no.2), which celebrates solar Huitzilopochtli's victory over the stars and invokes his college to the south of town. Thereafter, the rest of Matrícula records, page after page, the tribute payable to Tenochtitlan by its metropolitan and provincial tribute districts, which Mendoza confirms numbered 38 in all (also the original total of Matrícula's pages). The first of these districts is named after the *petlacalli* (which became *petaca* in Spanish), the woven rush basket referred to in *Coloquios* that corresponds neatly to the *fiscus* of the Roman exchequer.

Metropolitan Tenochtitlan amid its bastions and provinces
As the invading Spaniards gradually learned how to exercise socially the power they had gained with military conquest, heirs of the old order thought to assure a place for themselves in the new, in what Octavio Paz imagined as a Mexican raj that was still-born. A main literary result of this tactic was the Mendoza Codex, which incorporates the Matrícula in its entirety and despite its name has the hallmarks of a native proposition. The Mendoza text argues from (ex-)crown to crown, from authority to authority who understands the ways and means of power, and in certain respects it is comparable with the letter later

addressed to the Spanish crown by Guaman Poma from the vice-royalty of Peru. In each case, the authors of the text were after all the ones best qualified at the time to know what was going on.

In incorporating the Matricula, Mendoza turned its original sheaf of 19 sheets or folios into pages of a bound volume of 71 folios. It inverted the direction in which these pages are to be read – an ideologically significant shift – so that from-bottom-to-top is replaced by from-top-to-bottom (**Fig. 3.1**). It gave extra page space to the metropolitan districts and added both introductory and concluding sections, so that the 19 folios of the Matricula as such correspond to ff.17–55 of Mendoza's 71 folios.

At the start of Mendoza, the four provinces are laid out as on Tenochtitlan's shield (**Pl. 1**) in the classic quatrefoil time-map seen in Fejérváry (p.1), which throughout Mesoamerica (and indeed the entire continent) explicitly translates into political geography concepts and arrangements derived from genesis and the scheme of world ages. Centered on Tenochtitlan, this map appropriately has west to the top, the first of its four tribute provinces; nine patriarchs seated in the quarters ratify the founding of the city and its dynastic pretension and thereby prefigure the reigns of the nine succeeding conqueror-emperors, beginning with Acamapichtli. Enclosing the quarters, a canal of turquoise-water (*xihuitl*) flowing over 51 years (*xihuitl*) issues into the count of those reigns, and of these years, 2 Reed is highlighted as that of a New Fire ceremony. Dating to 2 Reed 1351, this in fact is the last of the four New Fires kindled by the migrant Mexica portrayed in Boturini, before they officially installed Acamapichtli as the first emperor (1376) and held their first supposedly autonomous kindling in 2 Reed 1403. The corresponding four previous Xiuhmolpilli or 52-year periods (1195–1402) are equal in number to the four volutes of smoke that emerge from the fire-drill in 2 Reed 1351. A wealth of further historical and calendrical information is legible in this inaugural page-map. For example, the leaf totals of marsh plants establish Series III C1–C11 year correlations, and volutes of smoke and breath mark the passage of Xiuhmolpilli from earlier calendar bases, which on the previous page are set into the longer story of genesis and world-ages depicted on the Sunstone. Like *Cuevas*, the Mendoza page map also shows skirmishes with established seats of dynastic power in Tenayuca and Colhuacan, to the north (west) and south (east) of what the Aztecs declared to be their new home and lake-island capital.

There follow the nine imperial reigns from Acamapichtli to Moctezuma II, each with its quota of conquests, among which two stand out, Tlatelolco and Coixtlahuaca, since their respective rulers are named, Moquihuix and Atonal. The defeat of the former (noted already in Matricula) assured Mexica control of the Basin; the defeat of the latter meant gaining Cemanahuac, opening up the eastern road to wealth greater than that provided by the rest of the empire put together, as Durán noted (2002, 1:238). Also additional, the concluding part of Mendoza deals with the complementary question of labour tribute and social control, in a series of thematic sections or chapters, paying particular attention to the *pochteca* tribute agents. If Matricula represents the hard economic core of the Mexica Feast system, then Mendoza makes explicit its cultural and historical setting.

As a text in its own right, Mendoza, starting with the quatrefoil title page, models itself on the Fejérváry screenfold, or some very close relative, even to details of the nine conquerors,

while in the additional concluding part we find the same norms of social control and attention to the *pochteca*. Mendoza's textual imitation of Fejérváry has the remarkable structural effect of highlighting the latter's 18-page Enigmatic Chapter (pp.5–22) as an antecedent to the pages that the former took from the Matricula; and indeed they show a common interest in hendecarchies and the Feasts of the year. This equivalence is explored below.

The opening pages of Matrícula, which specify the strongholds that protected the Mexica system and required staff and supplies in their own right, are no less susceptible than the rest of the text to both a practical and a literary reading. Listed in two sets of 11, inner/upper and outer/lower, these strongholds offer a kind of double hendeca guarantee, designed to protect militarily and to prefigure notionally. When we consult **Map 1** we see that the inner first set, starting with the 'star mountain' Citlaltepec, leads us from the north edge of the Basin in a gracious curve around the lake, and in so doing recalls the route followed by the Mexica after they had arrived from Tula-Coatepec and the northwest. Strung along the lakeshore, this first 11 epitomizes the metropolitan area, in the reading of subsequent pages (**Fig. 3.1**). Subjected thanks to the imperial campaigns begun under Acamapichtli, the outer second 11 defended the provinces surrounding the metropolitan area and are ranked by exposure and need, the most vulnerable regions lying in the 'hotlands' to south, east and north. The outer set begins (lower left on the first Matrícula page) with the caiman cave-mouth of Oztoma (**Pl. 2b**): this garrison defended the southern province and the western frontier of much of the system as a whole; and it oversaw settlement programmes organized by administrators sent out from four of the first 11 towns (Berdan & Anawalt 1992, 2:30–1). This detail may exemplify the relationship between the two sets of strongholds in general, respectively as inner resource centres and outer garrisons.

Prefatory, these stronghold pages specify just the geopolitical model to which the text as a whole adheres in going on to list 38 tribute districts, and without which it has to many seemed opaque or random. For the categorical distinction made here between metropolitan and surrounding areas is adhered to in the subsequent listing of tribute districts, and in the grouping of the surrounding districts into four provinces to west, south, east and north, each of which has its governor town: Atotonilco, Tlachco (Taxco), Chalco, and Cuauhtochco (**Fig. 3.2a**). At the norm of one per page, the first 9 of the 38 districts belong to the metropolitan area defined by the first 11 strongholds, and prefaced by the special temple district of Huiznahuac; by the same token the remaining 29 districts belong to the provinces defined by the second 11 strongholds, making two main groups of 9 and 29 (Fig. **3.2b**). Within this model, transitions in the listing, from metropolis to province, and then between one province and the next (from west to south, east and north), are indicated clearly, if subtly.

The initial move from the metropolitan area to the western province is prompted by the only repetition of a headtown name in the whole sequence, the two headtowns named Atotonilco (now missing in Matrícula, this folio is reconstructable thanks to Mendoza). The moves between the provinces to west and south (Atotonilco and Tlachco), and to south and east (Tlachco and Chalco) are prompted by shifts in page format which bunch up

Figure 3.2 Tribute geography and the sky: **a)** metropolitan Petlacalcatl and provincial capitals Atotonilco Tlachco Chalco Cuauhtochco. Mendoza; **b)** totals of towns. Mendoza; **c)** sidereal moon (109 + 137 = 246) and Hermes/Mercury (116; 88). Coixtlahuaca Map (upper left. Cf. **Fig.1.7b**)

a
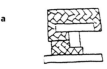

b

Gobernadores		Head towns		All towns										
Petlacalcatl	+123	centre	9	13	10	26	16	26	7	10	7	9	= 124
Atotonilco	+46	west	7	6	7	13	12	6	2	1			= 47
Tlachco	+69	south	7	10	14	12	14	8	6	6			= 70
Chalco	+82	east	7	6	22	11	11	3	22	8			= 83
Cuauhtochco	+45	north	8	7	6	7	11	7	2	5	1		= 46
	365		29										246

c

$$7 \times 3 \times 5 = 105 + 11 \quad = \quad 116 \qquad 7 \times 3 \times 4 \quad = \quad 84 + 4 \quad = \quad 88$$
$$7 \times 3 \qquad\qquad\quad = \quad 21 \qquad\qquad 7 \times 3 \quad = \quad 21$$
$$\qquad\qquad\qquad\qquad\quad 137 \qquad + \qquad\qquad 109 \qquad\qquad = 246$$

the last three of the districts in the western and southern provinces. Heralding a move from one province to the next, this placing of three districts on a single page, twice, is a formal decision that has nothing to do with quantities of towns in those districts or the amounts of tribute they rendered. In terms of Matrícula's pagination, it neatly reconciles the overall total of districts registered in that text (38) with the page total (38) of its 19 folios, the four pages thereby gained having been ceded at the start to the bastions and the Huitznahuac temple district (pp.1–4). That this alteration in format is not casual is further confirmed in the fact that as a result of it the overall page count of the text's three subgroupings, 4 + 9 + 25 pages, equals the sum of the first three primes squared: 2^2 (bastions, Huitznahuac), 3^2 (metropolitan tribute), 5^2 (provincial tribute). The final move, from east to north (Chalco to Cuauhtochco), is indicated by the modified frequency of payment accorded to Xoconochco, the last of the eastern districts, on account of its distance and the hazards of the road. In terms of tribute rendered, the shifts from one province to the next are underlined by the fact that the outlying districts to south and east, and all to north, were excused bulky loads of agricultural produce. Mendoza copies and reinforces the model, by allotting extra page space exclusively to metropolitan districts; within the surrounding provinces, like Huiztilopochtli's Hymn (*Icuic* no. 5, **Appendix C**) it also highlights the shift from the first of the four, the west, to the 'hot lands' of the other three.

Specifying its huge array of tributaries, Matricula amounts to the most precious early map of Mexico and much of Mesoamerica. It precisely defines what still today is Mexico's eastern border with Guatemala, along with provinces that largely coincide with its federal states, like Guerrero, to the south of the capital. By negative definition it reveals the autonomy maintained by areas like Oaxaca, in matters of economy and therefore calendar (as Rios and other compendia duly note), which in the larger pattern served to reinforce the inner borders between provinces (notably intermediary and sometimes enclave parts of the Sierra Madre Oriental, like Teotitlan, Tlaxcala, and Metztitlan). Yet more astounding, this wide-ranging imperial geography, though challenged militarily by such unrelenting foes as Tlaxcala, appears most often to have been acknowledged in international law, so that Tlaxcala's

account of the conquests it made after 1519 with the help of Spanish allies punctiliously distinguishes between towns within and without the Aztec domain. Separating the towns claimed by Tenochtitlan from those claimed as later conquests by Tlaxcala, the larger map of Mesoamerica fits together perfectly like pieces of a jigsaw.

The Matrícula is also informative about precedent, in incorporating strongholds and sources of goods and materials that had served empires prior to that of the Mexica. The exemplary case is Oztoma, foremost and lynchpin of the outer strongholds, which archeologically dates back to the Olmec: Durán notes Ahuizotl's decision to re-fortify and populate it (2002, 1:409). Oztoma is shown as a caiman cave-mouth (*ozto-*) in profile, with a blue nose, plus a hand affix (*ma-itl*, for the phonetic element *-ma*; **Pl. 2b**). The blueness of nose is striking, is cast as stone, and has the colour of the product for which the southern province defended by Oztoma was the major supplier, turquoise, precious stones being conceived of as the hardened snot of the caiman earth-beast. As depicted in Matrícula (p.20), the turquoise tribute appears to have been mined in the southern province, to which activity the hand may also point. Synonymous with the year for the Chichimec and Mexica, this mineral (*xiuh-*) was otherwise said to have been brought all the way from Pueblo mines far to the north, whence they had migrated.

Designating a frontier bastion in Mesoamerica, Oztoma's caiman head has the general western location assigned to Xiuhcoanaual in the Coixtlahuaca Map (**Fig. 2.7a,b**); it also lay cheek to jowl with the Purépecha over the border in Michoacan. Materially, this proximity fostered techniques of mining and metallurgy in the southern province of Tlachco, to which is testimony the range of metalwork (axe heads, bells) included in the tribute exacted from it. Culturally, it may help to explain the unusual emphasis placed on Oztoma's Feast cycle in the *Relación geográfica* of that town (1581. Acuña 1985, 6:283), given the huge importance of the Feasts in the Purépecha calendar, in which the Tonalpoualli is not a factor. Lying on this frontier, Oztoma, the first of the 11 outer garrisons and the focus of a major Mexica settlement programme, guarded the southern province, known for its axe heads. Exactly this cluster of concepts is prefigured in the story, told in the *Popol vuh* and reflected in Magliabechiano, of the 11 pioneers, the first settlers and house-builders, axe-bearers and drinkers who eventually became the first constellation of the night sky, the Pleiades.

Militarily, Oztoma had already served as a western bastion for the Olmec, who left much evidence of their presence in the area, not least in the image of the caiman cave mouth at Oxtotitlan (Grove 1970) that resembles that of Oztoma itself. Additional cranial and facial features of this painted image duly identify the cave mouth with its Olmec masters, the jaguar breed, while the feathers of its headdress intimate the Feasts and the Nemotemi (**Fig. 1.1**).

The profound resonance that Oztoma, first of the outer 11, continued to have, on all these and yet other counts, in the belief system and year calendar inherited by the Mexica from the Olmec is quite explicit in several sources. Perhaps the most dense and significant is the Hymn (*Icuic* no.14) sung every eight years at Atamalcualiztli, the ceremony that concludes the Feasts cycle in Tepepulco. The Hymn places Oztoma under the (Olmeca-Xicalanca) rule of Cholula (*on tlatoa Cholollan*), invokes the ball-game (*ullama*) of the Olmec 'rubber people' and the quartered ball-court found in the toponym Tlachco, Mexica governor of the Oztoma province, and celebrates the tribute it renders in exquisite objects of turquoise and gold (*xiuhnacochtla iteamic, xiuhmaquiztli iteamic*; Garibay 1958:150ff). These and other allusions echo those in the Hymn of Ixcozauhqui, wearer of the Xiuhcoanaual hood (*Icuic* no.6; see p.16 above)

In name no less significant than Oztoma and the bastions, are the 'governors' of the four provinces they guard. Atotonilco, governor of the western province, simply repeats the name of the penultimate metropolitan district, being contiguous with the metropolitan area and devoid of garrisons of its own. Governor of the first of the three hotland provinces, Tlachco to the south was guarded by the foremost garrison, Oztoma, whose snot is the turquoise that may denote the year, while its ball-court glyph denotes the principle of tribute quarters as such, in time as well as space. As a motif of quarterly tribute that is Olmec in origin, the ball-court attaches to New Fire ceremonies and methods of measuring the year in the annals of Tepexic and the Mixteca (Vienna pp.31, 31–4, 36, 40; Zouche pp.1–3). At the head of the eastern province or rather tribute road, the third governor Chalco, the place of jade located in the southeastern corner of the Basin, recalls (like Oztoma's turquoise) the mining of precious stones in its purview far to the east, and like Tlachco has a spatio-temporal definition. (It denotes the 80-year cycle noted in Chichimec annals – 1176 – 1256 – 1336 – linked to Acamapichtli's bid for power in 1 Flint 1376, and a factor in political life even after Cortés: see p.75 below; and Key p.21. For his part, Tichy has equated the years of Chalco's Jade with the 80 degrees of the Mesoamerican circle). Guarding the coast of the 'mar del norte', the fourth governor Cuauhtochco was ordered in 1519 to send emissaries to greet Cortés, on the main feast of his calendar (Easter; see p.8 above); among the the tribute it collected from its mountainous hinterland was the eagle of its name (Cuauh–, 5th of the Quecholli, the full name being legible as the day or year 5 Rabbit).

Semesters and quarters

The main body of Matrícula, which states which towns in which districts and provinces should pay which goods over the course of the year, consists of pages that have a standard format. Along the lower and right-hand margins there runs a chain of towns in a given district, the first being that of the Calpixque or collector. Rimmed by the glyphs of towns, the page itself shows the tribute due from the district they comprise. Categories of goods and items succeed each other from bottom to top of the page and have inherent in them three default frequencies; that is, the concept of the year was so deeply embedded in the system that items listed implied the frequency with which they should be paid, unless otherwise stated. Hence, according to the gloss in Mendoza, items in the first category, textiles (woven cotton capes, shirts, loincloths), as well as a great range of other products (paper, honey, wooden bowls, salt, shells, varnish) were to be paid half-yearly; in the second category, products of yearly harvests like maize and beans were due annually, along with costumes, artefacts of gold, jade and other precious materials; and third, metal goods like copper axe-heads, timber, and copal were due quarterly.

Because of its precise calculations of material detail, the Matrícula has long served as a scholarly guide to modes of production and supply in the Mexica empire; here it is important to recall the link between the corresponding schedules and the Feasts cycle. The first category, with its half-year frequency, also includes the greatest variety of goods, and in this sense is both first and predominant. How the half-year interval relates to the Feasts is stated explicitly. For, of the Mexica tribute districts, the one that lay furthest from the capital was Xoconochco, on the Guatemalan border in the eastern province, and the precious and exotic goods it supplied had to be transported along a hazardous route. Normally, most of these goods would have been due once a year, but Tenochtitlan preferred to divide the load 'en dos tributos' so as to halve any risk of loss. That is, regardless of their default frequencies all the goods were put on to the half-yearly schedule, and this decision is specified on the page (p.25) by the emblems of the Feasts in which the half years ended: the broom of Ochpaniztli (F1.9) and the conical hat of Tlacaxipehualiztli (F2.9) (**Fig. 3.3**).

At the end of the first tribute half-year, Ochpaniztli meshes closely with the phases of the solar year, its final day announcing the September equinox exactly. For this and other reasons, Ochpaniztli asks to be seen altogether as the major moment in the Mexica cycle, having similar prominence in the parallel years of liturgy, where its presiding deity is none other than the mother of gods Tlazoteotl/Teteo innan, matron of the thread (see Chapter 5). Moreover, as the hinge between the upper and lower halves of the sun's annual course, the summer and winter of the northern hemisphere, the equinoctial ending of Ochpaniztli (F1.9) led directly into Pachtli A (F2.1), also known as Teotleco, the arrival of the gods that was ritually marked by the footprints seen for example in Telleriano, Borgia and Tovar. More broadly, these footprints in Teotleco, at the start of the 'winter' half of the year, indicated no less the start of journeys then typically undertaken by *pochteca* tribute agents, and for that matter by hunters. A gloss in Rios makes the *pochteca* link explicit by referring the footprints to their patron Yacatecutli. One explanation offered for Ochpaniztli's tribute emblem, the broom, is that it served to sweep clean the roads that would be travelled in the following Feast. As for Tlacaxipehualiztli (F2.9) and the March equinox, the eponymous Xipe is said to 'drink night' ('youallauana'. *Icuic* no.15) in the Feast, as the days get longer.

Etzalcualiztli

Ochpaniztli

Panquetzaliztli

Tlacaxipehualiztli

Figure 3.3 Semesters and quarters: half-year Feasts. Mendoza f.47; quarter-year Feasts. Humboldt 1 (after Humboldt 1892)

With the Matrícula's first default frequency, half years, firmly tied to equinoctial Ochpaniztli and Tlacaxipehualiztli, what of the other two frequencies, the year, and the quarter year? All that has been said about Etzalcualiztli (F1.4; pp.21) identifies this Feast as the deadline for annual agricultural tribute, the bushels of maize and beans and the corresponding flours. In their copiously documented four-volume edition of Mendoza (1992), Berdan and Anawalt do not disagree; and they derive the concept of the quarter year from glosses that read 'de ochenta en ochenta dias' (literally, from one lot of 80 days to the next; 1992, 1:154–56). As other tribute documents confirm, these lots of 80 days lead respectively to the end of the pre-solstitial Feasts in each of the half years, Etzalcualiztli in the summer (F1.4), and Panquetzaliztli in the winter (F2.4). In this model, the endings of the halves and quarters of the year as a whole correspond, then, to the endings of the Feasts F1.4, F1.9; F2.4, F2.9 (**Fig. 3.3**).

In certain tribute texts these four Feasts are depicted so as to highlight the idea of quarters as such. In the Tlaquiltenango Codex (HMAI 22), they are subjected to a format which standardizes their end dates as quarter days of the year. Despite actual intervals of 80+100 + 80+100 days they are made to resemble the quarter days of the equinoxes and solstices of the year, which lie unevenly more or less 90 days apart. The standardized format of quarters is also found in the Tlapa screenfold I, a text which defines all payments as quarterly, no doubt thanks to the predominance of metals in tribute collected from that area: guarded by Oztoma, Tlapa lies in the southern province of Tlachco (Taxco), largely coextensive with the modern state of Guerrero and noted for its mines and metallurgy.

Tlapa I chooses a quarterly format in this way in specific contrast to its textual twin, Tlapa II. On their obverse side, both screenfolds record (in year Series II) the annals of the same part of Guerrero, yet each does so with its own thematic emphasis, which is reflected numerically in the grouping of years in the annals, and in the text on the reverse side. Hence, Tlapa I, which has an economic and political focus, groups its years in lots of 4+4 per page, registers conquest by Tenochtitlan, and details the tribute payments on its reverse side in quarters of the year. Tlapa II, which has a more dynastic concern, groups its years in sevens, and details genealogy on its reverse. Effectively, in depicting the tribute payments in this way, the layout of Tlapa I makes an explicit analogy between the quarters of the four-year

leap-day span (Nauhtetl; *cuatrenio* in Spanish) that is synonymous with both the four year-bearer Signs, and the four quarters of a given year. The same pattern is explicit in certain alphabetic transcriptions of such sources into Nahuatl, a signal case being the account of 'Realms, rulers and tribute' appended to the Cuauhtitlan Annals (f.65; Bierhorst 1992:129–34). There the main deliveries of woven goods to Texcoco demanded by Nezahualcoyotl and his descendants are specified by 'nombres de meses' which are the equinoctial Feasts (F1.9, F2.9) and the intervening quarters (F1.4, F2.4), along with two small supplementary instalments (F1.5 and F2.3).

Quartering of tribute in time and space is noted in subsidiary emblems that attach to the relevant Feasts and in the markers which distinguish the names of years (Number and Sign, like 2 Reed) from other Tonalpoualli days. In Borbonicus (p.34), a miniature version of the quatrefoil map of the system itself attaches to the quarterly Feast Panquetzaliztli (F2.4), while as we saw (**Fig. 3.2a**) the ballcourt design of Tlachco, with its two ends and two sides, identifies the southern member of the four provinces. As for the year markers, which denote the concept of year itself, of the nine or so different designs used for this purpose throughout Mesoamerica, more than half of them are structurally fourfold (**Table 3d**). This is the case with the foursquare box commonest in the Highland Basin, the Huaxteca, and Tlapa, and the diamond box (the square tilted through 45°) also found in the Basin as well as far to the east in Guatemala (in Fuentes y Guzmán, along with other key information about the year calendar in highland Guatemala: see HMAI 14:78; Edmonson 1988). As for the round marker known in the Teotihuacan valley, Cholula, Metlatoyuca and eastern Tlaxcala, it also exists in fourfold versions. Recalling the periodicity of metal tribute in the form of a coit, it may have quarters inset, like numerals on a clockface. Circular, these designs match those of shields, and of the solar disk itself, ancient versions of which have four sunray pointers inset into them.

In the account of the Atamalcualiztli ceremony that concludes the Feasts chapter in Tepepulco, quarterly patterning is likewise registered in a round marker, a turquoise ring to whose outer edge attach four small disks at the quarter points. In context, the purpose of these rings, eight in all, is to denote the timing of the ceremony, which takes place over 4+4 days every 4+4 years. The analogy established in Tlapa I between quarters of the four-year Nauhtetl and quarters of a year is, then, elaborated in the Atamalcualiztli time marker to include quadruple multiples of years and days (4+4). Tepepulco (II, 1) also defines the quarters of the day (see **Appendix B**). As a result, the summer and winter equinoctial halves of the tribute year, with the halfway solstitial moments that mark the quarters, come to be reflected in other dimensions of time, the 4 (+4) cipher applying to parts of the day, days, Feasts, and years. Through the Venus chapters in the screenfolds, this principle is affirmed in astronomy (4+4 days, 4+4 years), while the principle of the time shift as such is intrinsic to funeral ceremonies throughout Meso-, and indeed North America. On the Sunstone and in HM, the principle is extended to the Great Years of creation (viz. '102,000 years'), while 'Genesis' calculates the semester of 12,800 years.

In this way, the tribute year arrangement detailed in Matrícula and Mendoza, as the third of the three services (**Appendix E**), instructively complements the hours and years of nocturnal penance that govern the first. These texts take us far beyond what the west normally considers to be economics and recognizing the fact prepares us for further scrutiny of the time-space detailed in them and their literary antecedents.

Oztoma: caiman cave as military redoubt

Punctiliously respecting Matrícula's organization of Mexica time and space enables us to read it more intelligently as a text, and then to go on to correlate it to great advantage with precedents in the classic screenfolds. For the Enigmatic Chapters in Borgia, Fejérváry, Cospi and Laud (see p.26 above) appeal to the same model of the year in their own ways, a parallel of some consequence for assessing the role of the Feasts in the Mexica system and more widely. In the first instance, in taking solar semesters and quarters as its premise Matrícula matches the structure of the 18-page core chapter in Borgia, as we shall see (Chapter 6 below). As for the sets of 11+11 strongholds which guard and prefigure the system in Matrícula and Mendoza, Fejérváry provides the classic model in its 18-page 'Enigmatic Chapter', which in turn has close cognates with the corresponding chapters in Cospi and Laud. Fully exploring all these literary parallels is not on option here, given our Mexica focus. Nonetheless, the comparisons that follow offer to indicate how every one of the Enigmatic Chapters, which Nowotny could not relate to the Tonalpoualli, in fact belong to the Feasts and to the year of the night sky.

A representation of the Feasts no less choreographical than that in Borbonicus, the core chapter in Borgia (pp.29–46) is multilayered and rhythmically complex and reconciles in one statement the arrangements of Feasts in halves, thirds and primes that correspond to three services inherited by the Mexica (these Borgia Feasts are discussed in more detail below, in Chapter 6). Visually, the division into halves or semesters is the most obvious, since footprints mark out a road through the lower half of the year (a true 'Winterreise'), and are entirely absent from the upper half. Swept by the broom of equinoctial Ochpaniztli (F1.9, pp.33–4), the road begins with the 'arrival of the gods' in Teotleco (F2.1, p.35) and ends at the other equinox, at the emblem of Tlacaxipehualiztli's knotted cap (F2.9, p.42). Halfway, the quarter Feast Panquetzaliztli (F2.4, p.38) is noted as such in the quatrefoil emblem used to the same end at this Feast in Borbonicus (p.34; see p.56–7 below). The quarters in the upper half of the year are defined by the very structure of the text, since, as in *Cuevas* and 'Genesis', the year begins with the second quarter, marked by Tecuilhuitl's jade quincunx (F1.5, p.29), and ends with the first, marked by Etzalcualiztli's stew pot (F1.4, p.46). On the threshold of the summer solstice, Etzalcualiztli is the Feast of New Fire, sequel to one previously kindled in equinoctial Ochpaniztli (overloooked by Nowotny), and the mirror image of the Panquetzaliztli New Fire in Borbonicus (F2.4; p. 34).

Building on this division of the Feasts into semesters and quarters, Borgia then distinguishes between six Feasts (F1.9–F2.5) which are not dominated by Ilamatecutli's star-fringed body, the galactic womb named Tianquiz or Market in Tepepulco (II,i), and 12 that are (F2.6–F2.8). Above, Ilamatecutli's absence or presence dovetails below, though with a certain forward slippage, with that of the caiman earth beast

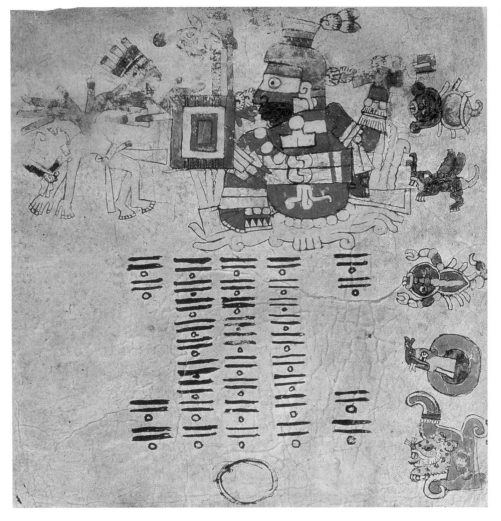

Figure 3.4 Caiman cave (bottom right) and elevens. Cospi p.21

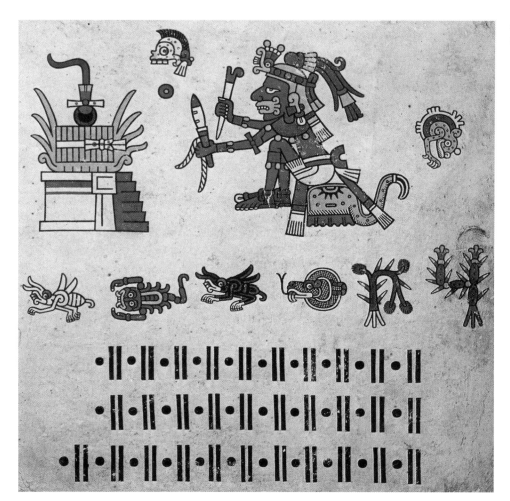

Figure 3.5 Caiman cave (top right) and elevens. Fejérváry p.5

Figure 3.6 Caiman cave, facing and below 11+11 walkers. Laud p.44

Figure 3.7 Seven Feasts, Micailhuitl B to Atemoztli: **a)** Fejérváry pp.15–22 (r–l); **b)** Laud pp.21–22 (r–l)

first seen in Ochpaniztli (F1.9). Seminal for the twelve-Feast planting season, just this trinary division of the year is declared in detail in Tepepulco II, ii (see Chapter 4 below). In Tititl (F2.6), the earth beast becomes the caiman cave of the Olmec jaguar; it acquires exactly the facial iconography seen in the Oxtotitlan mural (**Fig. 1.1**) and similarly indicates the 18 of the Feasts, and it initiates moreover a full correlation of the Tonalpoualli days with year Series I to IV, proper to Izcalli (F2.7).

Playing with the very notion of superimposed levels, the Borgia chapter goes yet further in parsing the 18 of the Feasts as 11+7, the sum of the stars that conform the two primary stellar signs named in Tepepulco (II,i): Yoalitecutli, the Lord of Night whose resplendent body lies deep within the earthbeast in Izcalli (F2.7), and Xonecuilli, the septentrion that bursts through the darkness with the hunters in Quecholli (F2.3. **Pl. 3**). By arranging the Feasts at these successive levels, Borgia invites the reader to contemplate the year and time itself in just the terms for which Cholula's priesthood was celebrated. Most relevant here, this core chapter stands as a copious antecedent for the model of the year developed in Matrícula and Mendoza.

Borgia's master account of the Cholula Feast system elucidates in turn the tight cluster of Enigmatic Chapters in Fejérváry (pp.5–22), Cospi (pp.21–38) and Laud (pp.39–44), which as a result prove to have more to do with the year of the Feasts than has hitherto been suspected (**Figs 3.4–3.8**). These three chapters share the following features. They all make calculations on number base 11, represented in Olmec fashion as two bars and a dot (5 x 2 +1), the arithmetical emblem known as 'palatine' (Tlacatecpan) that is set into an excessively steep pyramid in Tepepulco (II, iii; **Pl. 3c**) and which in years denoted the Ozomatli (Monkey, Sign XI) or sunspot span (*Historia tolteca-chichimeca* f.41v). They all depict presiding teams of 11 figures who link constellation signs with versions of the jaguar's caiman cave. And they all combine astronomical formulas, relevant to the sun, moon, planets, with references to political history. The caiman cave-mouth has just the jaguar affixes seen in Tititl in Borgia and a turquoise nose that recalls the toponym

Oztoma. Indeed, the turquoise has the same hardened affix as does the snot of Oztoma in Matrícula and Mendoza. The jaguar infixes, as ears and upper bodies, indicate an aging beast and display rows of (white) hairs corroborated by glyph-like markings on the skin which in each case total the number of Feasts (Laud, 18 in ear, **Fig. 3.6**; Fejérváry, 18 in beard, **Fig. 3.5**; Cospi, 11 in beard +7 in ears, **Fig. 3.4**).

On this basis, the parallel between Matrícula and Laud is notably close. Both array their sets of 11 in upper and lower registers: in each, the upper begins by invoking the stars (Citlaltepec; the Pleiades), and the lower begins or ends in Oztoma's caiman cave. Laud begins by vertically aligning New Fire with the Pleiades above. Through subgroupings of the elevens, both texts prefigure the quatrefoil map of four tribute quarters. In itself, the double set of 11 comes charged with a celestial reference explicit in the story of the Pleiades settlers, signaled by the first of the upper Mexica strongholds (Citlaltepec, Star Mountain) (**Fig. 3.1**) and detailed in Tepepulco II, iii. (The lower 11 in Laud, like the 11 in Cospi, carry the axes characteristic of these settlers on the Oztoma frontier.) This arithmetical insistence on 11 enriches the examples noted or alluded to above: Borbonicus images the 11 in the vertically halved disk that represents the time of the sun (right) and the night sky (left, 11 stars; p.11; **Fig. 2.5**); in Tovar, the eleven-fold bounty atop the pole in Xocotl huetzi (F1.8) was identified by Kubler and Gibson with the night-sky; the optimum number of stars in the constellations shown in Tepepulco is 11, and in the Florentine Codex this becomes the star number in general; in Mexicanus the hand loyal to Acamapichtli vows to restore the zodiac to its original 11 (p.36). In the *Popol vuh* (lines 3041–80), as in Amazonian texts, 11 determines the jaguar-led zodiac team which in the 'heart of night' reclaims for the wild the work done by day. And so on.

While the caiman cave has a terminal position in Laud, in Fejérváry and Cospi it is initial and is identifiable with Tititl in the year of the Feasts. The equivalence effectively established (thanks to Mendoza) between Matrícula and Fejérváry's 18-page

Figure 3.8 Females and males in Ochpaniztli: **a**) Fejérváry pp.16–17 (r–l); **b**) Tudela (l–r)

Enigmatic Chapter has been noted above. In Fejérváry, after the 11 begun in Tititl (pp. 5–14) seven further Feasts emerge explicitly as those of the solar year (pp.15–22), effectively establishing sequences of 11 'thin' and 7 'fat' units: this pattern is seen in the Round Dance in *Cuevas* (**Pl. 4**) and determines the very format of the Feast chapters in Borbonicus and Tepepulco (I,ii; see Chapter 5 below). In these cases, equinoctial Ochpaniztli is the grandest of the seven Feasts and in Fejérváry it boasts the presence of Teteu Innan, complete with spindle, broom, and the club-wielding male seen at this Feast in Tepepulco (I,ii) and Tudela (Magliabechiano group; **Fig 3.8**). In Fejérváry, Ochpaniztli (F1.9) comes after the mummy bundle of Micailhuitl B (F1.8) and the year runs on through Quecholli (F2.3; vertical arrow, severed bird's head) to the falling water-drops of Atemoztli (F2.5), to complete the span of seven Feasts that complement the initial 11 (**Fig.3.7**). In Cospi, the 11 likewise begin an 18-page chapter, the rest of which was however left blank. For its part, in a brief chapter (pp.21–22) that ends the first side of the screenfold just as the 11 end the second (pp.39–44), Laud features the same initial and final Feasts as those that begin and end the seven in Fejérváry (Micailhuitl B and Atemoztli, F1.8 and F2.5) drawing on much of the same iconography. Laud and Fejérváry also tie Micailhuitl B to the Tonalpoualli through the day 1 Water. In striking confirmation of this reading of the Feasts in these screenfolds, just this date 1 Water introduces Micailhuitl B in the Night Sky Grid in Mexicanus (p.13), which is likewise based on sets of 11 (**Table 4**).

Summary as this account of them has to be, these classic antecedents further validate the notion that Matrícula and Mendoza represent far more than a simple ledger and endow the tribute year with nothing less than a cosmic resonance. If we respect the map of bastions and provinces that they impose on Tenochtitlan's tribute landscape (and only then), we begin to see the remarkable logic that operates within it as a whole. At the practical level, this logic might enable the reader to remember, expect, and even reconstruct missing page-sheets in the file. For thanks to the campaign of conquests that began with the emperor Acamapichtli (and the reverses it suffered), the file must have been endlessly updated and modified; yet as represented in the Matrícula the whole system, its very

mechanisms, never fail to depend on ciphers derived from the calendar and the sky.

In these texts, the 11, in upper and lower ranks, usher in not just the Mexica tribute system but astronomical formulas, whose units are the very towns incorporated into that system (**Fig. 3.2b,c**). Providing the schedule for the payment of tribute, the year with its Feasts is commemorated in the fact that the towns throughout the empire subject to the capital and the four provincial governors number 365, the days of the solar year. An optional 366th or leap day is even provided by the preliminary toponym Huitznahuac. Complementing the commodity tribute determined by the Feasts, the labour tribute proper to the Tonalpoualli is prefigured in the totals of headtowns in the metropolitan and provincial areas, the 9 and 29 of the imperial shield, lunar factors which multiply to produce the count of 261 nights that enclose 260 days. Meanwhile, in the stellar domain of Citlaltepec proper, the individual towns in the four provinces equal the nights of nine sidereal moons (246). A yet further formula derives from the fact that the first of the four provinces (west, Atotonilco) differs from the rest by virtue of being entirely contiguous with the highland metropolitan area, not 'hotlands', and quite devoid of garrisons (all 11 occupy the provinces to south, east and north). That is, the distinction in principle between districts of the inner metropolis (9) and outer province (29) leads to this subdivision within the latter (7, 22), one which in turn has its astronomical correlative. Factors of one of the oldest formulas known to humanity, 22:7, these numbers correlate the years of the sun (7) with the synodic cycles of the planet Mercury (22).

Just this order of calculation is patent in the classic antecedents, in the Enigmatic Chapters. Fejérváry extends the lunar-solar count of tribute towns in an enhanced version of the Atamalcualiztli Formula, which includes the inner planet Venus and poses the total 2914 as:

8 years less 8 days = 99 moons less 9 days = 5 synodic Venus cycles less 5 days.

Focusing on sidereal rather than synodic cycles, Cospi multiplies by 10 the nine sidereal moon total given in Matrícula (246, 2460), and invokes the seven-year sun that correlates with the other inner planet Mercury (of which 22 synodic cycles equal 29 sidereal cycles):

2460 = 90 sidereal moons = 7 years less 7 days, less 1 sidereal Mercury cycle

The significance and practical relevance of the 90 sidereal moon period is stated in Tepepulco Part II (see chapter 7).

However such formulas are ultimately viewed or assessed, in Matrícula and the classic screenfolds alike they are set in the same numerical frame and respect the same ciphers and logic. Moreover in both sources the argument moves on from the 11 to the Feasts, so that in this sense the night sky prefigures and anticipates the solar year, just as the bastions guard the provinces and their annual tribute schedule. Apart from further illuminating the Enigmatic Chapters in Nowotny's catalogue, referring back to these screenfold antecedents enhances Matrícula's historicity and claim to be treated as a text in its own right. The signal example of this continuity proves to be the caiman cave of Oztoma, which the Mexica inherited from the jaguar Olmec. Celebrated along with Cholula in their Twenty Hymns, this place was made into a principle in their own tribute system, anchoring its arithmetic and ideology.

Exquisite, such an Aztec 'arrangement' might well seem fanciful, but it is easy enough to verify through simple arithmetic, and a reading of the text that follows *it* page by page rather than preconceived ideas about what it ought to be saying, or what Mexica imperial geography was really like. It affirms what the Mexica characterized as an ancestral loyalty to the equinoxes and the year of the sun, within a notable calendrical sophistication. In its day it doubtless had both beauty and strong practical advantages, and is eminently memorable, none of these numerical rubrics being random. For just these reasons, it provides a firm underpinning for conceptions of the Feast cycle which, while functional for the gathering of tribute over the solar year, are inseparable from the deeper time of cosmogony.

4
Planting Seasons

A model compendium from a good school, the Tepepulco Ms serves well to introduce the seasonal significance of the Feasts. It technically carries forward the competence of *tlacuilolli*, holding firm to the hermeneutics of the classic screenfolds, though of course with an eye to making clear alphabetically what it could to Europe. For this reason, in the Tepepulco Ms the alphabetic complement in Nahuatl has an authority never rivalled by the commentaries and glosses in Spanish added to the other compendia, by priests and scholars formed by Europe and therefore unable and unprepared from the start to comprehend the *tlacuilolli* original's intellectual wealth. The Tepepulco authors cogently affirm their knowledge and philosophy in the first person plural, referring to such matters as the source of rain ('we say it is Tlaloc...'; II, ii) and the calendar of 'our years' (*toxiuh*; II, iii).

The accounts of the Feasts provided in Parts I and II of Tepepulco are nothing less than indispensable. Paying close attention to them amounts to a hugely instructive *lecture* of the very best textbook. It is a true reading lesson, provided by a manuscript that illuminates (and is illuminated by) a dense cluster of native texts. Together, these pages of the Tepepulco Ms deserve to be recognized as an astounding resource for understanding the Feast cycle and its primordial place and role in the Mexica calendar. Part I concentrates on choreography and the service of the gods, and acknowledges the Otomi patron Otontecutli (see Chapter 6 below)

The four *tlacuilolli* chapters of Part II, which deal with the sky, seasons, politics and society, are cogent and subtly imbricated and interlinked (**Pl. 3a,b,c**). There is a lean, purposeful and ingenious appeal to the resources of *tlacuilolli* script, the logic of its layout, colour, number. Unique among surviving texts, this second Part reveals the practices and deeper logics proper to the calendar, through the *tlacuilolli* text arranged as it is on successive pages, and matched (or not) with statements in alphabetic Nahuatl. It would not be too fanciful to think of Part II as a small symphony in four movements, each with its measure, rhythms, themes, within multiple sound dimensions, that is, levels of resonance and reading.

The first two movements or chapters of Part II focus directly on the year and its Feasts – their nature, meaning, numeracy, valency – as manifestations of the time proper to sky and to earth. First come the celestial lights (*tlanextilia*), that is, Astronomy: the sun that emerges from the night sky (as on the Sunstone), faces the moon, and is conceptually matched by the stars of the zodiac Fire Drills and Xonecuilli's polar meridian (the model in Borgia), and by intermediary planets, comets and meteors (chapter i). It is here that the categorical distinction is made between the time determined by the movement of the sun by day and that determined by that of the constellations by night (**Pl. 3a**; **Appendix 2**). Then come Weather from above and facing Winds (*tlacpac eecaticpac*), Tlaloc's mountain, paths and

homes (chapter ii, **Pl. 3b,c**). With their focus on the year, these two initial chapters parse the 18 Feasts in subgroups, first according to the two primes 11 and 7 that, metronomic in the performance of the Feasts (Part I), here define zodiac and pole (Mamalhuaztli and Xonecuilli); and then in halves (9+9) that are upper and lower roads, and thirds (12+6) that correspond to planting and non planting seasons.

The worth of Tepepulco's account of sky and earth is strongly borne out through comparison with such classic statements as the Feasts chapter in Borgia and the Coatlan Inscription. The text was in this sense distorted by Sahagún when he adapted and transcribed its testimony into the Spanish prose of his *Historia general*. Moreover, Sahagún shared with Durán the strong Christian aversion to Tlaloc's fieldwork and cult of the crop-bearing caiman earth.

Weather and winds on Tlaloc's mountain

Completing the score of images that make up the first two chapters of Part II of the Tepepulco manuscript, Weather and Winds (*tlacpac eecatipac*, chapter ii; literally 'from above, in the wind') adds a further eight to the 12 seen in Astronomy (II, i. **Pl. 3b,c**). The structure is similarly intricate and is explained through overt reference, in the *tlacuilolli* images and the accompanying Nahuatl texts, to the 18 Feasts of the year. Moving down from the realm of Astronomy, we are now given the earthly coordinates of the Feasts.

The factor that obviously categorizes the eight images of Weather and Winds is hue, since the first four are coloured and the second four are not. Hence, as a set of 4+4, they respect the numerical paradigm which in ritual determines the Atamalcualiztli ceremony's 4+4 years and days and which in astronomy and tribute derives from the days and years of the sun and its and their quarters. In the cosmogony of 'Genesis', this pattern extends to primordial passages through darkness and the underworld, four harder than the other four (Rios f.2). Here, the four plus four correspond initially to halves of the year (coloured and colourless) each of which is introduced by a figure walking right to left (**Pl. 3b**). The first walker wears the wind mask of his name Eecatl and carries the staff of blue or turquoise (*xiuh-*) that ushers in the year (*xiuh-*). Enveloped by dusty winds, his cap pressed firmly on, he brings with him red and yellow zigzag lightning whose head is a steely bolt, and comes to face to face with Tlaloc's cloud-crowned mountain, which has dried to yellow but is now refreshed and greening thanks to huge drops of turquoise rain. At the end of the journey, the rainbow sums up its colours, as home and haven, in arches of turquoise, red, yellow and green. The Nahuatl glosses confirm that the first walker, whose turquoise staff may likewise denote the year, travels through its upper half, as this is experienced in the Mexica heartland and the Highland Basin, his winds bringing thunderstorms and then, halfway, Tlaloc's rains, whose ending is marked by the rainbow, the arched spectrum.

In this arrangement, Eecatl sets off from the same starting point in the year as that marked for first tribute semester in Matrícula, Tozoztli. He moves however in parallel time, attentive less to *pochteca* duty than to weather. He walks amid winds which stirring in this Feast (F1.1) in and near the Highland Basin acquire violent force by Toxcatl (F1.3), the warrior feast that preludes the monsoon (F1.4).

Announcing the other colourless half of the year, the second walker moves forward stiffly, pigeon chested; his high hat curls back so as to project a parabola of 3 x 3 shark (or filed) teeth. He is cold or frost and called Itztlacoliuhqui ('curved obsidian blade'), and the degrees of cold he brings are gauged in vertical black lines that spread from his temple across his face: in the Tonalpoualli chapter below (Tepepulco II, iv), this thermometer is applied to the tumescent face of Wind (Sign II). The three images of the weather brought by Itztlacoliuhqui – frost, snow, and hail – are all black and white, note wind direction, and include the hardest arithmetic (**Pl. 3c**). The mountain crown of clouds worn by Tlaloc (seen first in profile facing east) is seen now as if from above or in plan, with ledges in the gulley-passes between its five peaks intimating levels of permafrost, and its highest eastern peak now to the top of the page. The first of the three black and white circular diagrams introduced by Itztlacoliuhqui, the crown precedes the cyclonic snowstorm that all but obscures the seven stars and seven caves of its northern origin and whose fluffy flakes gently blanket the earth preparing it for good harvests. Frozen water like snow, hail in the next and final image compresses 3 x 3 x 3 to damaging density at great anticyclonic heights, as at polar extremes, in iceblocks crunched in a relentless spiral where only the strongest primes can survive (those that decorate the diagonal sash on Itztlacoliuhqui's chest, 2 and 3). The key significance of hail for rain-makers (*graniceros*) working in Mexico still today has been amply explored (Albores & Broda 1997). So, just as the first walker heralds the summer and its monsoon, the second threatens winter cold.

This first reading of the weather and winds on Tlaloc's mountain involves, then, two walkers, Eecatl and Itztlacoliuhqui, whose paths correspond respectively to the four coloured and the four black and white images which comprise the chapter, indicative of the seasons in the Mexica heartland. The reader's view of the mountain shifts accordingly, from profile to plan, enhancing the principle of calculation.

The horizontal and vertical scales of wind, temperature, and precipitation announced in the title of the Tepepulco chapter (*tlacpac eecatlapac*) principally gauge Tlaloc's water, the factor in half the images of colourful summer (clouds, rainbow) and three quarters of those of colourless winter (clouds, snow, hail). The rain-charged clouds that crown Tlaloc's high mountain head are shown twice, in summer in profile, and in winter in plan so as fully to reveal the fivefold positioning of the icy highland peaks which, snow covered and gendered, are accorded their own ceremonies as Tepictoton in Part I (ch. v). The water prisms of the rainbow notionally transfer their colour to the primordial plant, the maguey, whose leaves, maturing over 11 years (the sun-spot cycle), are said to be 'reddened' by them. The snow and hail are referred to their good and bad effects on harvests and crops.

The fullest of the accompanying Nahuatl texts attach to the two walkers, Eecatl and Itztlacoliuhqui. The first deals with the annual geography of winds and Tlaloc's crown; the second, with the rhythm of the agricultural year and its seasons. Eecatl's winds make a primary map of the earth, assuming coordinates brought down from the sky and enriching them with others of terrestrial origin. In the Nahuatl commentary, the winds are carefully numbered, named and characterized as five (Flo VII, 4 reduces them to four); visually coinciding with the five openings between the peaks of Tlaloc's crown, they blow in from or as:

1) Ciuatlampa (whence women)

2) Chalcopa (Chalco, the place of jade)

3) Mictlampa (whence the dead)

4) Chichimecapa (Chichimeca, the place of the Chichimecs)

5) Quetzalcoatl (Quetzalcoatl, the feather snake)

The name of the last wind is clearly egregious in referring not to geography but to a Tonalpoualli lifeforce, the bird-snake that weds the 13th of the Thirteen Quecholli (the feathered quetzal-) to the fifth of the Twenty Signs (-coatl, snake). This last wind is also the one represented by the walker depicted here, who wears the wind mask typically worn by Quetzalcoatl. Easterly, it blows in from the Gulf Coast, in summer with hurricane force, 'sweeping in the Tlalocs' into heaped storm clouds laden with warm moisture. Widespread, the cult of this Quetzalcoatl flourished particularly in Gulf Coast lands northeast of Tenochtitlan, signally Quetzalcoatlan (today Ecatlan) where the eponymous deity was honoured under the name Nine Wind (according to local Chichimec maps and histories from Tochpan and Itzcuintepec. PBM 91–7; **Map 2**).

As that of 'women', the first of the five winds blows in the opposite direction, from their house on the western horizon, and hence enters through the opening at the back of Tlaloc's crown, as he looks east. From Chalco, the second wind again enters from the east, in gusts that topple houses and trees, or more precisely just south of east, the direction in which Chalco lies from Tenochtitlan. In the Mexica economic system, Chalco (as we saw) is named as the third of the four provincial governors (Matrícula) and as the place of jade it served as gateway to the greatest of Tenochtitlan's tribute roads which brought in jade from its richest sources in distant Central America, again just south of east. Both easterly, Chalco's second wind is like Quetzalcoatl's fifth in arriving with great force, the two being separated by the frontal and highest peak in Tlaloc's crown and in Mexico (Orizaba) that majestically looms towards the Gulf. This is the huge easternmost Poyauhtecatl repeatedly invoked in poetry (for example, as a landmark in One Reed Quetzalcoatl's return to the eastern lowlands in *Cantares mexicanos*) and in rain cults (for example, its rattles of mist – ayauhchicauaztica – in the Hymn to Tlaloc, *Icuic* no. 3). Routed according to the plan of Tlaloc's five peaks, these winds suggest, then, an anatomy of head and limbs whereby just as the easterlies pass over either shoulder so the women's westerly comes in between the legs.

The remaining two of the five winds (3rd , 4th) complete the anatomy by blowing in from either side. The third is from Mictlan, the underworld and land of the dead; and the fourth from the Chichimeca homeland that likewise carries a deadly charge (*micoua*). In the geography of the classical lowlands where snow is unknown, Mictlan is to the south, the stifling underworld through which the epic Quetzalcoatl (having gone round its jade circle) opened a passage with his breath, as the Twins do through Xibalba in the *Popol vuh*. The Chichimec homeland, Seven Caves (Chicomoztoc), never lies anywhere but opposite to the north, beyond the safe passage of Mexica tribute and even beyond the northern tropical line ambitiously drawn in 'pecked circle' petroglyphs by Teotihuacan. The deadly charge of the Chichimec wind may have as much to do with this political history as with the starving mortality common on the cold northern steppes and in the Spartan Seven Caves, whose mouths are being obliterated here in Itztlacoliuhqui's whirling blizzard. (Before entering Mesoamerica, the Mexica had located their land of the dead to the north of Chicomoztoc.) Both these winds, from Mictlan and the Chichimeca, further have in common the fact that they lie to the sides of the great east-west current and body flow that runs to and fro between the other three across the highland Basin, backwaters as it were from the imperial Mexica standpoint, threatened with stagnation.

Numerically, this symmetrical distribution of winds is not only shaped by Tlaloc's five-peaked crown but calculated, the clue to the even spacing of their vectors being given by the easterlies, Chalcopa and Quetzalcoatl. As we saw, Chalco, in the southeast corner of the highland Basin was ritually besieged every 80 years, a year for each 80th or degree of the Mesoamerican jade circle of which that of Mictlan is the primordial example. As the second of the five winds, Chalco indicates then the $16°$ of this $80°$ circle allotted to each of them. Moreover, in this position, Chalco functioned successively in two directional patterns, as the second of the five winds, but also as the third of the four provincial capitals of the Tenochtitlan tribute system, being the gateway to the great eastern road. In the quatrefoil map of the tribute that nourishes the metropolitan heartland, the jade of Chalco becomes the in-flowing energy that has the colours of that mineral, green like precious water and red like blood, just as the four canals of liquid turquoise seen in Mendoza irrigate the Basin. Here the jade of Chalco, with its $80°$ and 80 years, arithmetically reconciles the value system of the five winds in Tlaloc's crown with that of the four tribute quarters.

As the names given to them necessarily indicate, these winds, on blowing towards Tenochtitlan and the highland Basin from five directions, carry charges that may signify on many levels, from deepest cosmogony (especially the easterlies) to current Mexica politics. The storms brought in from the Gulf Coast by Quetzalcoatl reenact the dialogues which this figure, submerged iridescent in water, has with Hurricane Sky Heart at the beginning of earthly time (in the *Popol vuh*). At this level, the Quetzalcoatl wind (image 1 in the sequence) (**Pl. 3b**) inheres in its namesake Gucumatz, the monstrous sea snake that communicates with Sky Heart via electricity, the vertical yellow-red lightning snake whose thunderbolt head (image 2) is divinely attired. The exchange results in the emergence of land in the form of Tlaloc's mountain top (image 3): brought by the summer storms that end in the rainbow (image 4), the water that annually runs off his face and body recalls this cosmic dialogue. A current in air and water, the original Quetzalcoatl's impulse becomes, then, that of the feathered snake of his name, the premise in turn of the vertebrate ascent recounted in the Mesoamerican genesis and the Twenty Signs. As such, it may violently devour, a monstrous serpentine swallower, protean with Xonecuilli markings (S on S) on its feathery scales, fish

finned and bird beaked, in the proto-Xiuhcoanaual image at Chalcatzingo which recurs 2,000 or more years later in the feathered snake monster swallower depicted by the Mexica in Borbonicus (p.14). In Tonalpoualli terms, as the twelfth of the Quecholli and the fifth of the Twenty Signs, Quetzalcoatl is legible numerically as their product, i.e. 12 x 5 =60. On the preceding page of Tepepulco (**Pl. 3a**), this calculation relates to the night hours of Quetzalcoatl's penance as Chalco's jade does to the hours of the sun.

In playing on Tlaloc's mountain, the five winds named in Tepepulco hark back to the creation story itself. In turn, facing east this mountain becomes the refuge and prototypical toponym of the human community, the 'altepetl' or water mountain, vividly depicted in Boban Wheel (**Pl. 8**). Defined by such a toponym itself a synonym for water, the jade wind commemorates Chalco as the recipient of value mined far to the east, ever alluding to the sun and its role in the formation of that precious stone in the earth's very crust, a notion confirmed in the previous Tepepulco chapter and on the Sunstone. In this way we are brought back into the realm of human activity, arithmetical factors, and the calendar.

Irrigation in Tititl

Just as the Nahuatl commentary on Eecatl, the first of the two walkers in the chapter, spells out the first annual anatomy and geography of the highlands, so the commentary on Itztlacoliuhqui, the second walker, does the same for agriculture. Through his figure, the 18 Feasts of the Mexica year are adapted specifically to the highland Basin, complicating the rudimentary and general model of 'summer' and 'winter' halves, and introducing the notion of human intervention. The threat of Itztlacoliuhqui's cold, we are told, may be anticipated already in the Feast that ends the upper half of the year, Ochpaniztli (F1.9), and this is precisely when and where this mincing figure is seen sidling in during the performance of the Feasts in Part I (**Pl. 7b**). Having arrived he projects his threat of chill for six Feasts or 120 days (this number could be deduced from the diagram of Tlaloc's fivefold crown, in which 11+13 liquid drops are seen to freeze and harden into a standardized 24, i.e.5 x 24 = 120). As Florentine Codex puts it (Flo VII, 6I):

> Frost is called Itztlacoliuhqui. Cold comes once a year, in Ochpaniztli, it begins in Ochpaniztli. And for six Feasts, six score days, the cold lasts. And then it ends, finishes, in Tititl. When that happened, they said: 'The frost has gone, now there will be sowing, it's sowing time, now earth will be planted, it's planting time; it's warm, mild, calm; the hour is good, right, at hand, imminent, here. They hurried and pressed on, restless, anxious, busy, worried, there was no let up; days would fly by. Anew they worked the fields and the soil, hoed and weeded, beans are set and planted, amaranth broadcast and seeded, chía broadcast, chiles planted; shoots are pruned, trained, nurtured.

Tepepulco notes that when Itztlacoliuhqui's reign ended in Atemoztli (F2.5), the arrival of the following Feast Tititl (F2.6) was greeted with the refrain:

oquiz in cetl	cold has gone
ye toquizpa	now come the green maize leaves
ye tlatotonia	now comes the warmth
ye qualca	now comes the good time

Itztlacoliuhqui's threat is then assessed with respect not so much to comfort of humans as to the survival of what they plant. Planting before Tititl is dangerous because as they emerge from the earth tender seedlings may be blasted by cold: only in Tititl can planted life be reliably renewed. In terms of human activity as opposed to just weather, Tititl becomes, then, the hinge of agronomy and the agricultural year, the time when a great range of vulnerable crops were and are seeded and planted: the chiles, beans, amaranth and the finer cereals are among those listed in the Florentine Ms. In this model, the key concept is not so much the monsoon (which in fact often proves too much for vulnerable crops when newly planted), but planting and irrigation in floating fields or *chinampas* (Broda 1983; 1991), immediately after the end of Itztlacoliuhqui's reign, without risk of frost. Thanks to *chinampa* and allied lacustrine water systems, the planting need not of course be delayed for lack of moisture: the water flowing from Tlaloc's mountain body intimates the springs that so abundantly fed the lakes in the Basin, especially from the slopes of the high southern rim, which are massively present in the Cozcatzin Codex and in Borbonicus's account of *chinampa* planting in Tititl (see Chapter 5 below).

In this scheme, the year falls not so much into halves (9+9 Feasts) as into thirds, that is, the six Feasts when there is no planting (F1.9–F2.5) followed by the 12 when there safely may be (F2.6–F1.8). With characteristic finesse these proportions, too, may be read off the *tlacuilolli* text. Walking in stiffly and pigeon-chested as he is, Itztlacoliuhqui proffers a left hand that shows a further deformity, a middle finger bent to take the space of two making a possible six, a statement fuzzily echoed in dots round the brim of his hat. Through sneaky hand gesture and hat brim, he alerts those he grimly greets to the span of his reign, the six Feasts that are then quite clearly and durably recorded on the rest of his hat, in six firm dots fitted within the nine-tooth parabola. The six Feasts allotted to him when wearing this hat are complemented by the other 12, which are likewise registered on the hats worn by the only other two characters in the picture: the other walker Eecatl, and crowned Tlaloc between them, with his lightning and rainbow. These three, the two walkers Itztlacoliuhqui and Eecatl, plus intermediary Tlaloc, act out their parts on the same page (f.282v), independently of the three cold non-human diagrams on the following page (**Pl. 3c**) which at this level of reading are left out of consideration or serve just as an appendix to Itztlacoliuhqui (f.283).

According to his tight-fitting cap, Eecatl's reign is a brief three Feasts, which is when he whips the winds during the first three Feasts of the upper half of the year and of the year itself (F1.1–F1.3), so as to sweep in the rain that arrives in the fourth (F1.4). Going down the page we see that Tlaloc's monsoon, caught by his five-peaked cloud crown, is recorded as a further five Feasts on his headband which like his curled upper lip catches and directs the rain falling on his mountain body. Then going back up after Itztlacoliuhqui's reign of six Feasts, the four planting Feasts begun in Tititl and fed by water that oozes and gushes from Tlaloc's body are recorded in a row of four larger dots set above the headband. In this way, the three hatted figures in this chapter establish sequences of 20-day Feasts within the year which may be read as a cycle, a shuttle going down and up between Eecatl and Itztlacoliuhqui, or a vertical palindrome whose literal inter-est stands midway in Tlaloc. That is, between Eecatl's three and Itztlacoliuhqui's six, intermediary Tlaloc accounts for the remaining nine Feasts of the year (3+6+9 = 18), in two instalments, five on the headband of his monsoon, and four on his crown which are those of the good

warm time that begins with Tititl. The overall cycle is then: 6 (no planting) +4+3+5 (planting).

Waved in as ever in Tozoztli (F1.1) by the wand of turquoise (*xiuh-*) held here by Eecatl, the year (*xiuh-*) in this hatted guise runs through wind and monsoon (F1.1–F1.3, F1.4–F1.8) to the cold that ends in Atemoztli (F1.9–F2.5) and the *chinampa* planting that begins in Tititl (F2.6– F2.9). For good measure, the last of the non-planting Feasts Atemoztli and the first of the planting Feasts Tititl and the all-important transition between them are identified in exactly these terms in the accompanying Nahuatl text, which is the antecedent of the Florentine passages quoted above. The suitability of these Feasts for planting is indicated meanwhile by the type of disk that counts them. Eecatl's three windy Feasts are open but small circles. Tlaloc's five monsoon Feasts, also open, are larger. Itztlacoliuhqui's six non-planting Feasts are closed, round dots that have no opening, while Tititl's four are easily the largest open circles. The disks that count the Feasts and show them as open or closed and less or more open may then reasonably be thought to evoke actual holes drilled for planting or seeding, of which the most capacious are the four that begin in Tititl. These four indicate the greatest yields of food, in copious colour transferred from the rainbow (as to the maguey) and set into the arches of flowers and fruit that still adorn the *chinampas* in Xochimilco.

The critical need for an annual calendar which would reliably schedule exact dates in the planting year is further indicated in a supplement to the Tititl Feasts set into Tlaloc's crown. For beside Tititl's four large open circles each of 20 days ('jewels in the crown'), there is an extra quarter circle, which indicates the Nemotemi or extra days intercalated in the Feasts cycle during just this planting season. Had the need for these extra days not been meticulously calculated, the intricate annual schedule of planting and non-planting Feasts would clearly have soon gone awry, as did the Julian calendar imposed by Europe (and the Egyptian calendar before it). In Mesoamerica, the basis for making this calculation existed, as Edmonson showed, in the 29-Round solar-year formula proclaimed there by 433 BCE at the latest.

Intermediary between the year's two walkers Eecatl and Itztlacoliuhqui, Tlaloc's two instalments of Feasts – his summer monsoon and his *chinampa* irrigation – are not just registered on his hat as five and four and a quarter disks, but are repeated on his face and body. During the monsoon, rain is collected by the characteristic curl on his upper lip, which functions like grooves of this shape actually carved by the Olmec into the sloping rock at Chalcatzingo (beside tender seedlings of squash and maize). At the end of Itztlacoliuhqui's reign in Atemoztli, water filtering down into and through his trunk and gushing from his notional 'armpits' (to use the *Popol vuh* term) is brought to the fields through carefully planned and constructed channels, some of which, on the Basin's southern rim, still work today. Inverting and concentrating the Sign Rain (XIX) – three round drops scattering from the ends of three liquid fingers – this irrigation is depicted on Tlaloc's side by three rounded springs above three channels, all bearing turquoise water.

Of itself, this image of downward movement or gravitational flow here denotes the Feast Atemoztli (F2.5, 'water coming down') when preparations were made for the *chinampa* planting that began in Tititl (F2.6). The emblem for Atemoztli in Boban shows the aqueducts carved in stone that were prepared for use

Figure 4.1 Tonacatecutli with crown and Xiuhcoanaual on maize-adorned litter. Rios f.1v ('Genesis')

in this Feast and are likewise still visible in Texcoco, on the eastern rim and lake shore. Atemoztli's emblem in Veytia 4 and 5 (pp.75–6 below) and in 'Encounter with Europe' (p.8 above) includes quite massive stone structures. Indeed, the descending footsteps that accompany these masonic versions of Atemoztli's 'falling water' emblem (**Figs 1.4, 7.4–7.6**) might be thought redundant were it not for this notion of human agency. In the Tepepulco text, the three dots (rounded springs) and bars (canals) of water supplied by Atemoztli numerically produce the sum of the year's Feasts in a kind of triple entry: $3(1+5) = 3+5+6+4 = 9+9 = 18$. This equation thereby might suggest that the yield of the *chinampa* planting begun in Tititl was worth that of an entire year of Feasts, including the labour required to construct and maintain the irrigation system. Arithmetically, it parallels the dots positioned as $12+6$, $6+6+6$, or $9+9$ around the leafy plant seen in the Sunstone, on Xiuhcoanaual's tail.

Introducing the idea of irrigation into the general and widespread model of halves of the year that stretch from equinox to equinox has the effect of modifying the phases of the Feasts cycle, and even the arithmetical model of the circle itself, replacing halves with thirds. For just as Tlaloc's wind-vane crown correlates with the quatrefoil of tribute flow within a broad concept of fivefold inflowing energy, so, in the field of human construction it correlates with the thirds typified by Itztlacoliuhqui. The need for some adjustment will be apparent from the simple arithmetical fact that while the jade's 80 is divisible by 2 and 5 it is not divisible by 3: in walking into his six-Feast season, Itztlacoliuhqui states the primes multiplied in that number in the 1, 2 and 3 unit-marker on the sash that diagonally crosses his chest. Nor in turn can the jade's 80 be a factor of the year of 360 days that is formally constructed by the Feasts (and was once paramount in the lowland calendar).

The clue to how this complementary circle is calculated is itself cryptic, and is found on a screenfold page that dedicates the Twenty Signs to Tlaloc (Laud p.45); Tlaloc's Hymn (*Icuic* no.3) offers a reading of this *tlacuilolli* statement, in celebrating this supreme dispenser of water as Ocelo-coatl, Jaguar Snake (PBM 135). That is, through his Rain mask or persona (Sign XIX), Tlaloc adds to his sceptre of Snake lightning (Sign V) a roar from his Jaguar headdress (Sign XIV; in other words, lightning plus thunder means rain; XIV + V = XIX). In the Tepepulco image, Tlaloc's cheek has jaguar markings and his underjaw has the lighter vegetation/fur that characterizes that feline in the Laud image, and generally. Roaring, Tlaloc voices the power and authority synonymous with his high five-peaked crown; and in opening his jaw in order to roar he exposes in profile half the teeth that make up his distinctive set of 12, three to the near sides of upper and lower jaw which modify the usual dental binary. When correlated with the five-factor, ever-authoritative crown this duodecimal set of teeth produces 60° rather than the previous 80°, 10° for each Feast of Itztlacoliuhqui's six-Feast reign (rather than a degree for every year of Chalco's jade circle).

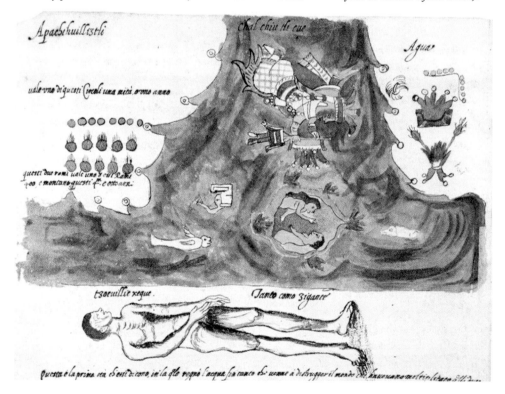

Figure 4.2 Food, four millennia, flood, and fish people; fallen giant below. Rios f.4v ('Genesis'. Cf. **Appendix A**)

Figure 4.3 Weather: **a)** wind in Toxcatl. Rios f.44; **b)** rain in Etzalcualiztli. Rios f.50

In the longer history of Mesoamerica, the link between water management and agriculture lies deep. The historically successive versions of the Twenty Signs suggest as much, as do the Coatlan Inscription and the account of the planting year initiated in midsummer by the Lord of our Flesh Tonacatecutli in 'Genesis' (**Fig. 4.1**). There, the roots of the planting season are traced back to the hunter-gatherers' 'Suckling Tree', when Atemoztli's falling water was still simply liquid nourishment falling from its branches, and to the flood and world age story out of which human agriculture emerged (**Fig. 4.2**; **Appendix A**).

The apportioning of the year's 18 Feasts into not just the halves of tribute (9+9) but thirds of planting (6+12) has been little recognized, though it is firmly enough stated here, in *tlacuilolli* and Nahuatl, in this second chapter of Tepepulco Part II. The lesson it teaches might be applied to advantage more widely. For, sharply defined in Tepepulco, the model of planting and non-planting Feasts is fundamental to accounts of the year within and even beyond the Mexica domain. Like tribute it has corresponding year markers, that typify monsoon rains or deciduous leaves (**Table 3d**). In Boban, Veytia 4 and Tovar, the seasonal import of Tititl is picked out by a hand that proffers seedlings, ready for planting, while within the planting season Rios vividly confirms the annual transition from dusty wind to rainfall, at just the right moment, in the meteorological backgrounds supplied for the corresponding Feasts (and no others): from a blast of grey wind volutes (Toxcatl F1.3) we move to a downpour of turquoise rain drops (Etzalcualiztli F1.4. **Fig. 4.3**). In the Tamazolco Map, the trefoil leaves of plants to either side of the irrigation system at Acolco ('where the water turns') make a similar statement (PBM 76–77).

As the hinge between non-planting and planting seasons (6+12 Feasts), Tititl (F2.6; **Fig. 4.4**) emerges as the whole principle behind the division of the year into thirds. Evidence of this can also be seen at Tepexic in the Coixtlahuaca Map, where the year is shown as 12 moons, four of which, starting with the equinoctial Ochpaniztli, are marked by falling leaves, thereby suggesting the same non-planting third of the year (**Fig. 1.7b**). In his discussion of the Feasts chapter in Ixtlilxochitl (in the Magliabechiano group), Carrera González notes that the ancient Mazatec calendar likewise divides the year into three seasons, two of which have to do with the milpa and planting, and one which does not. After the cold (*nýan*) come the heat (*ndoá*) and rain (*jtsí*) when planting occurs and produces respective kinds of maize. The significance of the match is perhaps enhanced by the fact that, in the Mazatec-Chinantec area (as among the Purépecha), the 18 Feasts may function in the absence of the Tonalpoualli (Doesburg & Carrera González 1996:174–75).

In Tititl, the choreographies of the Feasts (Borbonicus, Borgia, Tepepulco – see Chapters 5 and 6 below, plus Magliabechiano and Rios) all concur in commemorating a goddess whose complex array (*inechichiuh*) has led to her being identified with the whole cluster of fundamental earth deities, saliently the eponymous 'snake woman' Ciuacoatl whose ancient counterpart is Ilamatecutli (also the title of the consort of the Quetzalcoatl who was lord of Cholula when Cortés arrived). In this context, her distinctive features are a protuding tongue or a double-tongued head band, a skull mask, a weaving batten (*tzotzopaztli*) and a skirt and garments that may be distinctively edged in four colours and adorned with lattice, heart, skull and crossbone, flower and other designs (**Pl.9**). This goddess's chief function was to preside over the distribution of seeds and the eagerly-awaited start of planting in Tititl, when there were races up the pyramid steps to the temple that housed the grain bin (*cuexcomatl*) out of which the year's seeds and seed corn (*teosuchil*) were distributed. The Tititl scene in Borbonicus (**Pl. 6**) shows the 11 pyramid steps and an elaborate dance that involves her as the lavishly-attired goddess of *chinampa* agriculture, the 'diosa de la laguna' noted in the Spanish gloss. She then dominates the 12 planting Feasts that begin in Tititl, just as the 'other woman' of this screenfold, the mother of the gods Teteu innan, dominates the remaining six, beginning with Itztlacoliuhqui's arrival in Ochpaniztli (see p.52 below).

Figure 4.4 The cycle of planting and non-planting Feasts (cf. **Pl. 3**)

disks on hats	correspond to:
Tlaloc, upper band OOOO	irrigation during 4 planting Feasts, F.2.6–F.2.9
Eecatl ooo	dust storms during 3 planting Feasts, F.1.1–F.1.3
Tlaloc lower band ooooo	monsoon during 5 planting Feasts, F.1.4–F.1.8
Itztlacoliuhqui	threat of cold during 6 non-planting Feasts, F. 1.9–F. 2.5

Through Ciuacoatl/Ilamatecutli, the idea of seed and fruitfulness was carried over into human reproduction. For Tititl also celebrated fertilization, specifically through the figures of the five Ciuateteo, who were impersonated in what was called Illamateuh-chololoya, her 'leap' or dance, shown in this Feast in Borgia (p.39) and Part I of Tepepulco (f.253). That Ilamatecutli, furthermore, has a celestial nature is evident from the epithet commonly bestowed on her and registered in her attire or array: Citlalicue, the Milky Way with its hub or Market. In the Borgia Feasts chapter, the two thirds of the year specified for planting, from Tititl to Micailhuitl B, correspond structurally to just this celestial presence, as we see below (p.59 cf **Pl. 9**). Quiñones Keber (1995) notes how her appearance in Tititl weaves together threads of terrestrial and (via the 'white cloud-snake' Iztac mixcoatl) celestial significance.

That this very connection and its consequences remained significant in late 16th century is shown in Mexicanus. This text makes an eloquent comparison between the Mexica planting year, on the one hand, and the zodiac and system of four elements adopted by medieval Christianity, on the other. There, in the field of agriculture the planting stick (*huictli*) is plunged deeply into the earth during first two thirds of the year, from January to August (Tititl to Micailhuitl B), and withheld above it during the last third, from September to December (Ochpaniztli to Atemoztli. **Pl. 2a**). This is exactly the pattern of fieldwork recommended by Otontecutli in Tepepulco Part I, whose planting stick is similarly withdrawn from the earth in Micailhuitl B, at the end of the planting season. However, since it correlates planting seasons with the Christian months via the zodiac, the Mexicanus example shows how in fact the earthly thirds of the year steadily slip back (precess) against the thirds that keep time with the night sky. This slippage is already stated in the Borgia Feasts chapter, where the start of Ilamatecutli's celestial reign of 12 Feasts is shown no longer to coincide, as it once must have done, with the start of the 12 planting Feasts in Tititl. The specific distinction that Mexicanus makes here between the solar year of agriculture and the sidereal year of the zodiac is examined in detail in Chapter 8 below.

Coatlan: caiman cave as water source

Just as the fate of Tlaloc's planting seasons under Spanish colonial rule is noted in late 16th- century texts like Mexicanus, so their significance in pre-Mexica times, among the Chichimec of Yauhtepec, is celebrated in the magnificent Coatlan Inscription, a statement fundamental to understanding the Feasts of the agricultural year. Like the second chapter in

Borbonicus (pp.21–22), this stone text from Coatlan embeds the discourse of fertility common to plants and humans and conjoined in Tititl, under the aegis of Ciuacoatl-Ilamatecutli. Physically, it celebrates Cipactonal, wearer of the primitive Xiuhcoanaual and inventor of the calendar for the Chichimec, along with his partner: here, they are seen at and as a literal source, of water channelled towards well-tended fields (**Fig. 4.5**). Indeed, given its configuration and position in the landscape, the text might be consulted, like its Graeco-Roman counterparts, as an oracle. This ancient fountain at Coatlan, whose channels have today collapsed through neglect, resembles the many springs that ooze or gush from the southern slope of the Tepoztlan Ridge: a volcanic formation that runs west of Popocatepetl, this ridge rose to dam the Valley of Mexico, converting its northern end into the highland Basin much later dominated by Tenochtitlan (**Map 2**). Ubiquitous in Mesoamerica, the Nahuatl name Coatlan means place of the snake, which as number V of the Tonalpoualli's Twenty Signs conjoins notions of community that is vertebrate and reciprocal, and of the flow and current epitomized by channelled water.

Tripartite, the Coatlan text centres on the maw of a caiman that faces the onlooker and frames the water source; to either side, an aging human figure in profile turns to her or his task in hand. The gaping maw of the caiman (Cipactli, number I of the Twenty Signs) reveals a set of stalactite teeth and a rabbit head caught in profile: Sign VIII, Rabbit is qualified in unit dots by the number 2. In Nahuatl, this reads Ome Tochtli, Two Rabbit, the hero who was swallowed by the political Monster self-imaged in the late Classic city Xochicalco yet who triumphed to save his people and the tiny kingdom of Tepoztlan, of which Yauhtepec marked the southern rim (see Chapter 6). He and the mother who miraculously conceived him were celebrated in the equinoctial Feast Ochpaniztli, and still are, he on the fifth night and sixth day, today, the famous vigil and Día del Tepozteco, 7th and 8th September. Read as a Chichimec Series III year name *in situ*, 2 Rabbit at Coatlan would date the inscription to within 52 years either side of 1338 (i.e. after their assault on Cholula in 1235 and before Moctezuma I's intrusion in the 1440s).

To right and left, the caiman's glaring eyes refer us to the old couple of the calendar. Barefoot, she kneels clutching a stone-age masher; in sandals and seated on a plinth of cut stone, he writes with a fine-tipped bone. Back to back, they concentrate on their tasks and the head of each attaches to a metamorphic creature whose eye – a constant in evolution – reflects the caiman's. By this means she is identified as the Chichimec 'Obsidian Butterfly' Itzpapalotl, the moth of night that descends

Figure 4.5 Ome Tochtli in caiman cave of 9+9 teeth, between Cipactonal and Itzpapalotl. Coatlan Inscription (after C.A. Robelo in Nowotny 1961:52)

from the stars, slain avatar of the aging midwife Oxomoco (**Fig. 4.6**) and stellar Ilamatecutli (see Chapter 6). He wears the caiman's head as a proto-Xiuhcoanaual headdress, in a reptilian profile that in backing and protecting his own hinges on a beak and sprouts countable feathers. This proclaims him to be Cipactonal, whose being and power (tonal) belong to the caiman Cipactli. As the first Sign Cipactli, the ancient caiman is said to have emerged from the earth itself, the substance that is worked productively by human hands in the adjoining fields of Coatlan and watered by its mouth. Its stalactite teeth, four above and four below, are supplemented to either side by three plus three traverse molars, and by double drooling tusks at each end of the lower lip, making 18 teeth in all (twice 4+3+2).

Various in shape (plus one of the tusks is missing), the teeth are nonetheless quite symmetrical as units in defining as 9+9 the vertical halves of the mouth and head, nostrils and eyes, which are divided *in situ* by the path of the equinoctial sun. In the Chichimec and Mexica calendar, 9+9 Feasts to either side of the equinoxes in fact conforms to the basic model of the year which the latter propagated over much of Mesoamerica through their tribute system, as we saw in the previous chapter, 'Fiscal Acquisition'. Vertically symmetrical, the caiman's 18 Feast-teeth simultaneously signify in horizontal registers, in, above and

below the three plus three molars aligned with Ome Tochtli. As Feasts, this anomalous subset of six marks the third of the year when planting is not advised, before and after the 12 when it is, beginning in Tititl. The presence of Ome Tochtli between the 3+3 traverse molars signifies then not just his resilience when swallowed by the Xochicalco Monster but his capacity, in this role and predicament, to define the six non-planting Feasts by staunching the water flowing from the caiman mouth. By these means, the Tepepulco model of the Mexica planting year and irrigation, further corroborated, may be shown to have firm and exact antecedents in the Chichimec tradition.

Regulating the economy in tribute halves and planting thirds, the models of the year discussed in this pair of chapters (3 and 4) hinge respectively on the equinox in Ochpaniztli (F1.9) and on climate in Tititl (F2.6). In other words, the years in both cases depend on the sun. They are solar years and therefore to be distinguished categorically from the slightly longer sidereal year of penance and of stellar Itzpapalotl. In the interplay between these two kinds of year, of the sun and of the stars, there pulses the rhythm of the Feasts in performance, in glorious enactments around key personae, who also meter their civil and political authority in standardized quantities of days, as we shall see in the next pair of chapters (5 and 6).

Figure 4.6 Nine streams gush below Oxomoco (who has 11 toes and casts 9 kernels) and Cipactonal (equipped for night penance). Borbonicus p.21

5
'Like Waves Breaking': the Great Dance

More persuasively than the tribute collector and more merrily than labouring in the aqueducts, the dance, the celebratory *mitote*, brings populations together and synchronizes their feasts. As economics successfully dominate, so they incorporate sundry cults into the metropolitan scheme. So doing, they continue a catholic appropriation which the customs and choreography typical of certain Feasts indicate had been going on for a very long time in Mesoamerica, indeed since the birth of the calendar itself under the Olmecs, the mother and hence first metropolitan culture. While as a file of native paper sheets, the Matrícula deals in hard economic facts and the Coatlan Inscription sluices water flow, the pages of Borbonicus unfold to reveal brilliant performance of the 18 Feasts and the careful rehearsal of their older and local rhythms, albeit only where politically expedient and always, needless to say, under the watchful metropolitan eye. The offerings, costumes ('arrays'), liturgy, even massive architecture created for these Feast celebrations are detailed in *tlacuilolli* in several of the surviving Mexica texts, as punctiliously as their first performances must have demanded.

As the sole surviving screenfold representation of the Mexica Feast cycle over its full length, chapter 3 of Borbonicus deserves the closest attention, given its place and function both in the text overall, and in comparison with other classic texts. Its visual language acquires an especial edge when matched with that of Tepepulco Part I which depicts the performance of the Feasts, as well as detailing the central stage of the Great Temple and recording the Twenty Nahuatl Hymns sung to the gods, *In icuic*. All but three of these Twenty Hymns relate directly to the actors in the Mexica Feasts cycle: the rhythms of their stanzas echo the plan, angle and size of the stages these actors perform on, and their lexis matches details of their attires or arrays, the service offered to them, their cultural import, the lyrical and often enigmatic heart of their image (like the mask of Tlaloc, deciphered above p.45). As Luis Reyes has noted, the alphabetic glosses added to the *tlacuilolli* account can often help construe that enigmatic heart.

The Borbonicus Feasts chapter opposes and conjoins ancient and modern, female and male, mother and lover, noble and commoner, culture and ethnos, empire and subject, original and counterpart. Its *tlacuilolli* account celebrates life in and of the Feasts with great intensity, their costumes and dances, their smells, sounds and music, in a wealth of shape, colour, mode, measure and logics, that strictly cannot be transcribed into merely alphabetic script. Just because of this, we approach the chapter here ever recalling its place in the text as a whole, and holding firmly on to such basic theatrical concepts as its appeal to space on the page as space on the stage, its dramatis personae (gods as literal masks) and the sets these cohere into, and the drama itself as it unfolds (again literally, by the screenfold page) in time levels brought brilliantly together in the ritual moment.

Large and squarish, Borbonicus' pages once numbered 40, but Europeans cut off the first and the last two so that now only 36 are left. The screenfold is painted on one side and reads from left to right, the opposite direction to screenfolds from towns further east like Tlaxcala or Cholula which include the same thematic chapters. The opening chapter (pp.1–20) amply correlates the Trecenas of the Tonalpoualli with the Nine Night Lords, the Thirteen Quecholli and the Thirteen Heroes who emerge from their beaks (**Table 2**); chapter 2 (pp.21–22) is dedicated to the Xiuhmolpilli; and chapter 3 (pp.23–40) deals with the Feasts. The calendrical topics of all three Borbonicus chapters appear as cycles recurrent and persistent in society, predictive of fates and definitive of dues. Yet simultaneously they rehearse through custom and, in the case of the Feasts elaborate choreography, the profound and ancient experiences that gave them birth, as these are recounted in such seminal creation stories as 'Genesis' in Rios, *Legend of the Suns* and the *Popol vuh*. As the midwives' set of roots and origins, the Night Lords in certain cases become Heroes, and both in turn provide patrons for the Trecenas; the Night Lords also become the guardians of the years seen in Chapter 2. Critical for our purposes here, some of these Tonalpoualli figures go yet further and play major roles in the complementary cycle of the Feasts in Chapter 3.

In chapter 2 (pp.21–22), the 52 years of the Xiuhmolpilli are counted out in halves, as 26 plus 26; and they fall into subgroups of seven, thanks to the sequence of the Night Lords who guard them. The first half is allotted to the grandparent pair Oxomoco and Cipactonal, honoured by midwives, who through cross-fertilization produced the first common folk (**Fig. 4.6**). The second half belongs to Quetzalcoatl and Tezcatlipoca, epic Heroes (nos. 9 and 10) of the world ages and of Tollan or Tula, Mesoamerica's first named city, and genealogical prototypes for the aristocracy. These halves of the Xiuhmolpilli begin respectively with the Series III years 1 Rabbit (Sign VIII) and 1 Flint (Sign XVIII), the interplay between them being accounted for in Era datings in the *Legend of the Suns* and other genesis stories.

Page as stage

In a less tabular format, the Feasts chapter (pp.23–) continues in the same vein, alluding to the root concepts that gave birth to these 20-day periods in the year. They are identified principally by gods that dance and parade, the full figures also seen in the Feast chapters in the compendia (Tepepulco Part I, Telleriano, Magliabechiano, and to a lesser extent Tovar), all with the offerings, arrays, buildings and so on appropriate to them as rulers of time. The chapter starts in Izcalli (F2.7) presided over by Xiuhtecutli, the lord of the year itself, along with Ciuacoatl, the woman-snake who is honoured in the Twenty Hymns (*Icuic* no.13). It was Ciuacoatl's overarching and complex roles throughout the year, as the five-in-one deity in this chapter, that happily encouraged Luis Reyes to name the whole text after her.

At first sight the swirling colour and dance that fill the pages of this chapter are hard to construe. They in fact turn out to obey quite specific paradigms, once they are defined in the sense of being duly located in space, as on a stage, and in time, and once the actors or personae are identified, along with their roles in the drama. In Tepepulco Part I, these are concepts that are to some degree separated out into successive *tlacuilolli* chapters that deconstruct ritual in terms of offerings, masks and arrays, and location (stages and buildings).

In Borbonicus, throughout the horizontal left-to-right reading, transitions from one staged Feast to the next are always indicated by vertical lines; these may coincide with the page fold or edge, or may be drawn in ink about halfway across the page. The effect of this format in principle is to confirm the grouping of the Feasts in the pairs indicated in their Nahuatl names as 'lesser' and 'greater'(A and B in our notation). To begin with (pp.23–28), these pairs stand either side of the vertical ink line that divides a single page, sharing it, the initial lesser Feast being given slightly less space. The Feasts then go on (pp.29–36) to be given a page each, sharing an opening of two facing pages (at the close, p.37 reinitiates the cycle). Starting from Izcalli, this produces in practice a 'thin' sequence that is later complemented by a 'fat' one. There are few but telling exceptions to the rule of having either two Feasts or one per page. In the thin sequence, Tozoztli B (F1.2) is allotted a full page (p.25) although it is the second in a pair; this exception highlights the huge green mountain that represents this Feast, a landmark in itself, as we shall see. In the fat sequence, extra page space, that is, larger than usual stages are allotted to the two great women who preside over the Feasts that begin and end it: the mother of gods Teteu innan in Ochpaniztli (F1.9), and the eponymous Ciuacoatl in Tititl (F2.6). Both these Feasts take up more than a page: Teteu innan commands two facing pages for herself (pp.29–30), while Ciuacoatl incorporates the last seventh of the previous facing page (pp.35–36).

Simply respecting the Feasts' vertical borders over the 14 pages on which the cycle is depicted discloses a pattern within the 18 that is determined by the primes 11+7. Running from Izcalli to Xocotl huetzi and compressing 11 Feasts into six pages (F2.7–F1.8, pp.23–28), the thin sequence is succeeded by the fat one, which spreads over eight pages the seven Feasts that run from Ochpaniztli to Tititl, Teteu innan to Ciuacoatl (F2.9–F2.6, pp.29–36). In the corresponding action there is plenty to corroborate the significance of the 11, and of the great women's seven. At the end of the thin sequence of 11, in Xocotl huetzi (F1.8) the Feast of falling fruit, a huge pole was set up and adorned with paper butterflies, around which dancers turn to the sound of the drum. Ranged according to height, from smaller to larger, the dancers number precisely 11, and as such move in step with the count of the 11 Feasts visited so far. For the paper butterflies on the pole recall those seen in Izcalli, and only there, 11 Feasts or 220 days previously. Overwhelming confirmation of this Mexica choreography as such is found in *Cuevas*, where sequences of seven and 11 dancers are initiated respectively by the huehuetl and teponaztli drums, in an actual stage plan that has just this configuration (**Pl. 4**).

If respecting the vertical borders of the Feasts in Borbonicus begins to reveal numbers and logic latent in the cycle, then

noticing their reading direction clarifies things further. The Feasts begin and end with, and for the most part conform to, the horizontal left-to-right reading followed by the text as a whole. But there are four marked exceptions to this norm, when to look intelligently at the stage and the scene enacted requires us to turn the screenfold through 90° and read from bottom to top. At these moments, what were the upper and lower edges of the horizontal screenfold become its vertical left and right sides. The shift is most imposing when it happens the first time in Tozoztli A & B (F1.1–F1.2) and the fourth and last time in Atemoztli (F2.5), since the scene in these cases is of a jade mountain topped by Tlaloc's temple, so huge and solid as to affirm its own horizontal base. The 90° turn in the two intervening moments is significant in similar terms. In Tecuilhuitl (F1.5), rather than a mountain in profile there is a ball-court in plan with four players, one at each corner, who only after the screenfold is turned stand up rather than lie on their backs (exactly this effect is seen with the ball-court in the plan and guided tour of the Great Temple in Tepepulco, I, vii). The most complex case is the fourth mountain in the 'mountain' Feast Tepeilhuitl and its pair Teotleco (F2.1–F2.2), which symmetrically match those in Tozoztli A & B (F1.1–F1.2), though here the hill and temple are smaller and affected by the power of Ochpaniztli (F1.9), who anticipates the turn within her own two-page Feast.

As a set, i.e. disregarding for the moment the premature turn in Ochpaniztli rather than Teotleco, the four 90° turns readily correspond to the quarters of the tribute year, its Spring and Autumn equinoxes and the solstices that divide its upper (summer) and lower (winter) halves. That is, the turns indicate the start of the quarters whose endings appear as emblems in the tribute texts (F1.1–F1.4, F1.5–F1.8/9; F2.1–F2.4, F2.5–F2.9; **Fig.3.3**). So that physically moving the text around in this fashion, as the reading of it demands, obliges the reader to rehearse the apparent annual movement of the sun around the earth. In the depiction of the last of the 18 Feasts (Tititl F2.6), towards which the sequence tends and which celebrates the eponymous Ciuacoatl in her fullest self, these two reading directions, from left to right and bottom to top of the page, are uniquely and ingeniously interposed on her no less uniquely augmented stage (pp.35–6). Represented as it is on the page, the ball-court of Tecuilhuitl introduces a yet further spatial shift. For on the page this structure is defined differently from most other elements, which are seen in profile; rather the ball-court is seen in plan, as if from above. This amounts to an appeal to the third dimension, a third spatial complication of the text which recurs at the end of the cycle (and only there), adding still further force to the celebration of Ciuacoatl, in the grand finale of Tititl which, as we shall see, is also her grand debut.

Personae in gala performance

The page-stages on which the Feasts are represented in Borbonicus establish, then, key notions through format alone, frequencies denoted by sheer width, height, and viewing perspective. The same is true of the actors who appear on the stage, in many postures yet always in profile, facing left or right. It is of course fair to think of these figures, as many have done, as 'gods' of the Feasts. Yet it is not helpful to attribute to them the kind of fixed or essential identity attributed say, to the Greek pantheon, and it is still less so to try and assign a god to each

Feast. This is true for a variety of reasons, which have everything to do with the philosophy of identity and form inherent in *tlacuilolli* script. These figures are more numen than avatar, and meaning in them has rather to be untiringly deduced from such factors as sheer location on the stage-page, gender, company and rank (indicated by offerings received, frequency of appearance, grouping and so on). Also critical are the fact that person is literally persona or mask and may be pinpointed by the subtlest coincidence and variation in array and, not least, numerical and thematic definitions formalized in the Tonalpoualli.

Of the calendrical figures who, having multiple roles already in the Tonalpoualli, play no less a part in the drama of the Feasts, easily the most striking is Xiuhtecutli, whose name has meanings as multiple as he has roles. In each, he is primary. As the first of the Nine Night Lords of gestation who oversee the entire first chapter of Borbonicus, this figure engenders in the fire (*xiuh-*) sparked in coition. As the first of the Thirteen Heroes he conjoins fire with water that is turquoise (*xiuh-*). As the patron of the final Trecena of Chapter 1 (p.20), 1 Rabbit, he is the fire of the hearth and continuity, who achieves his fullest potential as lord of the year itself (*xiuh-*): his Trecena's Sign 1 Rabbit becomes the name of the first year of the Xiuhmolpilli seen in Chapter 2 (p.21), and indeed again in the Feasts chapter (p.23), where it is set in a square marker of turquoise. First on the scene in the first Feast of the year, Xiuhtecutli is succeeded by other embodiments of fire, who in turn lead up to four manifestations of the great Lord of Night himself Yoalitecutli, eleventh of the Thirteen Heroes, who perform the New Fire ceremony in Panquetzaliztli (F2.4).

For his part, as the last rather than the first of the midwives' Night Lords, Tlaloc releases the amniotic waters; in the company of the Thirteen Heroes (as no.8) he is the god of rain and precipitation, combatant with sun and wind. As a patron of the Trecenas he waxes as a god of vegetation and mountain storms, the main role he carries over into the Feasts, as we saw in Tepepulco. In addition to quarterly appearances in his mountain temple, in Borbonicus Tlaloc is invited and fed elsewhere, notably in Etzalcualiztli (F1.4), where a copious upright storage jar of maize and beans provides the 'good food' his rains helped germinate in the first place (in tribute ledgers, his mask denotes this Feast, which as we saw marks the start of the Mexica rainy season; **Fig. 3.3**). Other major players among the Nine Night Lords include Cinteotl (no.4) whose maize cobs denote the growth of flesh in the fourth moon of gestation. As a Hero (no.7), Cinteotl champions the superior intelligence of the seed that produced maize, and this is the main role he carries over into the 'upper' solstitial Feasts in Tecuilhuitl (F1.5, F1.6). Tlazoteotl, seventh of the Night Lords and white-faced like babies born in her moon, spins nothing less than the thread of life, and in this is conjoined with the mother of gods Teteu innan in Ochpaniztli.

Of the Heroes who are not the midwives' Night Lords, the pair shown fighting each other in Chapter 2, Quetzalcoatl and Tezcatlipoca (no.9 and no.10), have main roles, consistent with their world-forming activities recounted in the *Legend of the Suns* and related cosmogonies. Active and aggressive, Tezcatlipoca leads in both the warrior Feast Toxcatl (F.1.3), and the journey into the underworld or winter half of the year in Teotleco (F2.1). He is the guide endowed with unrivalled foresight, also in more recent time, in the great migrations from the north, where his constellation the Great Bear turns, the Septentrion Xonecuilli. Tezcatlipoca's respective roles and 'insignia' in these Feasts (F2.1, F1.3) are highlighted in Rios. By contrast, Quetzalcoatl, his equal and antagonist whom he deceived (as Telleriano notes, 'engañó a Quetzalcoatl'; f.3v) has a more modest role in the Feasts here, attendant to Huitzilopochtli's compadre Tlaloc. All these figures in turn rely on (and indeed may double as) a large supporting cast, which mostly features patrons of the 20 Trecenas who are neither Night Lords nor Heroes, but fishers, farmers, cooks, the flayed one Xipe, Xolotl the original canine companion, the pulque drinkers Mayauel and Patecatl, and several others.

On stage, certain figures are clearly more ubiquitous than others, though none appears just once. Sometimes one or other appears alone, while certain scenes, like those in Ochpaniztli, Panquetzaliztli and Tititl, gather many, in august galas, called dances (*mitote*) in the gloss. In these terms, feted in the galas of Ochpaniztli and Tititl, the two women Teteu innan and Ciuacoatl exude a quite special charisma (**Pls 5,6**). These two may be absent in name from the Tonalpoualli sets, yet they have a decisive role in the play of the Feasts, not least in opening and closing the sequence of seven determined by the very page formats of the chapter. As the mother of gods, Teteu innan receives the first fruits and has the ancient year marker in her headdress, when celebrated in her own gala (for which she borrows Ciuacoatl's skirt); and she attends the other two galas, Yoalitecutli's in Panquetzaliztli (she is the only woman to be invited to this otherwise male occasion) and Ciuacoatl's in Tititl.

For her part, Ciuacoatl does not return the compliment in not being Teteu innan's guest and indeed is seen with her only when this 'other woman' is on the sidelines, watching her being celebrated in Tititl. Ciuacoatl's Hymn (*Icuic* no.13) acknowledges Teteu innan only as the broom used to sweep the roads in Ochpaniztli. Moreover, in appearing four more times during the sequence of 11 'thin' Feasts, from which Teteu innan is entirely absent, Ciuacoatl has roles that her hymn suggests could or even should be also those of a politically potent man (owner of the bloodied eagle war feather; *Icuic* no.13), and which in any case embrace the 'coa-tl' community. As the 'five-in-one' celebrated in this Hymn, she dominates in every sense the period in the year that begins with her Feast Tititl (F2.6) and Izcalli (F2.7, jointly with Xiuhtecutli) and carries on through Toxcatl, Tecuilhuitl and Tlaxochimaco (F1.3, F1.5, F1.7), leaving Teteu innan to take over in Ochpaniztli (F1.9).

Celebrated in the Ochpaniztli gala, Teteu innan altogether heightens female being. During her Feast, women (though not Ciuacoatl) would sing in her honour for its 20 days (Tepepulco f.25v), and her power commanded each of her attendant 'papas putos' to display an erect phallos, huge but risibly only a stiff paper simulacrum. As her Hymn reminds us (*Icuic* no.4), she is the white-faced Toci Tlazoteotl goddess of childbirth, who spins the thread of life and has a spindle as one of her insignia, hence she provides the thread needed for the woven goods due as tribute at her equinoctial Feast. Borrower of Ciuacoatl's star skirt (*citlalicue*) that represents the Milky Way itself, she has enough cosmic force to bring the world (-ages) down to earth in Tamoanchan, the first great 'coming down' (*Icuic* no.4): this is the equinoctial site of moon and sun, the hanging down from the thread of the spider (ancient settler and colonizer), and the building of the first houses shown in Borgia. At the same time, her broom emblem shows her to be ever the sweeper of the roads, the lowly habit that gets to be mentioned in Ciuacoatl's hymn.

At her equinox, Teteu innan stands opposite Xipe, who is always male and who 'drinks night', urging on the day that will lengthen to become longer than the night as Tlacaxipehualiztli (F2.9) draws to its close (Reyes notes attendant means of calculating the light and shade of the equinox; 1992:195). In his Feast, the flayed one Xipe stands before his temple, wearing a reduced style of the conical cap seen in his array (Tepepulco f.269), but being offered objects that visually recall the Nahuatl root of his name in words meaning phallos, foreskin and testicles (Garibay 1958: 177). Besides confirming the male character of Tlacaxipehualiztli, these details also point to the deep concern with skin and skin covering seen in cosmogonical texts, the scales and feathers of the bird-reptiles and the snake that, emerging like a phallos from its sheath, sloughs its skin annually, in the case of the rattlesnake leaving a record of the fact in the number of rattles in its tail. Teteu innan's sexual definition as mother of gods may in these terms be prefigured within equinoctial Ochpaniztli itself, in the pair of male and female houses shown in Borgia, and in the matching of her with club-wielding warrior, seen also in Borgia as well as Tudela and, most vividly in Fejérváry, where outdoing the warrior she releases amniotic waters from a wrinkling belly (pp.17–18; **Fig. 3.8**).

Culminating in the equinox, hinge of the solar year, Teteu innan's Feast Ochpaniztli (F1.9) requires the most extensive preparations, over calendrical schedules of 4 (+4) years that conjoin the equinoctial sun with moon and Venus (said to be 'lujuriosa' in the gloss), and continues to impinge on the year even after the Feast officially ends. The chief image of her (p.30) is the prototype of 'our mother' Tonantzin-Guadalupe, the most revered Maria in America, whose Saint's Day originally fell in her Feast; the Borbonicus image is prominently quoted in the celebrated mural by Diego Rivera in the National Palace.

As we saw at the start, the pages that define the basic format and stages of the Feasts fall into two sequences, a thin 11 and a fat 7, numbered by the primes that likewise make up the 18 in other texts, determining the shape and choreography of the Feasts. Through 90°-turns in reading direction, these stages also intimate and modify the quarterly model of the tribute year, moving the start of the third quarter back from Teotleco to Ochpaniztli. These basic structures are however effectively overlaid and superimposed upon when the actors come on stage, populating it with their own designs. This is exemplarily the case with the prima donnas, Teteu innan and Ciuacoatl, first and last in the fat sequence yet at the same time each mindful of her own space and house, to the extent of deciding when her own season should begin. In this sense, as actor Ciuacoatl demands to be respected not just as the figure who in Tititl closes the fat sequence begun in Ochpaniztli by Teteu innan; in this position she also begins her own sequence of 12 Feasts (F2.6–F1.8), leaving Teteu innan with half that number (F1.9–F2.5).

Indeed, the dialectic between these two women, mother of gods or virile companion, tends towards mutual exclusion. Both produce cloth, yet each in her own mode: with the spindle she shares with the midwife Tlazoteotl, Teteu innan forms the delicate thread of life in the first place; with her batten,

Ciuacoatl weaves the exquisite skirts the other envies. Both foment agriculture, the former by blessing the harvest in Ochpaniztli, the latter by inaugurating seed-time in Tititl. Both bring sky down to earth: the former at the equinox in Tamoanchan which conjoins the Tlazoteotl's moon with the sun; the latter in Tititl, in the second coming down (*yancuic temoa*) of her leap or dance named and shown in Tepepulco, and in Borgia (p.39), where her worker-women Ciuateteo carry forward into the world the energy shed from above by the Milky Way Star-Skirt (Citlalicue, who in Tepepulco passes the weaving batten to Ciuacoatl).

As a result of this powerful interaction between the two women, each in her own space, the 18 Feasts are regrouped, so that the 11+7 of the format becomes the 12+6 of personae and social activity. In Borbonicus, the regrouping correlates perfectly with the seasons of the year declared in Tepepulco, whereby the 12 planting Feasts beginning in Tititl belong Ciuacoatl just as the six non-planting Feasts beginning in Ochpaniztli belong to Teteu innan. (Ochpaniztli's initial position here is reflected in the shift back from Teotleco F2.1 noted earlier with respect to the half-yearly tribute model also included in this manifold text.) Ciuacoatl's initial position in Tititl confirms her in the role as supervisor of planting and crops, especially in the *chinampa* context highlighted in this screenfold. Borgia and Fejérváry alike extend the correlation to include the night sky, recalling the arrangement in which Citlalicue, the hub of the galaxy, is seen above during the 12 planting Feasts, albeit plunging as a deadly *tzitzimine* in the twelfth, and disappears during the non-planting six. For its part, Borbonicus alludes to the night sky in Ochpaniztli in the 'S' image of the septentrion Xonecuilli, which is carried forward through the Feast indicating the forward movement of the constellations and the corresponding precession of the equinoxes. This exactly reflects the depictions of the same astronomical phenomenon seen in 'Encounter with Europe' (with respect to the winter solstice) and in Tovar (with respect to the summer solstice); thus paralleled, it serves as dramatic confirmation of the slippage between the years of the sun and of the stars that is calculated precisely in the Calendar Wheels and Mexicanus (see Chapters 7 and 8).

Drama

The formal criteria used so far in this analysis of the Borbonicus Feast chapter have ranged from sheer diagram of the stage itself to the numeracy, valency and gender that inhere in the personae who perform on it, the members of the cast. As we read through the chapter, the need grows to respond to the story itself, the full action and drama of the Feasts as they unfold in time, and to notice not just where and who but when and how. After the show is opened in Izcalli by Xiuhtecutli and Ciuacoatl (F2.7, p.23), the figures we initially encounter announce cults that are ancient and archetypal in Mesoamerica, and they do so singly, like Xipe, with his sheath of skin (F2.9), and Tlaloc selecting maize kernels, or receiving rudimentary homage atop his rainy mountain (F2.8, F1.1–F1.2). The offerings are basic and consist of firewood and food, while a newborn child will have its ear ritually pricked, a bloodletting which identifies this Feast with self-sacrifice of its name (*tozozoa-*). Things thicken in Toxcatl (F1.3), when Tezcatlipoca bursts in as leader in his team of four, to be revered with the incense produced by ceramic burners with the quatrefoil design. They thicken further in Etzalcualiztli

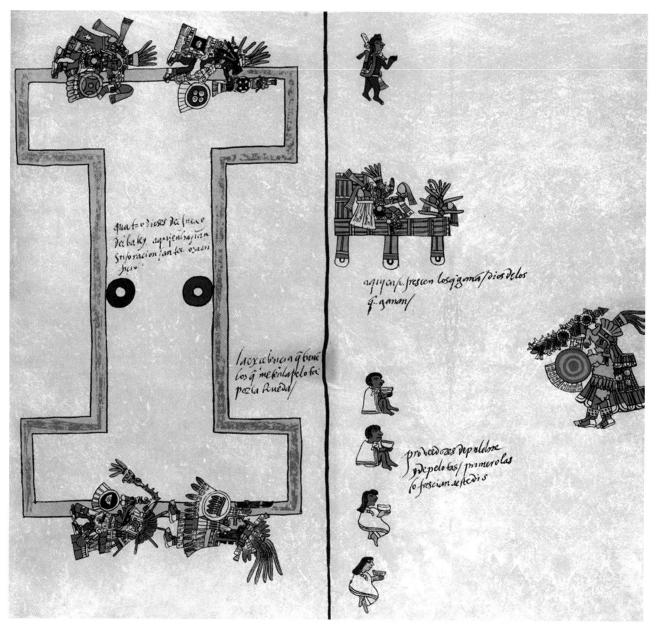

Figure 5.1 Tecuilhuitl A & B, with ball-court and maize-adorned litter. Borbonicus p.27

(FI.4), when Tlaloc's maize and bean feast is celebrated in a dance led by Quetzalcoatl and Xolotl.

But the major development in the story occurs with the turn of the page into Tecuilhuitl (FI.5), whose ball-court, positioned at 90°, demands the shift from horizontal to vertical as we pass the solstice and enter the second half of the upper year. Occupying facing pages, the two pairs of Feasts represented here, Tecuilhuitl A and B (FI.5–FI.6) and Tlaxochimaco and Xocotl huetzi (FI.7–FI.8, otherwise known as Micailhuitl A and B), play insistently with the notion of upper and lower, in terms of celestial origin, ancestry and descent, social class, and the year itself (**Fig. 5.1, 5.2**).

First of all, the ball-court of Tecuilhuitl A (FI.5) announces the rules of the game, as a durable (masonic) construct of stone that allows dialogue between players in their corners, the quarters of the year (as we saw) but now also of the town, in this primordial plan of environment. Calendrical systems that equate quarters of the year with the quarters of the ball-court are placed early in the Era in the annals recorded in the Zouche and Vienna codices (see p.34 above). Led here by Cinteotl and Ixtlilton (black patron of parties and games) at one end, and by

Ciuacoatl and Quetzalcoatl at the other, the godly players here preordain the upper social set, as the only ones 'excellent' enough (as the gloss puts it) to engage in the sport. For the game to happen, the players naturally need a ball, one made of the rubber exclusive to the American tropics (before Columbus), and suggestive in its unique elasticity of the most sophisticated philosophies of chance. For the people credited with both first playing the game and founding the first city are one and the same: the Olmec, whose name means the rubber people (**Fig. 5.1**).

In social terms, Tecuilhuitl B (FI.6) on the same page leaves no doubt about upper and lower, the former being denoted by very expensive clothing. Cinteotl, familiar of the flowery Xochipilli and guardian of the best 'seed' (*Icuic* no.8), is now seen being carried back from the ball-game in a litter, a privilege developed it seems in the east, in the lands of Olmec and Popoloca. As in 'Genesis', the east-west dimension of Mesoamerican culture as such is implicit in the pairing of red and black, the colours of the rings in the ball-court and of arithmetic and script itself. Invoking the pair of Tecuilhuitl Feasts, Xochipilli's Hymn (*Icuic* no.8) refers to both his place in

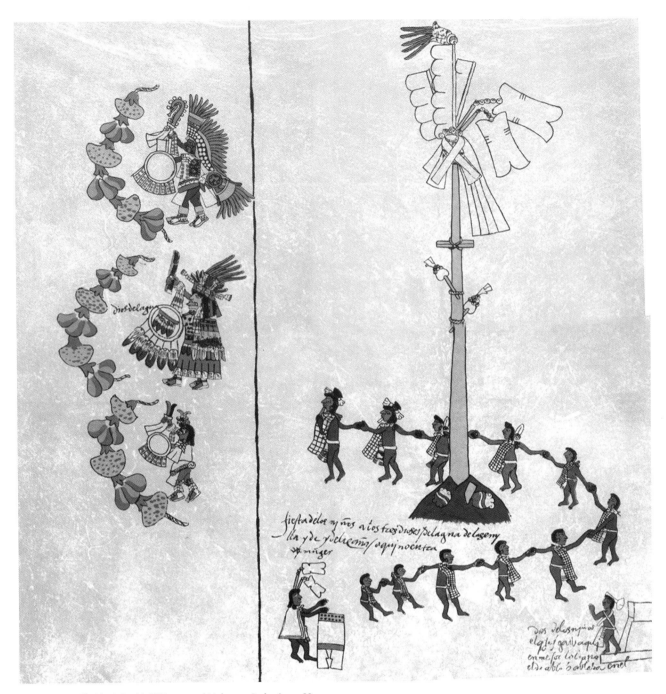

Figure 5.2 Micailhuitl A & B, with 17 blooms and 11 dancers. Borbonicus p.28

the ball-court (*tlachtli icpac*) and his familiar Cinteotl. For its part, Rios sets all this into deeper time, promoting Cinteotl-Xochipilli as the lord of our flesh (which is what the Night Lord Cinteotl is) who opens the 'Genesis' in that text precisely in Tecuilhuitl. In Edmonson's correlation of the Feasts with the Tonalpoualli, the Cholula year begins in Tecuilhuitl, its solar highpoint, as it does in *Cuevas...*, Tovar and, not least, Borgia.

The interest in the ball-game and seed indicates a thread in the story announced already by clothing and demeanour in Tlacaxipehualiztli which now becomes distinctive at the social court: ethnicity. For from the Yope with whom Xipe is associated, we have moved to the Olmec, widely recognized then as now as the 'mother culture' of Mesoamerica. The concern with seed and its social and ethnic – that is, cultural – derivation dominates the matching pair of Feasts on the facing page (p.28), Tlaxochimaco and Xocotl huetzi (F1.7, F1.8), which elsewhere and more widely are known as the Feasts of the dead Miccailhuitl A and B (**Fig. 5.2**). As alternatives, these Feast

names might at first seem anomalous or contradictory, since the Borbonicus Feasts invoke the merry gathering of flowers during midsummer nights (Tlaxochimaco F1.7) and fruit ripe and ready to fall (Xocotl huetzi F1.8). Yet Mesoamerican philosophy insists on survival through death in concepts like the flowering bone and the seed spat from the gourd skull, which derive from knowledge of vegetative reproduction and cross-fertilization inseparable from the notion that the star clusters around which our galaxy turns inseminate the earth. Here in Borbonicus, faced by three of the team seen already in Toxcatl, the seed-flowers of Tlaxochimaco rain down in the vertical half-page format (in just the total, 17, listed in the Florentine Codex, waiting to be inseminated by the 17-feathered Huitzilopochtli seen in *Cuevas* p.19; in Teotihuacan, 17 seed-flowers pour from the hands of the high priests in the murals of earthly paradise). The Florentine source offers brilliant accounts of how these flowers and seeds were gathered by couples under the stars of midsummer, when the heart of our galaxy dominates the Mexica night sky. The fruit

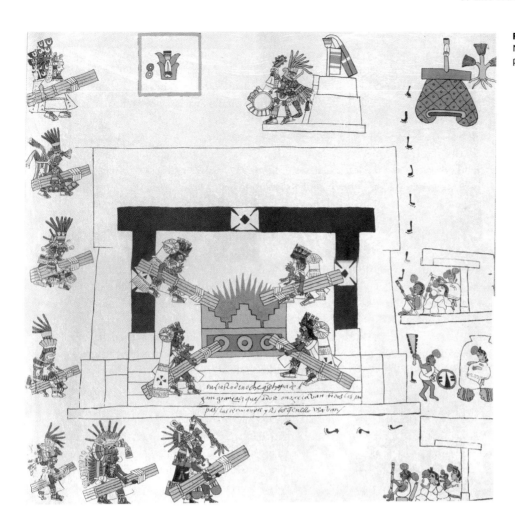

Figure 5.3 Panquetzaliztli, with the New Fire of year 2 Reed. Borbonicus p.34

in Xocotl huetzi is shown atop a high pole. In Tovar and elsewhere its 11 seeds, kneaded into dough, evoke the stars of the night sky (noted as such by Kubler and Gibson); here in Borbonicus the pole also holds high the mummy bundle of Micailhuitl. The image of an ancient tree, the pole belongs to the god of the Otomi honoured in the eleventh of the Hymns (Otontecuhtli icuic, *In icuic* no.11), which recalls the plants and seeds brought down to earth in the Otomi genesis, and whose prototype is the maguey (*me-tl*). In all, these seed Feasts draw on roots in agriculture, urbanism and ethnicity, in Teotihuacan and among the primordial Otomi, no less deep than those attributed to the Olmec on the previous facing page.

While the Feasts in the story so far nurture memories of founders deep in time, Olmec and Otomi, those coming after equinoctial Ochpaniztli turn attention to more recent role models, saliently the immigrants who during the previous 800 years (two *tzontli*) had set off from homelands far to the northwest, the Chichimec from Seven Caves and the Mexica from Aztlan. These arrivals are announced by footprints, the general motif of the following Feast Teotleco (F2.1), which translates as the 'advent of the gods' and is the first Feast of the lower half of the year. In some sources, Teotleco announces the start of the footprint road that runs right through the lower half of the year, through the underworld of the winter solstice, which is travelled by Tezcatlipoca and Quetzalcoatl in Borgia. Then, after acknowledging the intensely local mountain cults of commoners who had long dwelt among them (Tepeilhuitl F2.2), the cycle or story continues with the idea of migration itself, the epochal intrusions into the highland Basin of the Chichimec in Quecholli (F2.3) and then the Mexica in Panquetzaliztli (F2.4).

The moment of the 'fliers', Quecholli (F2.3) coincides annually with the arrival of migrant birds on the highland lakes, and the hunting of them at which the Chichimecs and their patron Mixcoatl ('cloud snake') excelled, having themselves arrived from the north as if in pursuit. Overseen by Mixcoatl and Tezcatlipoca, the activities and emblems of this Feast in Borbonicus include eminently mobile women carrying offspring in a net papoose (*matlahuacal*), serving pulque from a huge jar, dedicated reed-arrows, headband and head dress of duck or heron feather (*aztaxelli*), black facial markings that recall the ashes of the pioneer 'obsidian butterfly' Itzpapalotl, nets (also *matlahuacal*) for bagging game, and prey on spits that ranges from fish-like birds to skinned rabbits.

Migrating from their homeland Seven Caves (Chicomoztoc) from the 7th century onwards, the Chichimec ushered in a whole epoch or horizon in Mesoamerican history. On arriving, they organized the territories they had invaded into as many arenas, four to the west (including the Highland basin) and three to the east in the Sierra Madre Oriental. Prefigured in the caves in the *Historia tolteca-chichimeca* (f.16), this seven-fold settlement is indicated here in the distribution of headwear, arrows and other gear. As supposed 'barbarians' who swept in from the northern deserts, the Chichimec left records of their epic that are remarkably sophisticated in ways intimated by the Twenty Hymns and here by this arithmetic, which also inheres in such details as totals of pyramid steps, markings on the pulque jar (18), flags that count each Feast's 20 days. As the cloud snake, Mixcoatl has been seen as the male length of the Milky Way, and its hub the Market (*tianquiz*) that names his pyramid; his victim Itzpapalotl bears in her name the Chichimec calendar base in the Era (Round 72; Night Lord Itztli counting as two within the decade, Quecholli Papalotl counting as seven decades). The numeracy in Tezcatlipoca's attire conforms to the Riddle of the Feasts with which he first lured the Chichimec out of their caves (see p.12 above).

As they carry us forward in time, the Feasts condense ethnicity into politics. In Panquetzaliztli (F2.4), the story narrows to concentrate on the fortune of the Mexica, told in the annals in Mexicanus, Telleriano and Aubin, which culminates in the grand New Fire ceremony shown here, presided over by Moctezuma II at a specially constructed temple atop Huizachtepec dedicated to Huitzilopochtli in the year 2 Reed (1507) (**Fig. 5.3**). The ceremony was held in the Feast Panquetzaliztli (F2.4), confirmed by the banner (*pantli*) on Huitzilopochtli's temple, whence in deepest night and with all lights extinguished the New Fire was brought down at midnight to set alight the huge blaze seen below at the heart of the Great Temple, administered at the corners by four manifestations of Yoalitecutli, the Lord of Night and eleventhth Hero. The date 2 Reed is given above, in the square year marker inherited by the Mexica from the Chichimecs, and it is placed in the Chichimec Era through the 'fire-count' (cut firewood, flames, smoke) used in Mendoza and Boban. The 16 Rounds that have elapsed from that 7th-century calendar base equal the firewood *teas* or torches held by the each of the Yoalitecutli (4 x 4; food for the 16 flames); the *teas* held by the seven guests waiting in the wings anticipate completion of the Era's 100 Rounds (7 x 4; i.e. [72] + 28 = 100).

This event marked a major assertion of specifically Mexica power in the Basin and beyond. Retrospectively, the Xiuhtecutli who had announced the year itself wearing the Xiuhcoanaual in Izcalli is said (in a gloss) to have been impersonated by emperor Moctezuma, who foresaw doom and the Spanish invasion. Absent in this presentation, the tribal Huitzilopochtli could still be seen as a gate-crasher or arriviste at the august gala of personae, his solar power being contained here in any case by Yoalitecutli's all-encompassing night. As such, the New Fire date 2 Reed is designated in the *Legend of the Suns* as the year when, under the watchful eyes of the Star-Skirt and her entourage, a fire-drilling first 'smoked' the skies, and introduced the history of the Chichimecs. Year 2 Reed has a long pedigree in screenfold annals. Those of Tepexic point up its sidereal advance in the solar year; and it factors in turn into the whole complex principle (and reforms thereof) by which the Mexica measured and gave Series III names to years, here in Panquetzaliztli, and in Izcalli at the start, where the year and the Xiuhmolpilli both begin, having carried forward the initial year of the previous chapter, 1 Rabbit, placing it in its square marker. As for gender, like Chichimec hunting in Quecholli, Mexica fire-drilling is strongly male, in certain respects even more so. Here, women on the rooftops, especially if pregnant, shield themselves (inside urns or holding turquoise masks to their faces) from sight of the newly drilled Fire as it is carried down from Huizachtepec to the heart of the city.

Finally, irrupting into current time-space with cumulatively intense valency (in arithmetic, population, politics), the Feast cycle descends to the other side of the mountain Huizachtepec that establishes boundaries between it and Tenochtitlan to the north, and thence crosses the southern lake to face the water-rich southern rim of the Basin in Atemoztli, now in a finely

detailed map and chronometer. This means that we have reached the destination, the home page and probable provenance in Tititl (F2.6), of the drama of the eponymous Ciuacoatl herself, lady of the southern lake (of the 'diosas de la laguna'), mistress of millennial irrigation, and of the 'canoes' that until the 19th century continued to transport food throughout the year to the centre of Tenochtitlan/Mexico City. Doubly eponymous since, besides identifying her as 'woman-snake', this term can also designate a male official high enough in rank to be able to match or represent the emperor. This is the scene with which the chapter opens in Izcalli, when Xiuhtecutli/Moctezuma faces Ciuacoatl, both goddess and the imperial representative of precisely the part of the Highland basin where the Feast ceremonies start and end: the southern lake today residually visible around the *chinampas* of Xochimilco. The particular involvement of Tenochtitlan in this region, desirable for its water sources and its intensive *chinampa* agriculture, is revealed in the Cozcatzin Codex, a text written in the interests of allies whom the Mexica settled there (under Itzcoatl) and who may well have been acknowledged as 'ciuacoatl' officials. Its loss was sorely felt during the siege of 1521 (see p.10 above).

In the Hymns, this lakeland site is honoured as the home of ducks (depicted in Cozcatzin), their hunters and chefs, who came to remind everyone in the Basin of Itzcoatl's terrible humiliation of Tlatelolco to the north (Amimitl *Icuic* no.10). Geographically it surrounds the Chichimec bird-hunting shrine in Cuitlahuac, being *par excellence* the home of Atlahua, owner of waters (*Icuic* no.19) and *chinampatlalli* (*chinampa* fields), dweller in the basin to the left (*opochin*) or south of the sun's daily course and formerly subject to Chalco (*chalmecatl*). Amimitl's array exceptionally includes both the hunter's bag (*matlahuacal*) and the planter's digging stick whose obsidian tip is also that of the hunter's arrow (*itziuactlcuch*); as the hunters of aquatic birds adorned with the *aztaxelli*, he and Atlahua are especially able to reconcile the seasons of the sweeping broom, dried vegetation (straw and wicker) in the hand of Teteu innan (*in macxoyauh*) in Ochpaniztli, with the fresh shoots proffered in triumph and anticipation by Ciuacoatl in Tititl. This initial Feast of the planting season identifies her, in the fifth and grandest of her roles in this text and in the Hymns, with the Quilaztli-Ciuacoatl of the *Legend of the Suns* (Bierhorst 1992:146) who ground up the paternal manioc bones brought up from the underworld by Quetzalcoatl and put them into her jade bowl in order to form the human beings of our Era. Durán notes Ciuacoatl-Quilaztli as patrona of Xochimilco (1995, 2:131).

Needless to say, this alphabetic account in an un-American language of Ciuacoatl's Feasts can scarcely hope to respond to the kaleidoscopic music of the original or the subtlety of its propositions. In context it strives however to broaden understanding of both the aesthetics and the rigorous logic with which the cycle is expounded in this text. It tells the particular story of the Mexica/Aztec who entered the ancient arena of the Highland basin and Mesoamerica, and it tells it from a particular point of view, that of Ciuacoatl's *chinampa* settlements. The text as a whole is clearly designed not just to report but to affirm the antiquity and coherence of its authors' culture and beliefs. In just these respects this Ciuacoatl chapter usefully bears comparison with its literary kin, the Feast texts dedicated to Ilamatecutli, Tepoztecatl and Otontecutli.

6
Prior Hosts

Heroine and focus of the Mexica screenfold Borbonicus to the extent of giving it its name in Reyes' edition, Ciuacoatl is distinguished among the personae depicted in the Feast chapter we have just examined. Taking this figure as a yardstick enriches and illuminates comparisons between the Ciuacoatl chapter and other choreographies of the Feasts, set out in the core chapter of Borgia (pp.29–46), the panels *in situ* in Tepoztecatl's temple, and Tepepulco (I,ii). Like Borbonicus, these other three texts transmit their meaning not just through a principal persona but through the very stage that frames the action, and the larger drama. In so doing, they further reveal, through performance, the immense suppleness of *tlacuilolli* as visible language that is unavailable in alphabetic script.

As texts painted on deerskin and inscribed in stone, the accounts of Ilamatecutli and Tepoztecatl's Feasts antedate Borbonicus and Cortés alike, and self-date respectively to 2 Reed 1351 (or shortly thereafter) and 10 Rabbit 1502; they are true windows on to life in ancient America. Transcribed on to European paper, Tepepulco's account of the Otomi Feasts, especially those involving the 'Otomi Lord' Otontecutli, carries forward the spirit of dance into Spanish colonial times. It infuses life into the Feasts in the New Era begun in the New Fire of 2 Reed 1559, which is covertly kindled and consecrated elsewhere in that text (II, iii).

Ilamatecutli: palatine nights and days
As we saw above, the Borgia screenfold (**Figs. 6.1, 6.2**) has long been associated with the urban complex of Cholula, the 'Rome' of Mesoamerica. This great metropolis is significantly depicted in many native histories and maps from that area, above all, its own Codex, which features the consort rulers Ilamatecutli and Quetzalcoatl (González & Reyes 2003; PBM 119). The *Historia tolteca-chichimeca* precisely details its fortune after the siege and assault in 3 Reed 1235, when the Chichimec 'shot the face of Quetzalcoatl' (f.38v) and adapted as they could a calendar whose roots went back to the Olmec. The 1580 *Relación*

geográfica gives an unusually detailed account of its priesthood, the rites and temples that marked the year's passage. The Mexica emphatically acknowledged its precedence and cosmic significance in 'Genesis', in the opening chapter of Rios, and as we have seen Cholula is the core reference for those of the Twenty Hymns that antedate both Mexica and Chichimec. The site of vast and imposing architecture, despite the unending and wilful destruction that began with Cortés, Cholula is the provenance for Borgia favoured by Nowotny. (On recent enquiries into the history and power of this city, see McCafferty 2001.)

The Borgia account of Ilamatecutli's Feasts culminates in the New Fire held in Etzalcualiztli (p.46), under the post-1235 rule of the Chichimec (Nowotny brilliantly detected their northern cultural impact on this ceremony and the rites that preceded it). It corresponds textually to the fall of the 'Ozomatli' (Monkey) in the Chichimec New Fire year 2 Reed 1351, as this figure (identified by his Monkey Sign XI) is seen tumbling down the Great Pyramid seven pages later (p.53). This epochal event involved not just Cholula and the Chichimec but Olmec and Mixtec and is duly recorded at this 2 Reed date in the major Nahuatl histories of western Mesoamerica (*Historia tolteca-chichimeca* f.41v; Cuauhtitlan Annals p.26). The fall appears to mark the abrupt decline of the palatine system, whose emblem is the Olmec number 11, the Tlacatecpan device.

Even at a glance, the Borgia Feasts chapter announces its concern with the complex urban architecture and social hierarchy which Nowotny correlated with the yearly performance of rituals at Cholula. As stages, its pages contrive to encompass at one and the same time galaxy and innermost chamber. The 18 pages that comprise this chapter are read vertically, like Tepepulco, and begin like 'Genesis' and *Cuevas* in Tecuilhuitl (F1.5; **Fig. 6.1**), in a 'scene' that is Ilamatecutli's open starry body, galactic womb and hub. The downward continuum is radically interrupted, however, thanks to the fact that the first 10 pages and Feasts (F1.5–F2.5) run to the bottom on one side of

Figure 6.1 Tecuilhuitl A, with crown and jade coit above; and Etzalcualiztli, with maize plant and scaley Xonecuilli. *Cuevas* ... pp.31–32

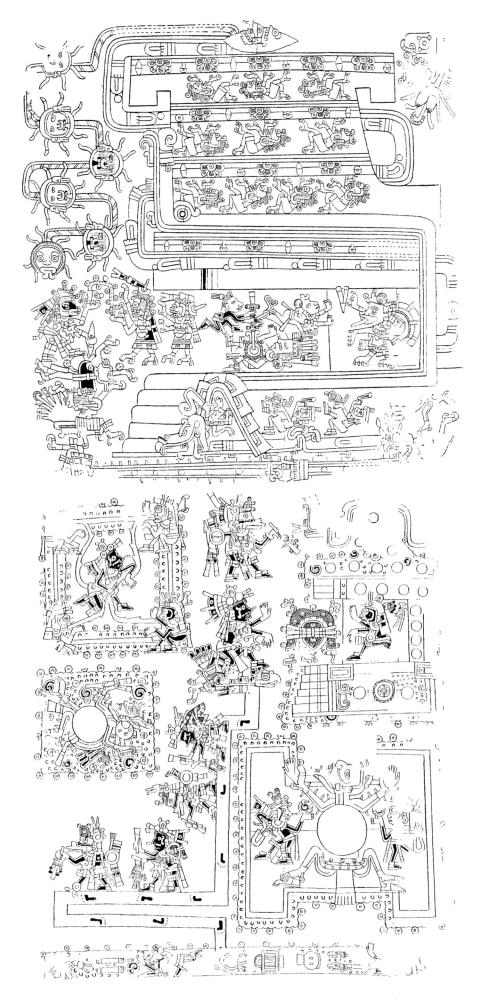

Figure 6.2 Ochpaniztli and house, firedrilling, Pleiades above and caiman below; Teotleco and footprint road. Borgia pp.33–35 (after W. von den Steinen, in Nowotny 1961)

the screenfold (issuing into the falling water of Atemoztli, F2.5), while the remaining eight pages and Feasts (F2.6–F1.4) initiate its other side from the top, beginning with the Planting Season in Tititl (F2.6), ushered in by the first of Ilamatecutli (Ciuacoatl)'s starry sky bands (cf. **Pl. 9**).

As for the ratio of Feasts per page, the norm is 1:1, and this is varied only twice, or rather in two ways. First, Ochpaniztli (F1.9) allots a page to each of its male and female houses (pp.33–-34). After the four opening pages (pp.29–32), which all feature the open star body in plan, these houses are seen in profile, as if in the scene of Teteu innan's equinoctial 'coming down' to earth (**Fig. 6.2**). The male house is the site of the first of the two New Fire ceremonies shown in the text, the primitive affair overlooked in Nowotny's description. The allotting of two pages to Ochpaniztli is compensated for immediately afterwards in the reduced space given to Teotleco and Tepeilhuitl (F2.1–F2.2). As the arrival of the gods that is evidenced by the footprints they leave, Teotleco is the Feast when the lower half of the year begins, right after the equinox: starting here in Teotleco, the footprints mark out a road that runs to Tlacaxipehualiztli (F2.1–F2.9; pp.35–42) and the March equinox. It is along this road that the norm of one Feast per page undergoes its second modification, this time in terms not so much of ratio (of Feasts per page) as of a superimposition that appeals to the third dimension, the two examples each being governed by a star figure resplendent in the night sky.

Irrupting in Quecholli (F2.3) (**Fig. 6.3**) into a recognizably urban Olmec landscape, the Chichimec wind bursts as night into the page, revealing the seven stars of the septentrion; the wind backs through three 90°-turns and thrusts southwards down the left side of the text, in parallel time to the former road of the Feasts soon to be revealed again to the right. This effect is matched further along, on the screenfold's other side, when between Tititl and Izcalli (F2.6, F2.7, **Fig. 6.4**) the road goes right in through the mouth of the Oztoma caiman cave of the Olmec jaguar, only to encounter the night sky within, in the optimal form of Yoalitecutli himself with his eleven stars. After Izcalli, in whose 'house' the Tonalpoualli is matched with year-bearer Series I to IV (Series IV being represented by the Olmec jaguar) the road emerges again, divides, and ends upon reaching Tlacaxipehualiztli and the equinox.

After this, still on the grounds of form, Borgia defines the last four Feasts, Tozoztli A to Etzalcualiztli (F1.1–F1.4), as a final subgroup. These four pages appeal to elaborate architecture, veritable building plans (except for Toxcatl) which moreover visually echo the format of the star bodies that framed the four opening Feasts. This formal parallel between the pages in plan at the end and the beginning is unmistakable, as Nowotny said, and they both concentrate rising Series of year bearers into kindlings of New Fire. This similarity highlights their thematic differences as life forms and architecture; and it has the further effect of contrasting both sets of four page-frames in plan with the houses of Ochpaniztli, which are seen in profile, and the meandering road map of the winter journey. Overall, these 18 pages anticipate the pattern of Feasts seen in 'Genesis' in Rios, which terminates precisely in Cholula: the initial descent from the life source (F1.5–), Tezcatlipoca's multidimensional epic of growth (F2.1–) and the installing of the urban architecture in F2.9/F1.1. The overall sequence of 18 pages in Borgia is, then, by page:

4 in plan (F1.5-F1.8)
2 in profile (F1.9)
4+4 footprint road (F2.1–F2.5, F2.6–F2.9)
4 in plan (F1.1–F1.4)

While it is possible at this level of sheer pagination to analyze Ilamatecutli's Feasts in the same formal terms as Ciuacoatl's, fundamental differences between Borgia and Borbonicus rapidly become apparent when we move on to consider the lead roles of actor personae, and the drama itself. In conjoining earth and sky, Ilamatecutli's very body becomes the womb of the Milky Way when overhead, filling the whole page (F1.5–1.8), while elsewhere it narrows into a celestial band (*streifenformig*) along the top of the page (F2.6–1.4), that is matched below by the terrestrial band of the caiman earth beast. Hence, this sky-earth pair pre-establishes as it were the pattern of planting seasons which is initiated by Ciuacoatl and Xiuhtecutli in Borbonicus and fully detailed in Tepepulco. Yet they simultaneously do far more than that: the very shapes and locations assigned to Ilamatecutli herself extend deep into the night sky and the galaxy while her caiman counterpart below epitomizes nothing less than the philosophy of life forms set and acted out at length in the *Popol vuh*. In this sense, the greater complexity of Borgia is daunting and can hardly be tackled here, for reasons of space and because in any case the Feast cycle in question antedates that of the Mexica, our main focus here.

In this perspective the most significant Feasts of all are those that most densely interfuse these orders of reality, upper and lower, outer and inner, through five images of stars that may be deciphered thanks in part to Tepepulco (II,i: Mamalhuaztli-Yoaltecutli, Miec and Tianquiz; Xonecuilli and Colotl onoc). In Tecuilhuitl (F1.5–; pp.29–), life forms start to emerge out of the dark pregnant body of the stars, in protean shapes and numbers, from the galactic womb deep within, that is the dream hub seen high above at midsummer, the *mundus patens* and the Market (Tianquiz). In Ochpaniztli (F1.9; pp.33–34), the group of bee-like pioneers builds the first house, drills fire and gets drunk within only to be shaken by the caiman earth, and rises heliacally to become the Pleiades (Miec). In Quecholli (F2.3; pp.35–), the Septentrion (Xonecuilli) turning round the pole projects into the story of metamorphosis, flight and migration which begins with the butterfly and that relies on bodily wings, fins, paddles and arms (the 'extended' insect-scorpion-turtle Colotl onoc). In Izcalli (F2.7; p.40), deep in the belly of caiman earth the Lord of Night himself (Yoalitecutli) is divided, his 11 stars showing as just over five to left and right, and glows resplendent as the sticks that will drill New Fire (Mamalhuaztli), pointing to their glowing tips at opposite ends of the zodiac, that is, its intersections with the Milky Way: Antares near the Market and Aldebaran near the Pleiades.

As a master exposition of the Feasts, the Borgia chapter explains the logic according to which Mexica choreography and science later reconciled the different rhythms of the solar year, the sidereal year of New Fire, and the civil year. In the Cholula text, New Fire is drilled when the Market is overhead near the summer solstice while in the Mexica text it is drilled when the Pleiades are overhead near the winter solstice; yet logic and principle remain the same. In the larger American perspective, the Borgia Feasts evidence the historical link between the tropical astronomy and that of the Mexica. The tropical norm is

Figure 6.3 Quecholli and the septentrion (Xonecuilli). Borgia p.37 (after W. von den Steinen, in Nowotny 1961)

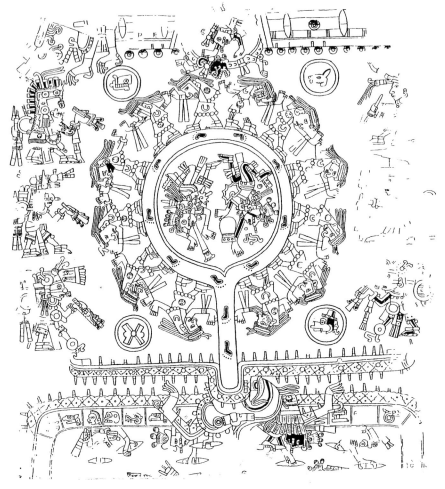

Figure 6.4 Tititl and Izcalli, separated by Olmec caiman mask (cf. **Fig. 1.1b**), Ilamatecutli above. Borgia p.39 (after W. von den Steinen, in Nowotny 1961)

for the Market and the Pleiades to function as the fundamental terms of celestial reference, at or near the zodiac intersections with the Milky Way. For its part, greater Mexica interest in circumpolar Xonecuilli hints at their own stronger links with the extra-tropical north; and the outstretched arms of Yoalitecutli, pointing to opposite ends of the zodiac, effectively privilege the Pleiades, obeying the Mexica notion that this constellation constantly 'quarrelled' with Market over the year, except for when the former disappeared from the night sky in Etzalcualiztli and Tecuilhuitl (as Telleriano reports; **Fig.2.1**). Market then had its brief moment of glory, only to become invisible itself at the other end of the year, when the Pleiades determined the moment of New Fire in Panquetzaliztli

Tepoztecatl: symposium under the stars

Fermented from the juice of the maguey plant, pulque (*octli* in Nahuatl) was the alcoholic drink most widely consumed in Mesoamerica before Cortés. The drinking of it was regulated by various rules that pertained to age, class, gender and, among the Mexica at least, the calendar. Over the year, certain Feasts were dedicated to the preparation and consuming of particular kinds of pulque. According Borgia, Tepepulco, Telleriano, Magliabechiano and other sources, pulque was drunk preferentially over a period of 220 nights and days, or 11 Feasts, 11 being the cipher that has a particular connection with the sky at night, the preferred time for drinking.

The enabling myth for these activities is set out, in concise but highly resonant terms, in the *Popol vuh* account of the pioneer house-builders, the first bearers of axe tools who cut wood for the roof-beam, get drunk, perish and rise to become the Pleiades (Miec). This link between axe, place of abode, drunkenness and the Pleiades is assumed in Mexica texts. Magliabechiano (ff.49–59) collectively attributes the name 'Two Rabbit' (Ome Tochtli) to the 11 pulque drinkers who carry axes and identifies them with place glyphs. Their astronomical nature is shown by a 'new moon' nose adornment (*yacameztli*) and by the fact that they number 11 (in this context, Riese speaks of them as 'die elf Götter der Trunkenheit'; 1986:99). The crude stone axes they bear as pioneers are adorned with white ties. These tools are highlighted by a hand pointing to the axe glyph (*tepoztli*, 'splitter'), and by the name of the first of their number Tepoztecatl, whose home is Tepoztlan, the 'axe place' (in this case, the axe is of copper; **Fig. 6.5**). The 11 also bear two types of fringed shield, round and square.

The place signs which accompany them (except for the presiding pair Patecatl and Mayauel, pulque gods *par excellence*) indicating their houses or abodes are an unusual feature for Mexica gods. Most of the abodes in question can be found on native maps and in some cases are themselves the source of native texts, not least Tepoztlan. For good measure, certain of them (Papaztac, Tlilhua, Tlaltecocoayan) reappear caracterized by lunar affixes in the Cozcatzin Codex, again confirming the strong link between the moon, pulque and the 'rabbit' Ome Tochtli. Another, Yauhtepec, the town which lies just south of Tepoztlan and still produces pulque today, invokes Two Rabbit in its Coatlan Inscription (**Fig. 6.5**). For its part, Borbonicus (p.11) shows the pulque-maker Patecatl under the 11-starred night sky, together with the emblems of new moon, axe adorned with quadruple white-ties, and the Monkey, XI in the Twenty Signs. Eleven is especially germane to pulque insofar as it equals the number of years it normally takes for the maguey plant to mature, or redden, as Tepepulco puts it (II, ii).

As for pulque Feasts in the year, both the Tepepulco Ms (I, ii) and Magliabechiano (ff.49–59) mark a beginning for Ome Tochtli in Pachtli, when even children got drunk on pulque, especially in the Tepoztlan area south of the Mexica capital (cf. Boone 1982:223 for the specific reference to Pachtli A [F2.1]: '... y en esta fiesta çelebrauan otro demonio q se dezia ometuchtli que es el dios de las borracheras'). Shortly afterwards, in Panquetzaliztli (F2.4), there was another main ceremony, when Patecatl prepared a 'divine' pulque (*teuoctli*) for the residents of the temple. Finally, in Atlcahualo (F2.8) and again in Tozoztli B (F1.2), everyone – children, women and men – drank a white pulque (*tizaoctli*) prepared by Papaztac. In Tepepulco and Borgia, main clusters of pulque drinkers, identified by the usual *yacameztli* affix, appear at the height and middle of this 11-Feast season (F2.5-F2.7). In Borgia (pp.39–41), they bear pulque, dance along a trail of 11 footprints, past the night lord Yoalitecutli 11th of the Thirteen Heroes whose body is inset with 11 stars, and descend from the night-sky of 11 stars. By contrast, in none of these sources is pulque a feature of any of the other 18 Feasts.

On this evidence, there must have been something like a pulque 'season', hitherto unrecognized as such, which in Mexica times lasted for 11 Feasts, or 220 nights and days, from Pachtli A to Tozoztli B (F2.1 to F1.2). Within the Feast cycle, this arrangement is marked by the two appearances of Tezcatlipoca with the same insignia ('le medesime insegni'; Rios), first in

Figure 6.5 Tepoztecatl Ome Tochtli: a) Magliabechiano (after W. von den Steinen, in Seler 1908); b) seed mural, Tepoztlan 1996

Pachtli A when he is said to have got Quetzalcoatl drunk on pulque ('engañó a Quetzalcoatl'; Telleriano f.3v) and again at the start of the seven complementary Feasts in Toxcatl (F1.3). As such, the structure concords with the patterning of Feasts in 'thin' and 'fat' sequences of 11 and 7, and it recalls the cases of inset 220-day periods noted above with respect to such other phenomena as year-starts, seeds and the celestial dominance of Market, though of course the pulque new moon period has its own start and end.

As the axe-bearing pioneer, Tepoztecatl is commemorated at the temple-pyramid dedicated to the pulque cult at Tepoztlan (**Figs 6.5, 6.6, 6.7**). In its day, the temple drew pilgrims from as far afield as Chiapas and Guatemala, and declares it was incorporated by the Mexica in 10 Rabbit (the sample glyph in Flo IV, 35) 1502, the last year of Ahuizotl's reign, in an inscription that also features the imperial feather crown of the Mexica (*xiuhuitzolli*). The Sign Rabbit recurs in Tepoztecatl's name Ome Tochtli, which we saw at Coatlan (pp.47–8 above), and is celebrated in the Hymn of the pulque drinking Totochtin (*Icuic* no.17). The building opens to the western sky of the new moon, a view that cannot be had from the town below. The inscriptions on panels in this temple, usually referred to today as the 'Tepozteco', potentially have enormous significance as a firmly pre-Cortesian statement *in situ* about a practice which brought together the time cycles of night and day, the stars with the Feasts of the year. They are however complex and demand detailed analysis, particularly with respect to how the pulque Feasts relate the overall year cycle.

A century ago, when they were better perserved than they are now, Eduard Seler offered an analysis of these inscriptions. He concentrated in particular on the two series of panels which respectively adorn the stone benches of the inner temple, to either side of the statue of the resident patron deity Tepoztecatl (Text I) which the friars hurled to the valley below, and the benches that line the north and south sides of the western anteroom (Text II). His study is still pertinent today insofar as it is the only serious attempt to integrate these inscriptions into the Mesoamerican calendar, while respecting the temple's west-east orientation, and the pulque-drinking cult of Tepoztecatl (**Fig. 6.6**).

Seler proposed, without fully vindicating, the following three ideas with respect to the inscriptions:

  a) on the grounds of layout and iconography, the 18 panels of Text I somehow correspond to the 18 Feasts of the year;
  b) at the same time, certain of these 18 panels appear to invoke not so much the 18 Feasts as the Ome Tochtli pulque cult;
  c) even at first sight, similarities can be seen between the glyphs in Text I and those in Text II.

In identifying the 18 panels of Text I with the Feasts of the year, Seler wisely bore in mind structure as much as iconography. He first established that the text falls into two halves, north and south, each of nine glyph panels. Then, observing the direction in which figures in the glyphs are facing, he suggested that the overall reading direction is from west to east, that is, from left to right along the north and east walls, and from right to left along the south and east walls. He then identified the open-mouth, closed-eye flayed face in the hinge position between north and east as that of the 'flayed one' Xipe,

the standard emblem of the equinoctial Feast of Tlacaxipehualiztli (F2.9). On the basis of this identification alone, he said, the northern and southern halves of Text I would culminate respectively in the summer and winter solstice Feasts, Etzalcualiztli (F1.4) and Panquetzaliztli (F2.4), an eminently Mesoamerican arrangement.

This hypothesis of Seler's was duly noted by Kubler and Gibson (1951:62–63), as not proven, though not impossible. The curious thing is that it is supported by details in the inscriptions that Seler himself failed to bring into play. The north half begins with a 'falling water' glyph which perfectly matches, as it should, the Feast Atemoztli (F2.5). On the south side, the other equinoctial Feast, Ochpaniztli (F1.9), is indicated as Tlazoteotl's, if not by her usual broom, then by her fibre threads and plaits (likewise shown at Ochpaniztli in Magliabechiano and other sources) (**Fig. 6.2**). The panel immediately before this one shows a skull, a normal emblem for greater Miccailhuitl B (F1.8), the Feast of the Dead which precedes Ochpaniztli (**Fig. 3.8**), and at the start of this southern subsequence a large feline characterizes lordly Tecuilhuitl (F1.5), just as it does in *Cuevas* (**Pl. 4**). Above all, these iconographic coincidences with other Feast texts are corroborated by structure; for to either hand, the panel sequences fall into halves, south being read right to left and north left to right, and hence determine midsummer (F1.5) as the beginning likewise found in *Cuevas*, 'Encounter with Europe', and Borgia.

As for structure, besides the division into northern and southern halves, there is a further one into quarters, the pattern we saw in tribute literature, determined here by 90° turns from north and south into the eastern end wall, at the equinoctial Feasts. Moreover, the panels that run in along the end wall to meet either side of Tepoztecatl's statue, from equinox to solstice in both cases, are further distinguished by displaying glyphs that are set diagonally rather than vertically, creating a 'V' effect either side of the statue. *In situ*, the sheer arrangement of the panels also ingeniously reflects the surrounding geography. The northern half of the text, which runs parallel to the high peaks of the Tepozteco range, culminates in the 'upper' summer solstice; the southern half, which runs parallel to the valley below, culminates in the 'lower' winter solstice.

Taken together, these details of structure and iconography can leave little doubt that Seler was indeed right in the first of his three hypotheses, and that there is indeed a correspondence between the 18 glyph-panels of Text I and the 18 Feasts of the year. On this basis, we may proceed to look for evidence of the pulque sequence within the annual Feast cycle.

In Text I, indications of the pulque cult include the liquid itself and its effervesence, axes, quadruple ties, round and square shields, the *yacameztli*, monkeys, and possible place signs. They can all be perceived more or less directly, allowing for what Seler recognized as deliberate visual play in the text, whereby a human head acquires the profile of an axe, and liquid can be water or alcohol (or even blood). This visual play, typical of *tlacuilolli*, has its verbal corollary in the riddles or metaphors recorded in the Florentine Codex (Book 6, chapters 42–43), especially in the anatomical register. In this source, we read how the pulque-producing maguey plant, points up to the sky with his thorns or 'fingers', and how the axe enters the forest with its blade or 'tongue' hanging out.

As for the distribution of this imagery within the yearly cycle

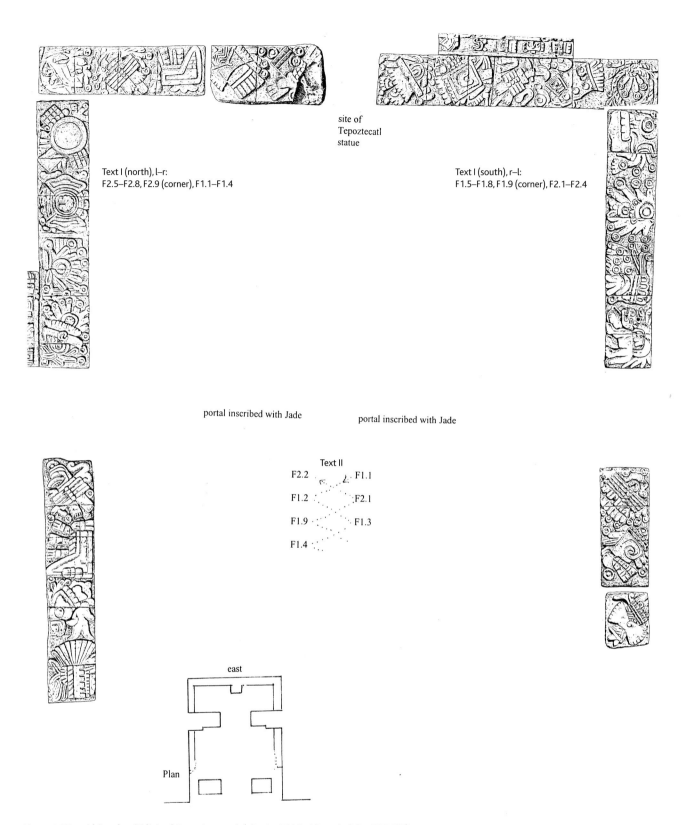

site of
Tepoztecatl
statue

Text I (north), l–r:
F2.5–F2.8, F2.9 (corner), F1.1–F1.4

Text I (south), r–l:
F1.5–F1.8, F1.9 (corner), F2.1–F2.4

portal inscribed with Jade

portal inscribed with Jade

Text II

F2.2   F1.1

F1.2   F2.1

F1.9   F1.3

F1.4

east

Plan

Figure 6.6 Texts I (above) and II (below). Tepoztlan temple (after Ing. F.M. Rodríguez, in Seler 1908:495)

in Text I, it is firmly concentrated in the II Feasts which we have identified above with pulque practices, that is, those that run from Pachtli A to Tozoztli B (F2.1–F1.2). The sequence begins with a pair of 'axe-head' glyphs inset in the double Feast of Pachtli, the start of the diagonal subset that leads up to Panquetzaliztli (F2.1–F2.4). These four opening glyphs sum up and arrange on the body, from head to toe, the pulque-drinker emblems shown in Magliabechiano. After the winter solstice and Atemoztli, liquid itself becomes the theme, notably in the effervescent Two Rabbit jar in which pulque was prepared

(identified by Seler as the *ometochtlamiztli*). After Tlacaxipehualiztli and the equinox (F2.9), the sequence ends with the splendid pair of Tozoztli panels, which ingeniously combine the motifs of the axe and the crown with the signs for temple and mountain/pyramid (*tepetl*), suggesting the toponymy of the place itself. This final pair of complex glyphs also includes flag infixes (*pantli*), which numerically indicate the 20 days of each of the Tozoztli Feasts.

This sequence of II pulque Feasts even comments numerically on itself, and visually highlights its start and end.

Figure 6.7 Tlacatecpan: HTCh f.41

For, the axe tongue of Tepoztecatl seen at the start in Pachtli A (F2.1) has the number 11 inscribed on it, the two bars and a dot of the emblem Tlacatecpan, in Tepoztlan the highest and principal of its *tlaxilacalli* or barrios (today San Juan Tlacotenco), in which the temple stands (**Fig.6.7**. In HTCh, the Tlacatecpan officer is overthrown in 3 Reed 1339, 88 years before the last year glyph, 13/3 Reed 1427). At the same time, the diagonal four-part axe tie seen at the start, in the double Feast of Pachtli (F2.2), reappears symmetrically at the end, in the double Feast of Tozoztli (F1.1), and occurs nowhere else. Thus defined by iconography, position and number, the pulque sequence of 11 Feasts inset here into the yearly 18 Feasts, from Pachtli A to Tozoztli B, corroborates the second of Seler's hypotheses about Text I in Tepoztecatl's temple.

Seler's third hypothesis proposes that Text I is reworked in Text II, of which the north and south parts are quite separate, running in parallel along opposite walls. Although now badly damaged, each of these parts or sides of Text II appears to have consisted of five or six panels. Seler's copy shows that the panels at the eastern ends, nearest to Text I and the best preserved, include the same iconographic feature, the quadruple tie, the very one which defined the pulque sequence within Text I. Only now they are switched between north and south. For the axe in Tozoztli A (F1.1) in Text I (north), whose head intimates a house roof, reappears as the first glyph to the south in Text II as a clearly toponymic glyph. The axe in Pachtli B (F2.2) in Text I (south), also head-like and likewise adorned with the quadruple tie, reappears to the north in Text II with a clearly profiled face, accompanying volutes being common to both glyphs.

The relative positions of other glyphs in Text II which can be seen to echo or derive from Text I indicate that the crossing-over between north and south that initiates Text II runs right through it, from east to west and back again, in plaited fashion, eventually having the effect of reconnecting it with Text I.(For example, the glyphs deriving from the sequence F1.9, F2.1, F2.2 in Text I weave a plait between north, south and north in Text II.) This sort of reading pattern is found in the screenfolds (Borgia p.56, for instance), and here, choreographically on the temple floor, it might intimate the 'swaying' progress for which the Two Rabbit drinkers were famous. Hence, what was the end of the sequence in Text I becomes the beginning in Text II, and vice versa, meaning that in the overall Feast cycle Text I and Text II mirror each other structurally, by starting after the autumn and spring equinoxes respectively (i.e. F2.1–F1.2 becomes F.1.1–F2.2). Highly eloquent is that fact that in this reading, and only in this reading, the glyph in Text I which reflexively defines the 11-fold nature of the pulque sequence as a whole (Tlacatecpan's tongue marked with two bars and a dot) recurs at what would be the 11th position in Text II, as if expressly to confirm both its plaited structure and its overall night-sky total.

In thematic terms, as we pass from Text I to Text II we go back in time. The axe of Pachtli B ages, its flint blade withdrawing into the haft, to the point of intimating the eye and the face of a Monkey. The crown-temple of Tozoztli likewise ages, recovering less artificial forms, exactly as in certain Olmec and other early place glyphs. Next, we see a more radical version of the handiwork of Toxcatl, which features the plait of the *petate* and the hand (with opposing thumb) that works it. As for the number 11 in Pachtli A, it explains more clearly the anthropomorphic tongue blade of the riddle (Florentine Codex Book VI):

Çacan tleino quauhtla calaqui nenepilotiuh? – tepuztli

What goes into the woods with its tongue hanging out? – the axe

In other words, the displacement of the 11 pulque Feasts within the year, which occurs between Text I and Text II, implies a regression in time, from later to earlier forms and concepts, from symposia in Mexica times to the very rock the temple pyramid rests upon. The stones that frame the doorway between Texts I and II are positioned as strata in colour and age, sedimentary and volcanic, and highlight massive square greenstones or jades to either hand.

As the patron of Tepoztlan, Tepoztecatl exists in a specific landscape, and at more than one level of time, the deepest or oldest concerning his role as pulque drinker.The axe-bearing pioneer is first encountered sitting by the foaming mouth of the volcano Chichinautzin, the cratered peak to the north of the town which serves still today as the first of its municipal landmarks: there, he enjoys the company of four neighbours, the first two familar from the Magliabechiano list: Tliloa, Papaztac, Cuauhtlapanqui and Tzocaca (Flo X, 29). In this cosmic landscape, the foaming lava of Chichinautzin (a name which itself indicates the notion of drinking or suckling) anticipates the foaming alcoholic drink, pulque. The sheer immanence of the mountains which guard Tepoztlan, high to the north, lower to the south, is invoked by Tepoztecatl when in a later life he survives the vicissitudes of the European invasion, in the play performed in Nahuatl every 8th September which groups them as 11. Recalling this, helps us to recognize yet a further dimension of the inscriptions in his temple.

Ranged six to the north and five to the south, the panels of Text II anticipate the account of Tepoztlan's guardian mountains given in the *Relación geográfica* of the town (1580). This source lists the Nahuatl names of the mountains, and makes the critical distinction between those of the north, which were named by the 'devil' Tepoztecatl himself, and those of the south, which were not.

Starting in the east, the northern set begins with Ozomaquila, the garden of the monkey whose profile some see in the cliff face. Next come Ehecatepetl, the 'wind' mountain, and the beacon Tlahuiltepetl, both part of the Tepozteco massif, and then Chicomocelotl, '7 Jaguar', followed by Cuauhtepetl, 'eagle mountain'. On the south side, starting again in the east, stand Yohualichan, the house of night; Ecauhtlan or Yauhtepetl, both places of magic herbs; the hand Ce Maitl; Cacalotepetl; and the jade mountain Chalchiuhtepetl, an abundant water-source. What remains of the glyphs in the north and south part of Text II fits well into this scheme, suggesting that at one level they may indeed be read as a microcosm of the surrounding orography. Clear parallels can be seen in the cases of the monkey and the wind peaks on the north side, and the dark house and magic herbs (hallucinating eyes) on the south side.

As the side named by the 'devil' Tepoztecatl, the northern names merit especial attention, since unlike those of the south side they explicitly invoke the Tonalpoualli, the calendar cycle complementary to the year's Feasts that was damned as devilish by all the early missionaries. Chicomocelotl, '7 Jaguar', is an indisputable case and serves as a marker for what turns out to be a whole sequence of embedded Tonalpoualli names, which rise incrementally from east to west, in the Series of year-bearer Signs (Rabbit derives from Two Rabbit Ome Tochtli):

Monkey	Sign XI	Series I
Wind	Sign II	Series II
Rabbit	Sign VIII	Series III
Jaguar	Sign XIV	Series IV
Eagle	Sign XV	Series V

This correlation of Sign and mountain suggests that Tepoztecatl's inscriptions represent a choreography of the Feasts whose calendrical movements are felt deep in time, a dance of equinoctial precession measurable in the very stone of the temple structure, notably the large squared Jades in the doorway between Text I and Text II (see p.73,91 below).

Otontecutli: tree haft

Tepepulco, the home of the compendium repeatedly drawn on here, has a population that stems largely from the Otomi, the ancient people who still today live in the pine forests and deserts that arch around the northern Distrito Federal, focused on towns named after them, like Otumba (Otonpan) or named in the Tepepulco Ms, like Xaltocan. Lying in Quetzalcoatl's wind corridor that links the Highland basin with the Gulf Coast to the northeast, Tepepulco is close enough to Teotihuacan for that great metropolis to have left lasting impressions. Just as Tepepulco was chosen by Sahagún as the source of his 'primeros memoriales', so four centuries later, in revolutionary Mexico, Otumba helped Angel María Garibay translate the Twenty Hymns into Spanish for the first time, Sahagún having left them in their 'demonic' Nahuatl. (In the 1880s, Daniel Garrison Brinton had published his grandly entitled English version, *Rig Veda Americanus,* in his Library of Aboriginal American Literature.)

In the Tepepulco manuscript as in Borbonicus, the main ritual representation of the 18 Feasts is choreographical (i, ii) though like Borgia it runs in vertical rather than horizontal sequence (**Pl. 7**). After it come detailed deconstructions of offerings (chapter iii), masks and arrays of male and female actors who number 18+18 in all (chapter v), and the setting of the performance which takes Tenochtitlan's Great Temple as the model (chapter vii), a plan of buildings and locations which in order to be read intelligently needs to be turned more than once through 90°.

The text is constrained by the fact of being written on European paper; it is formated with vertical groups of Feasts running down the righthand side of each page leaving room for the alphabetic commentary in Nahuatl to the left. Even so, it remains loyal to screenfold antecedents in appealing to the same numerical patterning of the Feasts seen in Borgia and Borbonicus. Exactly the year model of 11 + 7 Feasts is again established here, even if on a limited scale, by means of format, which Baird has closely compared with Borbonicus on these grounds. That 11 + 7 is indeed an annual pattern and a paradigm is confirmed by the fact that it recurs in both Borbonicus and Tepepulco Part I, starting respectively in Izcalli (F2.7) and Atlcahualo (F2.8). That is, the switch from 11 to 7 occurs at the same relative position with respect to the new-year Feast, corroborating the span in principle, and precisely not a fixed position for it within the year. Running vertically down the pages of Tepepulco, the initial 'thin' sequence of 11 Feasts is counted here as 3+3+3+2 (F2.8–F1.9) over ff.250–251v, i.e. 11 Feasts on four pages, while the proportionately 'fat' sequence is counted as 3+2+2 (F2.1–F2.7) over ff.252–253, i.e. 7 Feasts on three pages.

Overall, Tepepulco is less concerned with the positioning of major personae or interplay between them, of the kind we saw repeatedly in the Tenochtitlan screenfold with Ciuacoatl and Teteu innan. Rather the emphasis is on the community that produced the text, its very earth and terrain and the customs of its mainly Otomi inhabitants. This is quite evident in the Feast most known for rites that are communal (as opposed to directed from above), Tepeihuitl (F2.2), when the people use dough to make human models of their mountains and dress them up in paper garments, loving activities which are here further detailed on a special page appended to the Arrays chapter (f.267). In Eztlacualiztli (F1.4), Tlaloc devoid of mask lives modestly in a cave rather than being protected by a temple wall atop his mountain, and in Tozoztli (F1.1–F1.2) the fields invented from flowers and brilliant with blossom and burgeoning crops are explicitly defended as communal by the snake emblem (*coa-*). The communal fields of Tozoztli or Xochimanaloya (a name given to this Feast in Durán 1995, 2:252)are the more significant for the fact that, though 'simply agricultural', they are mapped in the same quatrefoil plan as Tenochtitlan's vast empire in Mendoza. Not only that, in order to be beheld properly, the communal snake and the fields it guards have to be inverted through 180°, that is, turned upside down, putting to the top those (socially) below and inferior (**Pl. 7a**).

In the version of the Feast named alphabetically as Micailhuitl A and B (F1.7–F1.8), visual attention is all on the more explicitly vegetative logic of its pair of local equivalents, Tlaxochimaco and Xocotl huetzi, the time of flowers and ripe fruit celebrated as 'Otomi' in Otonotecutli's Hymn (*Icuic* no.11). The flower and fruit tree dragged in and set up looms tall, huge and vivid green, not least because it belongs to Otontecutli, the god of the local Otomi, who make a dough effigy of him, as of the mountains, adorning it with paper cut-outs of Itzpapalotl, the obsidian butterfly, customs still much alive today. A rough customer, Otontecutli could uproot trees (HMP) and in his array a tree-trunk, held in his giant hand, serves as the haft of a rudimentary digging stick ([*i*]*tziuac mitl*), whose obsidian tip is raised to indicate that it effectively ceases to pierce the earth in this Feast (F1.8), at the end of the planting season (II, ii). Local vegetation repeatedly serves as a determinant of custom and culture, above all the 'divine maguey' (*teumetl*) of the moon (II, i). This hardy succulent provides pulque plentiful enough to rival the 'falling water' of Atemoztli (F2.5) and to enliven the 'house' of Izcalli (F2.7), as well as fibres strong enough to weave into workday clothing. Though serviceable, the maguey textiles seen throughout the text are coarse and as such are categorically contrasted with clothes of cotton imported from the Huaxtec hotlands to the north. In Ochpaniztli (F1.9) the equinox of night and day is expressed precisely in the opposition between appropriately clothed dark males and white females. Clad in maguey textiles like Ilamatecutli's rough pioneers, the men are forcing their way up a nine-rung wooden ladder from below to the upper register dominated by women dressed elegantly in cotton, Teteu innan chief among them (**Pl. 7b**).

Tepepulco values of this order are sharply defined when it is a question of Feasts adopted from other cultures and time-spaces. The roof architecture seen in Toxcatl (F1.3) suggests a nostalgic link with the metropolis Teotihuacan, nearby but ancient, and methods of astronomical observation common both to the *tlachialoni* held by Tezcatlipoca in this Feast and on the subsequent Atamalcualiztli page and to the 'pecked circles' characteristic of that city and found as far apart as the Tropic of Cancer (El Chapín) and the Maya lowlands. As for the Olmec, while in Tecuilhuitl (F1.5–F1.6) Borbonicus attributes to them the lords' ball-court and litter as tokens of early urban privilege, here the focus is on the sea not streets and on women not men, in the form of the coastal salt-water goddess Uixtociuatl also celebrated in this Feast in Telleriano, whose skirt has the blue-wave design (*atlacuilolli*).

The question of gender becomes acute in the Feasts proper to the immigrants from the north, the more recent Chichimec and Mexica, since their representatives in Quecholli and Panquetzaliztli (F2.3, F2.4) are unrelievedly male. Moreover, the Mexica are seen again at their equinoctial Feast Tlacaxipehualiztli (F2.9), where their practices are identified with the devil ('diablo'), a sop to Sahagún and the Christians no doubt (and directed at other gods), yet emphasized in the *tlacuilolli* text perhaps, by the apparent arrogance of Tenochtitlan's abnormally tall eagle and jaguar knights and by scenes of full-blooded sacrifice. Here in Tlacaxipehualiztli blood pours down steps from the bodies of victims, and from the designated loser in the gladiatorial combat (**Pl. 7a**) also depicted later in the plan of Tenochtitlan's Great Temple. Suggestive enough itself, this Tepepulco or Otomi view of bloodthirsty Mexica empire is traced back in these Feasts (and in Etzalcualiztli F1.4) to antecedents contemporary with Teotihuacan and with the Olmec, through emphasis on the sheer intrusive weight of urban architecture, its styles and crowning rooftop motifs.

Compared with Borbonicus, Tepepulco shows less interest in, even aversion to, social hierarchy and the cult of personae. Men and women of the community stand at similar heights, tend to cluster in groups, go barefoot, may paint their faces yet do not hide them behind masks. In these respects the subsequent chapters in Part I, which detail for the Feasts individual arrays, the Great Temple setting and the Twenty Hymns, should perhaps be seen not so much as supplementary as pertinent, like Part II, to wider imperial as opposed to local norms and customs.

Be that as it may, while Teteu innan retains something of her power, impinging (as in Borbonicus and again as Baird noticed) not just on her own but the following Feast, her female counterpart Ciuacoatl is largely relieved of the heavily political role she had among the *chinampas*. Rather than be allotted her own season of 12 Feasts, in which she appears several times, and rather than have multiple roles in her own Feast Tititl, in that Feast she is honoured in Tepepulco chiefly as midwife, holding her weaving batten, while her face-paint indicates the domestic grinding of maize she performed as Quilaztli in the creation story. As in Borgia, she is seen surrounded by six males at the hub of her dance, the Ilamatecuh chololoya, which celebrates human birth as the 'second descent' (Yancuitemoa), that is, after Teteu innan's in Ochpaniztli. Her key role in inaugurating the planting season is no more than hinted at in the arrays of the males, chiefly the yellow-faced Ixcozauhqui with his Xiuhcoanaual and the *tlachialoni* he passes to a companion. This

Figure 6.8 Otontecutli. Tepepulco f.262v

has the proportional effect of augmenting the Otomi Otontecutli as the one best qualified to measure the planting season, which he does, as we saw, when it ends in Xocotl huetzi (F1.8), by lifting his hoe from the earth before Itztlacoliuhqui appears in the following Feast with his threat of cold. This reading is confirmed by his Array (**Fig. 6.8**), and by his Hymn (no.11), which further links him esoterically with the Tonalpoualli Sign 1 Water, seen in this Feast (F1.8) in Fejérváry (p.14), Laud (p.21) and Mexicanus (p.13).

Much of this is summed up in the Atamalcualiztli ceremony that occupies a full page at the end of the Feasts cycle and was held every eight years, over eight days (f.254), a full and vivid surviving record of this occasion. Everyone is invited, as ever barefoot: Mazatec snake-swallowers like those seen among the Hopi today, an axe-bearing pulque drinker with his *yacameztli* nose adornment, astronomers of night and day with black and gold *tlachialoni*, the poor couple in ragged clothes who live under a leaky roof and beg alms from a passing aristocrat attired in a rich cloak, bird-men dancers three of the night and three of the day, and the smiling weaver-woman who dreams patterns on to her loom from the exquisite blooms and birds in the tree it is hitched to. Such designs continue to characterize artefacts from that area, saliently the embroidered cotton sheets sold to tourists, which to the sympathetic eye disclose the philosophies of life and calendar expounded in this text. The feathered bird dancers, face emerging from beak, strongly recall those depicted in the Annals of Tlatelolco, the last hearth and fort to resist Cortés in 1521 and venue of the Atamalcualiztli that accompanied the New Fire ceremony held in 2 Reed 1559, for which the memorial service for Charles V was used as a pretext and cover.

As its name shows, Atamalcualiztli means eating unsalted tamales out of respect for the maize of which our flesh was formed at the start of this world age. Much uncertainty has surrounded the question of when in the year it was held and how it was otherwise integrated into the calendar. Since 52 is not divisible by 8, it can have coincided with the New Fire ceremony only every 104 years, the 'ueuetiliztli' noted here (f.286) specifically with respect to the same 1559 occasion. The Nahuatl commentary (f.253v) notes that it attached preferentially to a moment between or in (*quemanian*) Quecholli (F2.3) and the communal mountain Feast Tepeilhuitl

(F2.2), 20 days earlier. (Particular links with Ixcozauhqui and hence Izcalli are otherwise suggested by Sahagún, as Nicholson and others have noted.)

Formally speaking, the footprints that define an anticlockwise frame for the Atamalcualiztli page indicate numerical and logical complexity of this order, since as hops and steps marking variable sets of toes they establish totals that intimate the Feasts, subtly modifying their norm of 20. As 11 and 9, the footprints in the vertical borders to left and right confirm that norm, while those left to right along the bottom and right to left long the top reduce it to 8+8, and require hops. The sets of toes to the sides conform regularly to four, while those below and above vary from three to five, so that the total of toe-print units equals the days of seven Feasts (140) plus five or possibly six extra days. This equals the 'fat' sequence plus intercalated days, acknowledged in the very format of this text and Borbonicus, as well as in the arithmetic in the corresponding chapter in Fejérváry and Cospi which refine the Atamalcualiztli formulae with respect to sun, moon and the two inner planets (**Fig. 3.2c**).

Of the Twenty Hymns, the one corresponding to Atamalcualiztli (*Icuic* no.14) is perhaps the most complex, since besides calling on a large cast of characters some of whom are seen here, it invokes Cholula before the Chichimec and Mexica rose to power. Along with the closely related Hymns 9 and 18, Atamalcualiztli comes then to broach the dichotomies between birds of night and birds of day, gold and turquoise, the great coming down at Tamoanchan, and the pushing of *pochteca*

endeavour to its western limit in Oztoma, the ancient frontier fortress later commandeered by Tenochtitlan as the first among its lower 11 bastions. In this deeper immersion in the story of the year and the Feasts, Otontecutli himself even recovers his reputation as a primordial god of fire, especially for the third member of the Triple Alliance Tlacopan/Azcapotzalco (which was most often dominated by the other two, Tenochtitlan and Texcoco). He becomes the lightning axe that clears the field for planting, as in the poem attibuted to Nezahualcoyotl and published – in Otomi – in the 18th century; and he goes east to consult superior Popoloca intelligence about fire-drilling, and how they 'cut the hair of the sunwind' (HMP chapter 3).

Focusing first on Borbonicus, this pair of chapters (5 and 6) has explored what can be gleaned from those texts which concern themselves with the Feasts in performance, their staging, choreography and enactment. In this context and setting, the year that governed the tribute and agricultural systems of the Mexica is made to resonate explicitly as the measures of the dance that supremely infuses the moment with time, syncopating rhythms of sun, stars, and social seasons. Drawing on *tlacuilolli* resources unavailable to the alphabet, these animated pages allow us to glimpse the surge of life which historically has quickened the very idea of the Feast and the year among the Mexica. Myriad in colour, sound and pace, this movement nonetheless responds to calculations of time that can be assessed and correlated in fine arithmetical detail, as the final pair of chapters (7, 8) goes on to propose.

7
Anniversary Wheels

Representing the Feast cycle literally as a circle or ring, definitive in the case of the calendar wheels associated particularly with Texcoco and Tlaxcala, is a convention that endures today (**Fig.7.1**) and has in practice had consequences both formal and thematic. Figuring as cogs or between spokes in the wheel, the Feasts acquire a certain uniformity in being reduced to emblems basic enough to fit in the space available. At the same time, this very uniformity better allows for arithmetical correlation with other calendar cycles and hence augments the types and scales of time that they may articulate, as it were mechanically. Contrary to a tenacious prejudice, the wheel itself was not a European import but had long served as a fundamental reference for Mesoamerica before Columbus, both in the practical sense indicated by the wheeled toys that Diego Rivera enjoyed including in his paintings, and conceptually, the Mexica Sunstone being a justifiedly renowned example (**Fig. 7.2**).

Wheels known to include the Feasts cycle all have the same format. A disk or face-dial in the middle indicates the scope and theme of the text, and dates it to a given Series III year. Around it are seen further rings or halos that widen like ripples, which may appear to enclose the face, or the centre may radiate through them in rays or lines or step into them along a trail of footprints. The face may also record the changes wrought on it by time, its temporal fortune, in diachronic modes ingeniously reconciled with the cyclic frames around it. While, as this description may imply, these texts are normally read outwards from the inner face, they are no less comprehensible when read inwards from outermost rim. Indeed, the more complex examples are read outwards from within and inwards from without, in accounts that meet or pass each other in the middle.

Apart from the Feasts, the cycles that enclose the central disk are either astronomical and register the movements of the moon and other bodies, or they are calendrical and count out the Twenty Signs of the Tonalpoualli, the 52-years of the Xiuhpoualli, and other year multiples. All of the Wheels appeal specifically to the idea of the year embodied in the biped walker, whose footprints always 'count', numerically and semantically,

and/or the metamorphic reptile Xiuhcoanaual, whose main body is a snake of numerate and numerable coils and scales but whose tail retains insect or crustacean features and whose head evolves into that of the caiman.

Concentrated around their cameo dials, the Wheels delve succinctly into the teaming imagination that produced the Mesoamerican calendar, every one of whose cycles has quite specific origins, functions and rationales, and in this format they amount to a superbly sensitive philosophy of the forms and phases of time. Why otherwise elaborate so many cycles in the first place? The Wheels are all also forcefully ideological and political: they state a strong particular case while reflecting on a general situation or condition, dating it as an epoch, an anniversary worth remembering. Hence they are Anniversary Wheels that register specific year dates that are historical within the cyclic wheel: appealing to the three origins and services of the year and the philosophy inherent in Xiuhcoanaual, they place these dates in time by invoking year multiples characteristic of the kind of time in question. As at Pahuatlan, the solar year of growth tends to fall into the heptad seven and the lifetime 70 proper to midwifery and genealogy (Borbonicus, pp.21–22, Mendoza f.71, Tlapa Annals I), the sidereal year into star-eye multiples of 13, and the civil year into vigesimal multiples or Xiuhmolpilli volutes of voice or flame-smoke (*mimixcoa*). Moreover, these year counts start from Series III base dates privileged by the Mexica, those of Acamapichtli's official installation in 1 Flint 1376, the departure from Aztlan in 1 Flint 1168, the Chichimec antecedent in 1 Flint 648 (C11, 632 C1), and the beginning of the Era itself in 13 Reed and 1 Flint, 3113 and 3112 BCE. This much is to be presumed in the reading of the Anniversary Wheels and their concept of chronology.

Here, main examples of Anniversary Wheels are read in chronological order of production, of the year dates they themselves specify and identify with, which range over half a millennium from 13 Reed 1479 to 10 Rabbit 1978. In every way the classic model, the Sunstone prominently displays the year 13 Reed between the tails of the Xiuhcoanaual on its upper rim and is customarily thought to be self-dating to 1479 (13 Reed C11), Tenochtitlan's hey day. Through that year name it no less casts back to the homonymous year (C1) at the start of the current Era, 3113 BCE, and to aeons before that. The concentric disks at the centre spell out the year 1 Flint (successor to 13 Reed in the Xiuhmolpilli) in three images which correspond to the three lengths of year, solar, sidereal and civil, each being placed by appropriate year-multiples as the year when Acamapichtli founded the empire in 1376. Written on native paper rather than inscribed on stone, the Boban Wheel of Texcoco (**Pl. 8**), like the Mendoza Codex of Tenochtitlan, seeks to defend upper-class rights threatened by the first Viceroy (installed in 1535) in the year 7 Rabbit 1538, the seventh of the heptad begun in historical fact in a year 1 Flint centuries earlier; starting from the same

Figure 7.1 Equinoctial half circles. Pahuatlan screenfold 1978, title page

Figure 7.2 Sunstone; diagram and detail of Xiuhcoanaual tail

base dates as the Sunstone, the whole is enclosed in the ring of the Feasts.

The triennium that spans Cortés's arrival and the fall of Tenochtitlan, 1 Reed to 3 House 1519–21 was commemorated as such in several texts (notably in 'Encounter with Europe') and was meaningfully recalled one Xiuhmolpilli later (1571–73) in Veytia Anniversary Wheels nos.4 and 5. The former offers a wry assessment of this later triennium, the 'spiritual conquest' (as it has been termed) made murderously more efficient at that time by the 'second coming' of Europe, in the form of a reinforced Spanish Inquisition. Surveying the same 1 Reed to 3 House anniversary from a Tlaxcalan viewpoint, Veytia no.5 makes a perhaps less agonized assessment of these years; at the same time, it anticipates the great solar eclipse and aftermath of 1691–92, at that point still 120 years into the future (Key 53). The 5 Flint 1692 date is predicted in the annals of Tlaxcala and the Cholula plain (Dehesa), and as 8 Flint C1 in those of Tepexic and Coixtlahuaca (Selden Roll). Historically, this eclipse in fact precipitated the uprising known as the 'Corn Riot' that all but put an end to Spanish rule in Mexico.

Published in Italy in 1579 in the same decade that Veytia

Wheels nos.4 and 5 were conceived, Wheel no.2, which in fact consists of two wheels one above the other (they are inverted in HMAI fig. 73), serves as a decisive term of negative definition. Printed in a European book (as Mendoza would be 40 years later), the Valadés copy of the text known as Veytia no.2 seeks no doubt to respect the original (now lost). The Wheel of the Feasts is appropriately placed at the top of the page above a spiral arrangement of the Tonalpoualli and the Xiuhpoualli, and their clockwise and anticlockwise sequences and their division into 9+9 surely result from that original (**Fig. 7.3**). However, printing and the European world-view between them reduce subtlety and intelligence it surely had, ordering these cycles with a rigidity more appropriate to the mechanism of a clock. By contrast, as a direct and often agonized response to the style of violence introduced by Cortés and reinforced by the Inquisition, the Wheels unemended by Europe follow the Sunstone in preaching not immutability but a succinct and immensely sophisticated articulation of time that repeats yet is never quite the same.

In Mexico today, the philosophy inherent in the manuscript Anniversary Wheels remains resilient and continues to inform

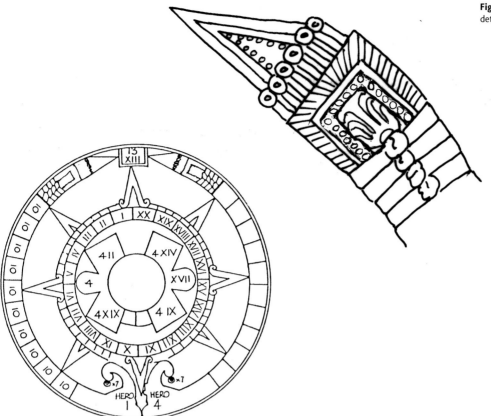

Figure 7.2 Sunstone; diagram and detail of Xiuhcoanaual tail

texts fashioned in the native tradition. As the Nahuatlato Mexican scholar Luis Reyes notes (1992:20), the three self-dating native-paper screenfolds issued in Pahuatlan in 1975, 1978 and 1981 acknowledge in *Coloquios* terms the time elapsed since the end of Moctezuma's last Xiuhmolpilli (also the start of the Mexica New Era, 1 Rabbit 1558/ 2 Reed 1559). That is: eight 52-year Xiuhmolpilli of political life (416 years), six 70-year lifetimes of planter and peasant (420 years), and, astoundingly, nothing more or less than the 423 years (likewise specified in *Mexicanus*) which produce 6 days of stellar-solar slippage (i.e. 6 x 70.5 years; see p.90–1 below). Each screenfold commemorates the time elapsed not just in appropriate multiples but appropriate *tlacuilolli* forms: in the 1978 screenfold the solar or lifetime seventies are imaged as sevenfold leaves of growth sprouting from branches, exactly like the count of the 210 Mexica years that runs from Aztlan to Acamapichtli (Boturini screenfold; **Fig. 2.2**). The title page of this 1978 Pahuatlan text returns us to the source of this intelligence: the Wheel of 9+9 Feasts. Aligned with the equinoxes and centred on a Janus face, this recent Anniversary Wheel numbers the Feasts as cogs and darkens those of the double Feast, Micailhuitl (F1.7–F1.8), whose interstice (dated to 'agosto' 10th or 12th) was invoked by Cuauhtemoc's surrender in 3 House 1521 (**Fig. 7.1**). In 13 Reed 3113 BCE, this interstitial Feast date had initiated the Era itself.

Imperial Sunstone

Waggishly dubbed 'Moctezuma's Watch' at the Mexican Exhibition in London in 1823, the Sunstone had shaken to its foundations the Spanish viceroyalty overthrown by the creoles in 1810. For in 1790 it had been excavated at the corner of the cathedral and what is now being recovered as the site of the Great Temple, where it had served as the Cuauhxicalli depicted

in Tepepulco (I,xiv). Like the poetry that Ovid and Virgil wrote for the Roman emperors, it casts cosmogony, the story of creation, as prefatory to imperial power. Unlike the Roman poets, however, the authors of the Sunstone were less constrained by the vanity of a human individual and were certainly better at astronomy (the *calmecac* or academy in the Tepepulco plan is connected by a direct path to the Cuauhxicalli). Since excavation, its immense story of how evolution culminated in Mexica power has been steadily recovered thanks to comparison with other *tlacuilolli* carvings and manuscripts, and to the alphabetic transcriptions in Nahuatl annals like those of Cuauhtitlan (Appendix A). Its quincunx of world ages copies that of the Coixtlahuaca Map; its seven levels of relief carving follow those on the pyramid at Xochicalco. It is probably the most resonant icon of the America that Europe invaded (**Fig. 7.2**). The reading that follows pretends to little more than meditating further on the often neglected function of the Feasts and the Xiuhcoanaual in the overall design, and in the intermeshing of solar, sidereal and civil years. It supplements what has been said so far about the multiple readings of the Feasts proposed on this stone disk, notably the pair of Xiuhcoanaual on the rim and their distribution on the dragon body itself and the ingenious disposition of them around the maize plant on the tail. There they are arranged in proportions that are legible as those of the tribute year (9+9), or those of the planting seasons (12+6), or yet again in the Quecholli sequence stated in *Cuevas* (5+6+7; **Table 3c**).

As we saw in the first Chapter (p.17 above), the Feasts are represented on the Sunstone in the Xiuhcoanaual bodies that constitute the rim of the text to right and left, while the innermost face is framed by the quincunx of the world ages or Suns, a circle inset into the Sign of this Era, Four Ollin (4 XVII) (**Fig. 7.2**). With their respective appeal to the three kinds of year

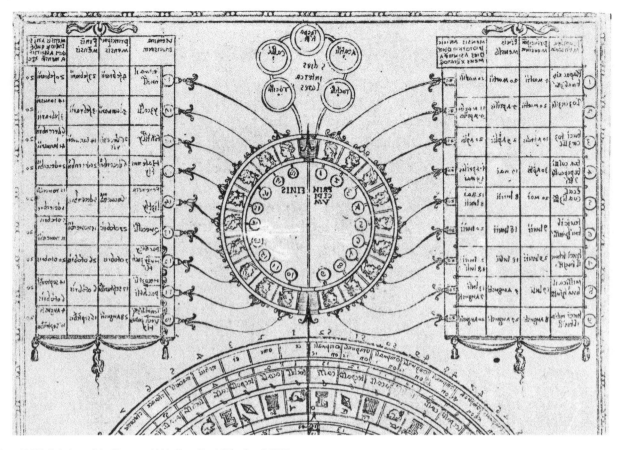

Figure 7.3 Half circles and the Nemotemi. Valadés or Veytia Wheel no.2, 1579

defined by the Feasts and the three correlations of the years 13 Reed/1 Flint, rim and core share a certain numerical logic. For their part and in addition to confirming the distinctions between kinds of year already noted, the three segments of the Xiuhcoanaual body at the rim also appeal to the model of the sky seen in Borgia Feasts chapter and explained in Tepepulco (II, i; see p.41 above). That is, the 11 plus 7 units attaching respectively to the Xiuhcoanaual tail and head correspond numerically to the stars in the ecliptic and circumpolar constellations specified in those sources.

Midway between rim and core, halfway in or halfway out, there appears the ring of the Twenty Signs, regularly segmented, and read anticlockwise from the top. In this position on this of all disks and Anniversary Wheels, these Twenty Signs epitomize concepts in the story of creation narrated at length in the *Legend of the Suns* and the *Popol vuh*. From the cosmic forces of Wind (II), and precipitation (Rain XIX), lateral and horizontal, the earth wet with Water (IX), hard as Flint (XVIII) or elastic as Earthquake (XVII), comes through the Signs to implant its flora of Reed (XIII) and Flower (XX), and to raise its vertebrate fauna of scaley Caiman (I, initially the earth itself), Lizard (IV), Snake (V), the furry /hairy mammals Deer (VII), Rabbit (VIII), Dog (X), Monkey (XI), Jaguar (XIV), and the feathered Eagle (XV) and Vulture (XVI), each with its skin covering, locomotion, diet, blood temperature, breeding habits and sexual tastes, all prefiguring in their way the distinctively human Skull (VI) and Toothed and muscled jaw (XII) and the handling of primary tools like the Flint knife (again XVIII) and the shafted Reed arrow (again XIII), within terms that are both primeval darkness and well-built dwelling House (III).

On the disk, between the ring of Twenty Signs and outer Xiuhcoanaual rim there lie four concentric circles, which further appeal to the substance and arithmetic of this creation. Indeed thanks to close parallels with the sun disk depicted and described along with the constellations in Tepepulco (II, i), these four bands may be read in registers that correspond to rock and mineral strata (sedimentary sandstone or volcanic *tezontli*, metamorphic jade, fossil limestone, gold); vertebrate body (blood, jade lymph and snot, bone, excrement); human tool, product and adornment (awl, ear-spool, needle, pierced-nose coin); and (moving finally from faber to factor) vigesimal and binary arithmetic. As for the concentric circles which lie between the ring of the Twenty Signs and the face at the core, in highlighting the year names 13 Reed and 1 Flint they graft on to the creation story, via the year calendar, anniversaries in the history of the Mexica and Mesoamerica. The structure of the face, its neatly parted hair, teeth, and adornment of jade ear-spools and necklace suggest the multiples of years involved, for which the structure of the four outer bands serves as double entries.

Through imagery too complex to explore fully here, the Sunstone locates in this way the three 1 Flint years inscribed on the central face, as the inaugural year of the empire 1376, two Xiuhmolpilli before the commemoration of the text itself in 1480. This inaugural year is shown to fall 4 Xiuhmolpilli after the start of the migration from the rustic western homeland of the Mexica in 1 Flint 1168, and 14 Xiuhmolpilli after the base date in 1 Flint 648 (632 C1) inherited from the Chichimecs. This earlier 7th-century calendar base is shown to have been common to both east and west: it is the base of the eclipse tables in the Dresden Codex, for example, and falls in the 72nd Round of the Era. Historically it marked the end of the Olmec inscriptions and the 'hiatus' in those of the Maya, during the political upheaval depicted in the Tepexic Annals around 1 Flint C1 (632). In the west, in CII (648), the same year date locates the official emergence of the Chichimec from Chicomoztoc Seven Caves. This calendrical agreement between eastern and western history is commemorated on the Sunstone in the 7-star crowns that adorn each of the two Xiuhcoanaual caiman heads to right and left, while the 7+7 stars actually count out the sidereal Xiuhmolpilli that run from 1 Flint 648 to 1 Flint 1376 (14 x 52 = 728).

Fundamental to calendars both eastern and western, the 1 Flint on the tongue at the very middle of the Sunstone identifies the beginnings of the Mesoamerican Era with the year 13 Reed named on the rim in CI (3113 BCE). For the flint-tongue names the following year 1 Flint, the first of the first Round of the Era in Series III CI (3112 BCE) . More ancient on the central face, this common base date originates the long count to 1376 AD as 5 + 5 hair-strand *tzontli* (each 400 years) plus the six Jade beads of the necklace (each 80 years), one of which is one tenth longer than the other five, i.e. 1 Flint CI (3112 BCE) +4,000+ 480+8 = 1 Flint CII (1376). In the double entry, this count is confirmed within the 5,200-year Era by the 10 x 10 volutes of New Fire numbered on Xiuhcoanaual's scales (100 x 52 = 5,200). The 1:4 ratio in the digits of hand/foot placed beside the face reinforces that of the faces emerging from the Xiuhcoanaual caiman heads to left and right below, which belong respectively to Xiuhtecutli and Tonatiuh, Heroes 1 and 4. Between them, these statements, on the face and rim, confirm in arithmetic and through the five human senses that the Era is the Quinto Sol, a fifth of the precessional Great Year proposed as 25,750 years here and in Mexicanus (see Chapter 8 below, p.91). At the centre, this Great Year is stated as 25,600 years in the classic formula 'twice twice 80²', legible in the two Jade faces of each concentric ear spool, as it is on the two faces of squared Jades in Tepoztecatl's doorway. In turn, the Great Year becomes the year-unit in calculations of cosmic time, for example, the Atamalcualiztli or octaeteris denoted on the Sunstone by its 4+4 solar rays and the hundreds of millions they project into, which are quite explicit in the Maya inscriptions and the Madrid Codex (BFW 303). In calculating these anniversaries, the Sunstone draws out the consequences of the discrepancy between the solar and sidereal year setting the whole within the pair of Xiuhcoanaual figures that define the rim, and whose vertebrate bodies celebrate the year of the Feasts as they emerge from insect or crustacean tails and culminate in caiman heads.

Altepetl Texcoco

In Texcoco, across the lake from Tenochtitlan, the year 1539 saw a shocking application of European justice to Mexican affairs, Christian and secular in the best style of the Inquisition. An heir to the Texcoco royal house, Don Carlos Ometochtzin had been arrested, tried for heresy, and found guilty; and in that year he forfeited all his lands, possessions and rights and was burned alive, along with his library. In the process, fellow heirs Don Antonio Pimentel and Don Hernando de Chavez, sought to confirm the status they had enjoyed since the year 7 Rabbit 1538 as officials under Spanish rule. To that end they produced the Boban Wheel, a circular leaf of native paper beautifully framed by the 18 Feasts, which ingeniously juxtaposes synchronic and diachronic time and proposes anniversaries of multiple significance.

In this Anniversary Wheel, the circumference consists of the ring of 18 Feast emblems (**Pl. 8**). These are displayed like hours on a clockface, between an outer red frame, and an inner turquoise frame divided into 4 x 13 segments; both legible as *xiuh* and therefore synonymous with the year, these colours may indicate the energy of fire and water that issue from Tezcatlipoca's foot in 'Genesis'. Further intermediary circles appear between the Feasts and the turquoise frame; the first consists of the numeral 20 repeated 18 times, the other is a trail of footprints that number, per quarter: 20, 18, 18, 16, an average of 18 (in the 1994 Porrúa 'facsimile' one of the footprints is missing).This is 'the walk through the year' noted by Dibble and described by Durán (1995, 2:245). Within these five concentric circles (Feasts, numerals and footprints between fire and turquoise), we see a particular history, recorded by the Texcoco officials two decades after Cortés arrived, in the face of growing Spanish greed and violence. Intertwined with that of Tenochtitlan after Nezahualcoyotl and the founding of the Alliance early in the 15th century, this history begins long before and includes the Chichimec migrations from Seven Caves. In this arrangement, the enclosing frame of the Feasts becomes the guarantee of a system that has roots deep in time, and which after the invasion continued to work demonstrably better than the flawed Julian calendar imported from Europe. Simultaneously, the 18 Feasts are made to serve as an arithmetical factor in calculating this depth in time, from Chichimec beginnings in the 7th century, and then within this Era and world age.

In the Wheel, the two Texcocan heirs Chavez and Pimentel found their claims on their dynastic predecessor Nezahualcoyotl, the city's famous 'poet-king', and his Mexica ally Itzcoatl, who in turn are preceded by a pair of remoter Chichimec ancestors, female and male. Calendrically, these three pairs of people live and travel (*nemi, nenemi*) upwards through the heptad of years that runs from 1 Flint to 7 Rabbit. The seven Series III year-names of this heptad are established through details that attach to the second member of each pair, reading right to left and moving forward and upward in time: the Chichimec woman seen beside her Seven Caves abode points with two fingers to the year 2 House, Nezahualcoyotl's crossed-arrow insignia indicates 4 Reed, and Chavez's municipal water supply is so regulated as to suggest 6 House. Uppermost, the year 7 Rabbit (*chicome tochtli*) is written out unambiguously in Nahuatl and corresponds to the Christian year 1538:

		7 Rabbit
Chavez - Pimentel	6 House	[5 Flint]
Nezahualcoyotl - Itzcoatl	4 Reed	[3 Rabbit]
Chichimec woman - man	2 House	[1 Flint]

This is however a heptad of seven quite special years, which elapses not in one but over 18 Xiuhmolpilli. This span runs from the Chichimec 1 Flint base (648 AD) and is stated in a double entry by the volutes of smoke and speech rising between the pairs and in the count of the 18 Feasts around the rim.

The Chichimec are placed first, that is lowermost. Clad in animal fur, they live in the wild northwest at Chicomoztoc, whose Seven-Cave format prefigured (or was reconstructed on the basis of) the seven arenas of power established by their descendants when they migrated southeast. As branches of this family, the seven are prefigured in the branches of the tree that here overshadows the cave. These Chichimec live as a family couple. A hunter, he has lit a fire under a low sun, blackening his hands so that they look like the hooves of the deer (*mazatl*) or commoner (*macehual*). Looking out from the cave, she welcomes him, extending a hoof but also a hand, indicating by two joined finger units the calendar name of their home, 2 House. These transformations at Chicomoztoc are alluded to in the most Chichimec of the Hymns (*Icuic* no.4 and no.7)

The couple are cooking rudimentary fare al fresco, and the smoke of their fire rises in volutes; these are arranged so as to signal Xiuhmolpilli arising from the 1 Flint calendar base, 'in chichimeca yeliz' (Cuauhtitlan Annals; Bierhorst 1992:24) acknowledged in texts from every one of the seven arenas claimed by the Chichimecs, and extended further eastwards on the Sunstone (632 CI, 648 CII). For 12 volutes carry us up, over 624 years (12 x 52), to 1272, when the Chichimec leader Xolotl, still fur clad, laid claim to Texcoco and founded its dynasty. The 624 years are corroborated in exactly the kind of double entry seen in the Fejérváry Feasts chapter where, as here, the 52-year Xiuhmolpilli rise as volutes from material previously defined as lengths of cut firewood, cross-laid diagonally four times, i.e. 5^4 or 625.

Thereafter, a further three volutes (15 in all), uttered as speech by both Nezahualcoyotl and his Mexica ally Itzcoatl, register the moment when these two agreed to set up the Triple Alliance in 1 Flint 1428 (exactly 15 x 52 years from 1 Flint 648), which issued into Texcoco's *annus mirabilis* 4 Reed 1431; this year is indicated by the four ends of the diagonally crossed Reed arrows before Nezahualcoyotl, and is celebrated in the Quinatzin Map and other Texcocan texts. As emperors, one of Texcoco and the other of Tenochtitlan, each now wears civilized cotton clothing, the latter's history of migration from the wild northwest being subsumed for these purposes into that of the former (as in *Cuevas*). Visually, in *tlacuilolli* terms, this play with the Series III year-bearer Signs is comparable with that seen in Tepepulco II,iii (the House's stone quarried from rock strata that compress Flint, Rabbit's hand gestures and seasonal furcoats, Reed's arrow/hoe apex that resists becoming socially that of the steep pyramid, and so on).

A final quota of speech volutes between Pimentel and Chavez carries us up to the years 5 Flint and 6 House (six dark swirls in the water below Chavez hint at the latter year), already in the 18th Xiuhmolpilli after Chicomoztoc, and to the date of the text, 7 Rabbit (1538), written alphabetically above them in Nahuatl (cf. Sullivan 1997:190). At this date in Tepepulco (II, iii), Pimentel and Chavez are depicted as heirs of Texcoco's empire, along with their contemporaries in Tenochtitlan and Colhuacan. The pair acknowledges Spanish colonial rule in the hats they wear, the wands of office they hold and in the rounded arches awkwardly incorporated into their architecture. Yet they still wear the tilma cape and claim prior loyalty to the local community (*altepetl*), seated as they are above vivid glyphs of water (*atl*) and mountain (*tepetl*), the largest in the text. Also, they go barefoot and make footprints, precisely as they mark the bounds of their Altepetl, like the 'idea of the year' ('Xiuhcayotl'; Dibble 1990:17) shown to walk through the Feasts around the circumference.

The ratification sought by the pair in this Anniversary Wheel goes, then, beyond diachronic western notions of simple precedence. As the outer cycle or circumference, the Feasts, reading clockwise, affirm the passage of time through the turning year, and each of the 18 Feasts is confirmed as 20 days by

the Texcocan version of the *pantli* glyph. Beside the Xiuhcoanaual head at the top of the Wheel, space is opened out of which the Xiuhcayotl emerges to begin his walk through the Feasts in Atlacahualo (F2.8) and to which he returns at its end in Izcalli (F2.7). He leaves footprints whose toes affirm their days (18 x 4 x 5 = 360), which are complemented by the Nemotemi shown between the start and end of his journey. These 'useless' intercalated days are named by the Tonalpoualli, in six columns of year-bearer Series (III IV V I II III). The first column terminates in the year Rabbit, specified in the date 7 Rabbit 1538.

Meanwhile, the statement as a whole is further grounded in the inner concentric frame of the Xiuhmolpilli, turquoise blue, inset as 13 segments per quarter, 52 years in all. Along the path between the outer and inner rings, the footprints stride at an average of four per Feast, which correlate numerically to either side, with 20 days of the Feasts to the left (as we saw), and now with the 52 years of the Xiuhmolpilli to the right. In this way, Xiuhcayotl's 18 footprints, in treading the bounds of the Altepetl and living through the year's Feasts, come to echo historically just the 1:4 ratio of Xiuhmolpilli seen on the Sunstone. For on the one hand, they confirm the 18 x 52 years that run from 1 Flint 648 at Chicomoztoc to the Xiuhmolpilli in which Chavez and Pimentel live (1 Flint–13 Reed, 1532–83). On the other hand, the footprints establish the Chichimec base date within the Era (1 Flint CII of Round 72, 648 AD) from which these Xiuhmopilli are counted, the base being set solidly now in the inner ring of 52 turquoise years, 4 x 18 x 52 years after the Era base 1 Flint CI (3112 BCE).

In so turning, the Feasts enter time long prior to the Christian Era imported by Mexico's new rulers, and (at that date) scarcely imagined or articulated by them.

Second coming and eclipse

Little studied, the Anniversary Wheels known as Veytia numbers 4 and 5 (**Figs 7.4, 7.5, 7.6**) are closely akin to each other , and they recall in common the 'Encounter with Europe', the fateful triennium 1 Reed to 3 House that brought Cortés and destroyed Tenochtitlan (1519–21), in years with those names one Xiuhmolpilli later, 1571–73. The changed circumstances in which the authors of these texts were by then living, recounted in Mexicanus, Aubin and other annals, is evident in wry commentaries legible as in 'Encounter with Europe' in the Feast emblems, the year-bearer Signs, and other standard iconography. Xiuhcoanaual, on the rim of no.4 and coiled at the quarters (albeit with fuzzily marked scales), unwinds in no.5 as the emblem of Coailhuitl (F2.9), the coils visible still as bends in the long enduring body of the community.

In the civil arena, both of these Veytia Wheels note the impact of the European style theatre (Cuauhteocalli) that was opened in Mexico in 2 Flint 1572, according to the annals in Aubin. Hence, Toxcatl, the Feast of the performance that had been for real 52 years earlier in 2 Flint 1520, becomes illusion on stage, indicated in this Feast by blonde wigs, and the effect of vanishing point and perspective in the theatre building. These years also disturbed the rhythm of political succession, which had carried on constantly, even if reduced, since Cuauhtemoc's surrender in 3 House 1521. A crisis arose with the premature death of Francisco Ximénez, the governor or *juez* from Chalco, 'Chalco chane', who had enjoyed general respect as successor to Tenochtitlan's emperors. His dying before the end of his official term in 1576 somehow enabled the Spaniards further to reduce the power transmitted in this line of governors, when Antonio Valeriano was installed in 3 House 1573: in denoting this year, Veytia no.4 makes the Sign House look neglected and run down.

According to Aubin, Ximénez's demise meant the premature celebration, in 3 House 1573 rather than 6 Flint 1576, of the 80-year Jade ritually identified with his town Chalco, a calendrical custom begun as early as 11 Flint 1256, according to the *Historia tolteca-chichimeca* (from this 1256 date, 1576 completed 320 years, or four 80-year Chalco Jades; see p.34 above). In depicting the Jades that represent Tecuilhuitl A & B in the ring of Feasts, Veytia no.4 draws out their calendrical significance, in subdivisions that correspond to the quarterly tribute installments of twice 5 plus twice 4 Feasts; but it also shows that these native calendrical mechanisms are worn; in Veytia no.5, they are displaced by patently theatrical rulers in western guise.

In Veytia no.4 (**Figs 7.4, 7.5**), just as the House Sign (3 House 1573) is also made to indicate political loss, so the Flint Sign (2 Flint 1572) is quite restructured to indicate technological change. From being flint knife and primeval tool, this Series III Sign is proposed as the rim of a stone wheel, seen in three-quarter view. This corresponds to the fact that in that year of 1572 a water-powered millwheel was installed in the San Juan aqueduct, entirely in the interests of nascent Spanish capitalism, and with no regard to native water needs or patterns of agriculture. In fact, neglect of agriculture is indicated in the ring of Feasts at the start of the cycle in Tititl, which as we have seen coincides with the start of the planting year; and it becomes a persistent motif. In this Veytia Wheel and its companion no.5, seedlings wilt or wither exposed on the roof still in Izcalli, bread 'freezes' in Toxcatl, yields and offerings are thin in Etzalcualiztli, and uncleaned irrigation channels overflow in Atemoztli.

Most deadly of all was the second coming of 1 Reed 1571. The arrival in that year of a posse of Inquisitors is anticipated in the Texcocan annals known as the *Códice en Cruz* (1 Reed 1415–13 Rabbit 1570; in fact, less of a 'cross' than a swastika) as they head for Mexica in their boat. Involving secular encomenderos, denunciation, torture, forced confessions, the dunce cap, their sadistic programme was intense over these years (Aubin, Mexicanus) and led to the deaths of many political leaders (possibly Ximénez himself). The Inquisition's grotesque ideology and mission are impishly satirized in an ecclesiastical version of the year-bearer Reed (Veytia no.4).

A common feature of these Veytia Anniversary Wheels is their interest in the moon. In the Gemelli version (**Fig.7.4**), Wheel no.4 depicts moon cycles in an inner ring, in a lunar *tlachialoni* divided this time into six as in Tovar. The face at the centre of no.5 is that of the moon eclipsing the sun. Though surely Europeanized, this lunar imagery in both Wheels nonetheless testifies to the same body of local knowledge that is found in Tepepulco's account of sun, moon and constellations (II, i), 'Genesis' in Rios, and Mexicanus (see next Chapter). In turn, it may be traced back to observations recorded already by the Olmec and much refined in the Maya stone inscriptions, and in the Dresden eclipse tables.

As the ring of moons in Veytia no.4 shows, indispensable to this knowledge is the distinction between synodic and sidereal cycles. In this and the other *tlacuilolli* sources, the profiled face

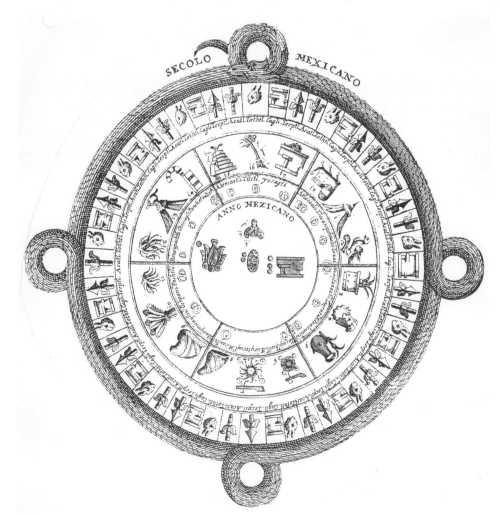

Figure 7.4 Feasts clockwise in six sections, Tititl uppermost, enclosing moon and four Series III year bearers (1 Reed, 2 Flint, 3 House, 4 Rabbit), within anticlockwise Xiuhmolpilli, 1 Rabbit uppermost, and clockwise four-coiled snake. Veytia Wheel no.4, Gemelli version

Figure 7.5 Veytia Wheel no.4 (cf. **Fig. 7.4**)

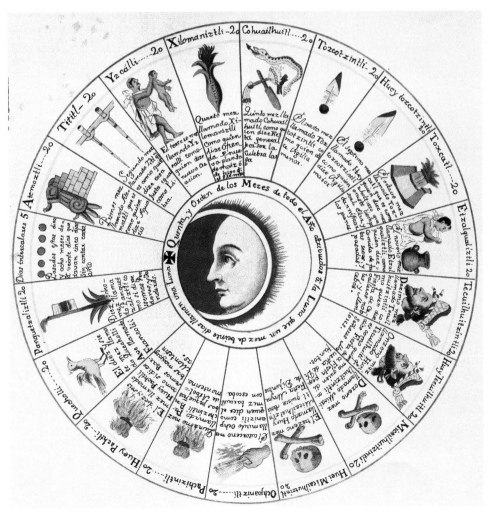

Figure 7.6 Feasts clockwise, Nemotemi to left between Panquetzaliztli and Atemoztli, enclosing solar eclipse. Veytia Wheel no.5

of the moon is made to contrast with the more evenly drawn back of the head, making of the latter a measure in its own right. Indeed, it may denote the moon in its own right, independent of light and shadow cast upon it, the smoky disk of Tezcatlipoca's 'obsidian mirror'. This is the body that treads relentlessly along its path around the earth, along which it may occlude the sun in an eclipse at any time, may occlude a star when entirely in shadow and invisible, and reveals where it is with extreme precision when appearing in the west adorned with the very first sliver of the new moon (Tepoztecatl's *yacameztli*). To complete a cycle in this mode or behaviour, that is, to return to the station along the star road where it set off, the moon takes 27.32 rather than 29.54 nights, its sidereal rather than its synodic period of its phases of reflected light. The classic formula stated in the opening chapters of Borgia and Cospi (pp.1–8) elegantly reconciles a half of theTonalpoualli's two lunar counts as Tlazoteotl to her own square within that of the Night Lord set, i.e. $2 (7^2 \times 9^2) = 260$. As such, the sidereal moon's career through the stars is still closely observed in Mesoamerica, particularly its parlous passage through the Great Rift in the Milky Way (Tedlock 1992:31), and in the Tonalpoualli the 27.3 nights of the journey are likewise commemorated by the nine Night Lords, this time in their unending count of nights. The practice of counting an extra night every 3 sidereal moons ($3 \times 27.3 = 9^2 + 1$) needs adjustment only after 90 moons (the 2,460 nights seen in Cospi), the precise length of one such moon being 27.32 nights.

All this might explain why in the inner circle in Veytia no.4 (**Fig. 7.4**), a hastier sidereal moon appears to chase its synodic counterpart around the year defined by the Feasts. It also informs the context in which to assess the massive solar eclipse depicted in Veytia no.5 (**Fig. 7.6**). In this latter Wheel, the first two of the Feasts, Atemoztli and Tititl, are identified alphabetically with the imported zodiac, although in a most unusual and revealing way. For while Atemoztli (F2.5) is identified with Aquarius as in Mexicanus and Tovar, Tititl (F2.6) is connected not with the following constellation Pisces, but with Libra, the ninth of the 12 zodiac signs. At the first time level,

this forward leap corroborates the claim made at the center of the Wheel that the Feast is in some sense to be understood as a moon ('que un mes de veinte dias llaman una Luna'), its 20 days roughly corresponding to movement from Aquarius to Virgo within a single lunar cycle. At the second time level, the forward leap has the effect, within the year, of establishing the by now familiar pattern of thirds, dividing it into the periods of 8 plus 4 months that correspond precisely to the 12 plus 6 Feasts of the native planting seasons. At yet a third time level, the 120 days of the latter season are exactly equal to the number of years that would pass before the greatest solar eclipse seen in Mexico for centuries, famous for the uprising against the Spaniards which it provoked (1691–92). As 5 Flint (C11; 8 Flint C1), the year of this eclipse was made to coincide with the terminal date projected in several native texts contemporary with, or earlier than the Veytia Wheel no.5, among them, the Tlaxcala Annals, the Dehesa Codex (which Edmonson identifies as Olmec), the Tepexic Annals, and the Selden Roll (see Key).

On the evidence available, it is impossible to say whether the anniversaries noted in Veytia no.5 extend into the future, to the eclipse of 5 Flint predicted in other texts. To be sure, the lunar face that eclipses the sun at the centre of this Wheel is nothing if not enigmatic.

Texts that depict the Feasts cycle as one of a series of concentric wheels constitute a particular group, little noticed as such hitherto, and when noticed most often suspected to be extraneous to the native tradition. Comparing extant examples and starting with the firmly pre-Cortesian Sunstone reveals a remarkable homogeneity in the group, and it yet further vindicates the importance of *tlacuilolli* as the medium indispensable in the study of the Feasts. For these Wheels, on the one hand, deploy format in the interests of concision, much concentrating Mexica philosophy and measurements of time. On the other hand, they value 'play' and resist the reduction and lifeless mechanism that after the 16th century came increasingly to characterize comparable western models, along with the deadly binary opposition between the synchronic and the diachronic.

8
Mexicanus

Of the names bestowed on Feast texts by Western scholars, Mexicanus must be deemed one of the more fortunate, since in fact it deals comprehensively with things Mexica and Mexican (Mexicayotl). Housed today in Paris, the 102 amate pages that comprise this text make a most authoritative statement about the Feasts, the philosophy implicit in them and their relationship with the Christian calendar. This much has been indicated by those few who have made extensive commentaries on it (Mengin 1952, Galarza 1966, Prem 1978), having wrestled with its blotches, possible lacunae, and above all its strong penchant for riddle and pun. Here it is considered for its articulation of, and reflection on the Feasts, in just the terms taken as categorical in this study. Mexicanus is a *tlacuilolli* text, which draws also on the Roman and other alphabets, and on Roman and Arabic numerical notation. It offers clues to its provenance and argument in two Nahuatl glosses. One refers to the arrival of the Christian mission in San Pablo Teipan, site of the imperial Mexica palace; the other, to loyalty to the pagan line of emperors begun by Acamapichtli, whose descendants lived in the same quarter of the city.

Correlating Mexica and Christian years on page 9, the first gloss ('sand acosti teopixque ualcallaque sa paollo') notes the arrival in 5 Reed 1575 of the Augustinians in San Pablo, the southeastern barrio of a nascent Mexico City (it is seen in this position in the quincunx *traza* in Osuna Codex pp.196, 257). At this date, the Augustinians took over the Christian mission in this *tlaxilacalli* or barrio from the Franciscans, who in their day had been helped financially by Inés de Tapia, descendant of the royal Mexica family and owner of the huge palace that can be clearly seen in San Pablo in the Tlatelolco Map of 1550. On the eve of the Gregorian Reform of the Julian calendar, introduced into Mexico in 1583 and a main theme in Mexicanus, the Augustinian college of San Pablo was renowned as much for its library, maps and astronomical instruments (Grijalva 1985:327), as for its desire to convert native intellectuals.

As the southeastern quarter of Tenochtitlan, San Pablo had previously been known as Teipan ('on the stone'); to the south of the Great Pyramid, this is the area of the royal houses, and of the college Huitznahuac, which is featured in Matrícula (f.4) and in the Twenty Hymns (*Icuic* no. 2). What appears to be the glyph of Teipan is seen in the dynastic map in Mexicanus dedicated to Acamapichtli (pp.16–17), whose cause is revered in the other gloss (p.36), by an initiate who names himself Tlacotecpatl and says he is determined to defend and ransom Mexica values, not least those articulated in the calendar and the night sky.

The overall argument proposed in Mexicanus hinges on the thought that in overcoming the Mexica militarily, Christian Europe had been defeated intellectually, above all in its understandings and calendrical organization of time. This defeat was not just technical, in the sense of the inaccurate Julian measurement of the solar year, but conceptual, since

missionary instructors Franciscan, Dominican and Augustinian alike, were unable effectively to distinguish between the solar and other kinds of year, let alone trace and codify their phenomenological roots. This implied an intellectual limitation which by definition Europeans could not be aware of and which they did nothing to resolve when they learned to measure the solar year less ineptly than they had done and removed the 10 superfluous Julian days in the Gregorian Reform. Indeed, the European insistence on accuracy had the effect of privileging a particular 'scientific' precision and of leaving to one side and to blind faith such questions as custom (the Eastern Orthodox point), our origins in time, our inner and outer space, the star-bright womb of life.

Stated in *tlacuilolli*, the argument draws on all the resources of this script, in emblem and image, embedded and free-standing number, and layout. In facing Christianity, the text takes on the scripts, arithmetical notations and icons through which that religion had spread itself over the world and was then attempting to habilitate itself in Mexico. The result is challenging for the modern reader, to say the least, yet more legible when compared with the Feast texts that have been studied here and to which it in turn becomes a useful guide. As always, argument is inseparable from structure, that of Mexicanus having an intricacy that is as delightful as it is informative.

As with any *tlacuilolli* text, no discussion or analysis of Mexicanus is feasible without prior agreement about exactly how it is to be read, its reading principles, format, and chaptering. Although the overall left to right reading direction is clear enough, the interconnection and imbrication between pages and groups of pages tends to be less so. Among other factors, this is due to the poor condition of the opening and closing pages, and the deliberate smudging, effacing and re-use of others. This led Hanns Prem in his commentary (1978), the most expert to date, to have a poor opinion of the work, although he conceded he was unable to examine the original in Paris and had to make do with Mengin's inadequate 'facsimile'. Prem believed there were missing pages (e.g. 'falta por lo menos una hoja' (p.277)), complained of messy detail, here and there an 'anotación confusa' (p.279 fn 28), and declared that overall Mexicanus was a failed attempt at correlating the local and imported systems: 'un intento, malogrado en lo esencial, del dibujante indígena de correlacionar el calendario indígena con el cristiano' (p.287). Yet drawing in part on information he himself provides, a less hostile reading reveals that all these and other supposed defects, faults and errors in the text may stem rather from sophisticated play with reader expectation. It makes it possible to trace the threads of the complex argument, which falls into three parts. The first concerns the end of the Julian Era and the origins and ideologies of the Mesoamerican year (pp.1–15). The second – the bulk of the text – consists of annals that recount six lifetimes of the Mexica (423 years), on the road from Aztlan and in power in Tenochtitlan (pp.16–88). The third, barely legible, records the Trecenas of the Tonalpoualli (pp.89–102). In each part, and especially in the first, the Feasts have multiple and indispensable roles. In the discussion that follows, reasons will also be suggested for believing that the text is in fact not missing any pages and stands complete as it is. Amidst ostensibly Christian apparatus, it begins (p.1) by announcing its faith in Tezcatlipoca, whose all-seeing *tlachialoni* is held high in the Feast of Toxcatl, as it was in 2 Flint 1520, when the Mexica rose up against the Spaniards.

All-seeing Tezcatlipoca

Daring to depict Tezcatlipoca's *tlachialoni*, the opening page of Mexicanus deals with the Christian months and establishes the format adhered to in the first chapter (pp.1–8), which covers the span from May to December (**Fig. 8.1**; cf. **Fig. 1.2**). In the most basic reading, this first page is seen to divide into three fields, a column at the left margin, and two horizontal registers on the main page. The column is defined by a vertical line, which separates it on the page in the proportion 1:10, i.e. a first 11th (on odd-numbered pages this proportion tends to be obscured by the European binding at the spine). The horizontal registers are divided equally by a narrow band that extends to the right from the left-hand column and consists of a double row of alphabetic letters, 31 above and 31 below, each in its own sequence. The horizontal division is effected, then, by elements which, as banded sequences of letters, give information of themselves. In the column vertically assigned to the first 11th of the page, this order of information is enclosed in that space in emblems, signs, and lettered phrases and words. From top to bottom, we may read (or reconstruct from the blotches) the zodiac sign and the word Gemini, an upright lunar crescent, glyphs and letters that suggest phonetically in Nahuatl the syllables of the month of May, and the total 31, in *tlacuilolli* numerals.

Aligned with the horizontal dividing band halfway down the column, the glyph of moon, named and counted as a month in Nahuatl syllables and numerals, initiates the two sequences of letters that derive from its movements. These are the quarters of

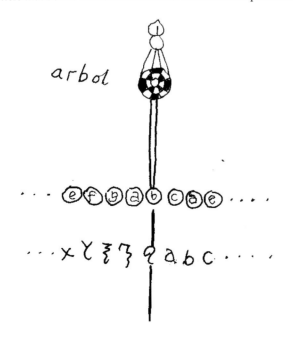

its synodic phases, each cast as the seven letters of the week **a** to **g**, and the 27 night letters of its journey through the stars, for which purpose the 24 Roman letters are augmented to 27 by an extra **r** and two extra **z**s, derived from other alphabets. Indispensable to Christian liturgy before the Gregorian Reform and variously named (in Asian as well as European languages), these letter sequences are referred to here as dominical (of the synodic moon's four phases) and (lunar) zodiacal (of the sidereal moon's hastier journey through the stars). Permutating throughout the year, these letter sequences serve to determine the date of Easter, the greatest feast of the ecclesiastical year. On this opening page, May Day is recorded by the dominical or Sunday Letter **b** (which shows there was no leap day that year) and by the lunar letter **n**. By the end of the month, 31 May, they have permutated respectively to **d** and **q**.

Forming the band that separates the horizontal registers of the page, the dominical and zodiacal letter sequences serve to identify, through linking threads, images and emblems, sometimes whole figures, that are placed above and below them. Those above are to Christendom as those below are to Mexicayotl. In the Christian space above, on 1 May we detect traces of a head or heads that denote St Philip and St James the Less, this being their Saint's Day in May, and they are followed on 3rd by the Holy Cross, in triple trefoil.

Below, along the bottom margin run the Mexica Feasts, marked at mid- and/or end points ten days apart by their emblems, so as ingeniously to allow for the correlation identified above as 'TTTM', in which indeed the letter M stands for Mexicanus, as we saw. On this page we have Tozoztli B (now effaced), 5 May; Toxcatl at the *tlachialoni* midpoint (thus highlighted in Tepepulco I, ii) on 15th (Julian end, Gregorian middle), plus a terminal upright line on 25th; and the start of Etzalcualiztli, whose emblem appears on the following page. In their own system, the Feast emblems are correlated with the Series III year bearers (except VIII, Rabbit) and their qualifying Numbers. As in the Tepepulco Xiuhmolpilli (II,iii), in the process the Signs acquire added meaning. For example, the House (III) in Micailhuitl becomes the house of the dead, from which they journey in the afterlife, leaving footprints like those seen at the same Feast in Laud (p.21). They travel in their own time and their destination is the interstice of this double Feast of the Dead which signified alike at the birth of the Era and the surrender of Cuauhtemoc (see p.10).

No doubt laborious, this formal introduction is unavoidable since in any competent reading of Mexicanus much hangs on sheer layout. For in the first instance, the initial May/ Toxcatl page sets the template for the first chapter that is strictly adhered to on the following seven pages, which go on to treat the months from June to December in the same terms, being literally superimposed above the Feasts from Etzalcualiztli to Atemoztli. Over this span, two thirds of the year are duly registered as 35 dominical cycles or weeks, that is the 245 days that are enclosed in nine Lunar Zodiacs of 246 nights, from the eve of May Day (Walpurgisnacht, 30 April) to New Year's Eve (31 December). Meanwhile, the gallery of Saints that opened with Philip and James extends to include Christ himself, in the Christmas hay, and three cohorts of 11 who commemorate the years of his life. These include his contemporaries, disciples and scribes; forerunners like John the Baptist, and Michael plus two fellow archangels (whose name glyphs, as three of the maguey's seven leaves, fathom shamanic depths); and the founders of the Church proper, doctors, popes and martyrs. In all, month by month these cohorts of 11 propose a model of construction akin to that protagonized through the Feasts in earlier *tlacuilolli* texts by the likes of Ciuacoatl, Ilamatecutli, Tepoztecatl and Otontecutli. Only now, mostly males with shaggy beards, they edify, protected by, and as, the walls of abode bricks that phonetically spell Saint in Nahuatl (*xantli*). They clutch their books of scripture and rise from them not to dance but to remonstrate and even slay with sword, Michael in this singularly representing his shapeshifter archangel trio. Collecting tribute at the September equinox Matthew reveals what could be a Mexica ledger of 9+9 entries; at the solstice, Thomas, travelling far to the east, becomes Nahuatl phonetically and culturally as the tomato grower. The few moments of feeling belong to the few women, in wonderful *tlacuilolli* portraits rich with water and shells, like that of Lucy.

The founder males come sarcastically to include Cortés, in Quecholli 1519, and Viceroy Suarez de Mendoza who arrived in Pachtli B (St Francis's day 1579) and died in 1583. Between them, this fashionably attired 16th-century Spanish pair complete the 64-year span over which the Julian year count slipped a further half-day (12 hours) behind the sun, as we saw (p.7). The continuing lag is indicated above by splits in the connecting lines to the dominical letters, while below it appears in shadow lines at one- and ten-day intervals beside and between the Feasts, notably in Toxcatl, in Pachtli B (when the 10 days were historically excised), and Miccailhuitl A, in the footprints of the dead.

Starting the chapter off, the May/Toxcatl page has certain distinguishing traits. For as the first Feast to be named, it is the only one whose midpoint aligns with that of the month, at the Ides. Given the text's comparative agenda, this coincidence acquires some significance, especially since, although the Gregorian Reform changed the position of Christian month dates in the solar year, it did not change the nominal dates of the Saints (Philip and James stayed at 1 May regardless). Most striking, the staff that supports the *tlachialoni* thrusts it so high as to pass right up through the band of dominical and zodiacal letters into the Christian superstructure (**Fig.8.1**). While the emblems and vertical lines of the other seven Feasts may connect with the those coming down from the Saints and other Holy days above, this is the only case of direct flow and surge from below to above. Historically the triumphant *tlachialoni* must recall how its owner Tezcatlipoca was reinstalled after the Spaniards were thrown out of Tenochtitlan after the Toxcatl uprising in May 1520. The staff is glossed 'arbor' (Latin) or 'arbol' (Spanish), the tree whose sap ever rises, like that in Pahuatlan, the living original of Christ's Cross.

While expressed through Christian months, May to December, the two-thirds of the year covered in the opening chapter has abundant native precedents as such, not least in the system of planting seasons, while the specific span of Feasts from Toxcatl (p.1) to Panquetzaliztli (p.8) is prefigured in Borbonicus through the fire-bearing Yoaltecutli (p.56 above). Again, the 35 weeks or 245 days of the dominical letters echo the Atamalcualiztli count in Tepepulco and are effectively enclosed by just the 246 nights or nine sideral moons of the Lunar Zodiac, which we have seen are fundamental to tribute arithmetic in Matrícula and Cospi (p.33 above). Yet again, in concentrating on

fixed holy and Saints Days, the eight months in question avoid necessary reference to that part of the year which in both the Christian and the Mexica calendars is most affected by moveable feasts (Easter; the Nemotemi), and which is dealt with subsequently. Indeed, this has the further effect of highlighting the one moveable Christian feast that is featured here in the eight months from May to December, namely Ember Day, the Wednesday that marks the very end of Eastertide, which is placed here on 1 June.

The only moveable Feast noted in the opening eight-page chapter, Ember Day is translated as 'Head bowing' (*Cuatollo tempora*); this ingeniously naturalizes the Latin term *quattuor tempora* (which became quarter days) while emphasizing that there were originally three not four Ember days, born of pagan harvest, vintage and planting. Weaving Eastertide back into the solar year, the other two Ember Days are duly placed on Wednesdays in September, near the other Holy Cross (14th) and prior to the equinox, and in December, near St Lucy when the sun sets earliest (13th, in the northern hemisphere) and prior to the solstice. In context (and contrary to Prem's assertion), the fact that Ember day falls here on 1 June means that the text, like the Anniversary Wheels, speaks from historically significant years even while juggling calendar cycles, Mexica and Christian. Between 1519 and 1583, Ember day fell only three times on 1 June, in years 11 years apart, 1547, 1558, 1569, the middle year being the one identified by the Era wheels on p.9. The huge significance of Ember Day itself is examined in the Eastertide triptych, which alerts us to its identification with Hermes/Mercury and to the deep time cycles inherent in its Saxon etymology.

The correlation with the Christian year offered in the opening 8 pages is developed in the following 7, which further contrast the cycles of the Julian and the Mexica calendars, including now respective eras, night skies, and body time. The edifice of the church constructed by the Saints, adobe bricks of its walls, is revealed as the world system that rests on St Peter, the rock of the papacy. Accordingly, power radiates from this centre through the cycle of dominical letters, which are roman and have a pagan origin in the calendar of Julius Caesar. As a 28-year wheel, this Julian cycle is juxtaposed with the 52-year Xiuhmolpilli, in a consideration of the eras of temporal power and empire (p.9. **Fig. 8.2**). Then, the two great Christian feasts, equinoctial Easter and solstitial Christmas, are analyzed as the main hinges of the Julian year, eccleciastical in March and civil in December. Located by the zodiac signs and lunar letters recorded on the previous pages, these are critically assessed against the planting seasons that hinge on Atemoztli (pp.10–11. **Pl. 2a**). Finally, monastic doctrines of yearly penance and self-sacrifice are epitomized in the human body of Corpus Christi, parsed here as the blood that courses through it in time with the stars and the aeons of genesis over which it evolved (a notion formerly commemorated by Rome at Septuagesima; pp.12–15). Literally central to this blood analysis is its middle leaf (pp.13–14): in a double 66-unit Night Sky Grid, this contrives to interrelate the calendrical and astronomical cycles and progressions of Mexica time – Feasts, Tonalpoualli, sun, stars, planets – in ways that the Christian calendar, Julian or Gregorian, could not hope to match (**Fig. 8.3**).

The further comparison of Christian and Mexica years aims not so much to insist on the superior mechanisms of the latter as

Figure 8.2 Xiuhmolpilli and dominical wheels on the 'naupoalxihuitl' base. Mexicanus p.9

to continue to vindicate through them a whole worldview and belief system. For marking the very end of the Julian Era in Mexico, in the year 13 Reed 1583, this response to Rome's mission was written six decades after the Mexica had verbally rejected The Twelve Franciscans in the *Coloquios* of 1524, and it follows the very same argument, working out now in technical detail from a more colonized present. Having exactly stated the TTTM correlation, Mexicanus enshrines it just in the philosophy of the three origins and services of the year stated in the *Coloquios*, offering thereby a comprehensive if cryptic critique of western theory and practice. (The intervening bonfires that the Christians had made of books and people no doubt favoured a preference for the cryptic.) The imperial drive that derives from the 'acquisitions of the hunt' is typified in the image of Peter, the first pope, and the temporal power that radiates from Rome like spokes in a wheel (p.9), in the political construction of time and its eras. Then, in the second service Tlaloc's agricultural year is measured as the cultivated field under the stars (pp.10– 11). Last, the nightly penance of bloodletting, the ancient 'first service', is identified with bleeding practices and Christ's self-sacrifice (pp.12–15). As in *Coloquios*, the tripartite statement is a masterpiece of concision, and it relies fully on the Feasts for its

articulation.

Taken together, these opening 15 pages of Mexicanus may be regarded as a necessary prelude to the specifically Mexica history and experience of the world to which the main length of the text is devoted (pp.16–88). Although it occupies only a single page (p.9), the disquisition on eras and political power is so dense as to require attention in its own right.

Whose era encompasses whose?

In being considered first of all as the expression of political power, of units in imperial eras, the respective years of the Christian and Mexica are formed as contiguous wheels, whose rims touch (p.9. **Fig. 8.2**). One is the Julian 28-year cycle of first Sundays in the year, derived from the dominical letters seen in the previous chapter. It runs here from letters **d** to **e**, translatable into years AD as 1551 and 1578 thanks to the fact that the Augustinians' arrival in San Pablo is noted in the year **b** as '1575' (arabic numbers also made to resemble the uncial cipher 'IHS'). The other wheel is the 52-year Series III Xiuhmolpilli, the year-bearer members of the Tonalpoualli days seen in the previous chapter, and it touches the Julian wheel, roughly, at **b** (1558) 1 Rabbit, so as to suggest age-old slippage. Centering the Julian wheel with key in one hand and book in the other, St Peter determines its position to the left of the Xiuhmolpilli. For its part, the Xiuhmolpilli asks preferably to be seen as uppermost, thanks to its alignment with the base placed beside/beneath Peter's wheel, which effectively turns the whole page through 90°, laying the saint pope out flat, head to left. Set at a right angle, these positionings of the wheels relative to each other on the page are further confirmed in the base by the vigesimal place-value operative in the two cohorts of numbers given within it. In the upward reading, large-disk 20s below are followed by small-disk single units; above, *tzontli* 400s are followed horizontally to the right by *pantli* 20s. The upper calculation yields '1540' (4 x 400 less 3 cancelled 20s, or 1,600 minus 60); the lower calculation affirms the prime significance in all this of the Feasts cycle (18 x 20 plus 5), together with the 52-year Xiuhmolpilli (2 x 20 plus 12).

Breathtaking in its elegance and concision, the page epitomizes more than any other the argument of the whole text; found inscrutable, it has been subjected to diverse interpretations. A Nahuatl gloss in the base placed directly above the Feast count of 365 (18 x 20 plus 5) offers valuable advice. It reads *nauhpoualixihuitl*, that is, literally 'four count year'. This term has been assumed to confirm the four-year structure (Nauhtetl, *cuatrenio*) common to the Mexica and Christian calendars and visible here in the wheels above the base, in the unvarying double-lettered leap years, seven in all, in the Julian cycle; and in the four Series III year bearers of the Xiuhmolpilli, House, Rabbit, Reed and Flint. Being to their left, the gloss 'nauhpoualixihuitl' has also been taken (a little less redundantly) to refer to the four *tzontli* that yield 1540 (4 x 400 less 60), confirming them as year units. It may well do both things, and yet further (and to more purpose) tell us that the whole page may be read four times or in four different ways. Standard in the screenfolds, this possibility is strengthened by the only other item on the page not so far accounted for and indeed otherwise not accountable for: the notable emblem comprising reed-arrow, bird and pot that is set lowermost in the base, between the Feasts count that dominates from the left-

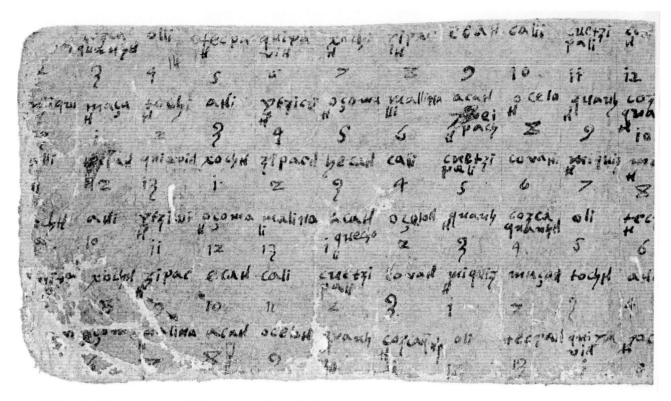

Figure 8.3 Night Sky Grid, from Teotleco 3rd 2 XV to Panquetzaliztli 8th 2 XX. Mexicanus p. 14

hand corner (18, 5) and the corresponding large and small disks to the right (2, 12). For this emblem is legible in four ways, phonetically, then as the year name 2 Reed, or 12 Reed, and, not least, as the initial Feast Tozoztli (F1.1); as a result, it offers to assess, correlate and enhance the year information noted so far (1540, **d** as 1551–, 1 Rabbit 1558). The four readings prompted by the arrow emblem take full account of every item and detail in the page design, and they reconcile and build on interpretations made by scholars hitherto. As for alignment, for the pot to be set upright requires the Xiuhmolpilli to be considered above rather than to the right of St Peter's wheel (that is, vertically, as with the two wheels in Veytia no.2. see **Fig. 7.3** above).

Made up of three elements like the prongs of St Peter's key, the emblem can be read first of all phonetically in Nahuatl, as it was by Galarza, as the dominant syllables of *to-totl* bird, *mi-tl* arrow, and *co-mitl* pot, whence *tomico*, for the Latin or Spanish *dominicus/domingo*, whence in turn the dominical letters in that wheel. The same procedure is followed with the Saints' names in the previous chapter, like San Francisco, where co- is also the pot *co-mitl*, and here it points us to the wheel of dominical letters that begins with **d** 1551. Then, taking the two large disks right beside it as qualifiers, the reed arrow in the emblem can be read as the Series III year bearer 2 Reed, Ome Acatl. Hence, it may be understood as the Mexica New Fire year, much commented on by Mengin, which follows directly on from the 1 Rabbit 1558 highlighted above in the Xiuhmolpilli, being the second of two consecutive dates, like the 1 Flint that follows 13 Reed on the Sunstone. Covertly kindled under the noses of the Spaniards at Charles V's Tenochtitlan funeral (see p.4 above), this Mexica New Fire in 2 Reed 1559 is depicted in similarly hybrid fashion in the Tlatelolco Annals account of the event, in an image of 2 Reed that appeals to Christian iconography on the one hand and the Xiuhmolpilli on the other. Or again, deferring to the ever greater calendrical complexities analyzed by Prem, the year name can

be encoded arithmetically 2 XIII and integrated into the larger Mesoamerican system, according to the Mexica C11 and Cholula C1 correlations determined by the 2:12 ratio of the accompanying large and small disks, eliciting corresponding time depths in the Era. Fourth and last, the emblem can be identified as that of the Feast Tozoztli (F1.1), as precisely the arrow and bird that, as Prem also saw, denote that Feast in this very text, in the Tonalpoualli chapter below (p.95), in Tovar and in Boban (**Pl. 8**). This time, the bird of *do-mingo* (*tototl*) becomes more specifically the parrot (*toznene*) which in this and the other depictions of Tozoztli that we have seen (*Cuevas*; 'Encounter with Europe') schedules the penance begun on the first day of that Feast (*tozoa*; F1.1.1).

The four readings of the year suggested by the 'four year count' 'nauhpoualixihuitl' gloss on this page, with its twin wheels and base, are then conveniently summarized as: i) *domingo*, ii) Ome Acatl, iii) 2 XIII, and iv) Tozoztli. To engage in detail with what they have to teach about political origins would take more space than is available here, especially given the extent to which they cross-reference with each other, with the other two origins that follow, with the text as a whole, and with cognate pages in other Mexica texts. Relying on **Table 4**, what follows attends chiefly to the indispensable role played in all this by the Feast cycle, which controls the page from its (lower or upper) left-hand corner.

Rigid as the spokes radiating from Peter's Rome and perpetual in the Julian calendar, the 28-year dominical-letter cycle did not allow for leap years to be suppressed every 128 years (the undislodgeable 32nd four-year tooth, as it were); hence the need for the Gregorian Reform and the removal of the 10 days. Tied to the annotation '1575', the page shows the last of these cycles, which as such was rendered redundant by the Reform, running from year **d** (1551) to year **e** (1578. The final four years **d cb a g** 1579–82 are examined in their own right in

Table 4 Calculations in Mexicanus

Mexicanus	Feast	22 & multiples	Tonalpoualli (Trecena)	Hermes/Mercury
a) p.1 Tlachialoni/Ides of May	F1.3.11			
	+ 3.6	22 x 3 = 66		
Night-Sky Grid (p.13)	F1.6.17		1 IX (17)	
b) p.2	[F1.1.1]			
	+ 3.6	22 x 3 = 66		
	F1.4.7			
[Septuagesima]	[F2.8.11]			
	+5.16			synodic cycle
Ember Day ('Quatolo')	F1.4.7			
c) p.9 1540 years		55x28 years		
1551 AD		22x70.5 years		
d) Night-Sky Grid p.13	[F1.1.1]			
	+5.16			synodic cycle
	F1.6.17		1 IX (17)	
	+2.4	22 x 2		½ sidereal cycle
	F1.8.20/F1.9.1		5 XII/6XIII (20)	
	+1.2	+22 = 66		
	F2.1.2		1XIV (2)	
p.14	F2.1.3		2XV (2)	
	+3.6	22 x 3 = 66		
	F2.4.8		2XX (7)	

a–d) 22 = Nine Wind in Telleriano (f.9); 66 = total of numbers up to and including 11
b) F1.4.7 (Etzalcualitzlti 7) = 1st June Gregorian = 22nd May Julian (inaugural date of Legend of the Suns, 66 days from its Tozoztli start date, F1.1.1)
c) 1540 = 1600−60; 1551 = start of 28-year cycle; 70.5 years = one day of precession
d) Grid dates presume inclusive counting. New Fire date 2 XIII (Reed) F2.5.1 lies 7x20 units from 5 XIII F1.7.1

the conclusion; see pp.88–9 below). Besides initiating the 28-year cycle, in Julian practice this year 1551 signifies in the count, by centuries AD and their fractions, of jubilee years, with which the Augustinian arrival in 1575 was in step. Made explicit through a papal reference to the Augustinian foundation in that year in Aubin (f.59v), the jubilee count is noted here in St Peter's book, in the roman L comprised of five dots that denotes 50 (the friars referred to the 52-year Xiuhmolpilli as the jubilee). Yet further, with (rather than as) its five constituent dots, the roman L in the book states just the number of cycles (50+5) that produces the total given in the base, each of these two calculations arriving at the same figure by its own route and means, letter cycle, and addition of vigesimal multiples: 55 x 28 = 4 x 400 − 3 x 20 = 1540.

However, satisfying as it may be arithmetically, in context this preliminary equation serves rather to point up the lack of concordance and correlation that has plagued the Christian calendar historically. For while the 1540 years may be deemed years AD if counted from Christ's supposed birthday and hence warn of the calendrical crisis in the colony noted later in the annals (1541), the lettered years of the dominical cycle for their part inherit older Julian practice from the pagan Roman era (Ab Urbe Condita) and among the faithful began to be Christian under Diocletian in 284 AD (1038 AUC), 13 centuries prior to the Gregorian Reform (the 10 x 128 years that produced the 10 extra days), that is, ten or so dominical cycles before years AD were

themselves invented, in the 6th century AD. Rome never successfully reconciled these various year counts and eras with each other, let alone with the astronomical rhythms of sun and stars and time depths integral to Mesoamerican calendar, while Christ's birthday has been variously located in the decade from 4 BC to 6 AD. Inconsistency of this order is indicated in the fact that the dominical wheel begins not in 1541, following on from the base, but 10 years later, in 1551, setting up exactly the play between 10 lost days and 10 lost years developed below with respect to the final four Julian years. For its part, the extra year seen falling from below 1540 in the base might indicate the notorious Christian failure to acknowledge the year zero between years After and those Before Christ, years BC being a flawed invention that came even later (necessarily remedied much later again in the astronomer's year count used and noted here as BCE).

Turning now from Rome to Tenochtitlan, we may exchange years named by dominical letters for those of the Mexica Xiuhmolpilli, focusing on the 2 Reed which produces New Fire. As 'Ome acatl', 2 Reed takes us from Rome's red and black spokes to the suppler red and segmented turquoise of the Xiuhmolpilli and to the moment highlighted by the contact between the two wheels. This is the end of the 52-year cycle inaugurated by Moctezuma, 2 Reed 1507 to 1 Rabbit 1558. Of the large disks lowermost in the base (2, 18) to either side of the emblem, those to the right (2) qualify it as a year name when it is read as the Sign Reed (as we have seen), while those to the left, the 18 of the Feasts seen in the corner, may now confirm its distance in years from 1540. From the Chichimec base respected by the Mexica, these 18 may further count as a distance number when taken to be Rounds, exactly like those counted from 1 Flint 648 in Boban (which explicitly recognizes the 18 as both Feasts and Rounds; cf. also the 17 Rounds from 1 Reed 635 to 13 Rabbit 1518 narrated unbroken in the Cuauhtitlan Annals, p.6 above). Moreover, the internal grouping of the 18 as 15+3, seen also in Boban, distinguishes the New Fires kindled under the emperors (2 Reed 1403, 1455, 1507, i.e. after Acamapichtli was installed). In all, Ome Acatl enables Mexica self-location, firmer and more consistent than any possible in the Christian apparatus.

In turn, by encoding Ome Acatl as '2 XIII', the third reading of the emblem integrates the Chichimec-Mexica Era into that of the Olmec and Mesoamerica, again with notable consistency, this time by using all the numbers in the base. First, the 18 large disks to the left that mark the interval from the base to 1559, 2 Reed CII, are matched to the right by the large two that, having qualified the year Sign Reed, now simultaneously mark the interval to 1543, 2 Reed CI. Then, as further qualifiers of the same Sign the corresponding smaller numbers to right and left above (12, 5) complete the correlative statement: 2 XIII CI : 12 XIII CII : 1559 :: 2 XIII CII : 5 XIII CI : 1543. Mexica and Chichimec CII years are similarly integrated into the larger calendrical whole in Rios, while as the last year to be depicted in the *Historia tolteca-chichimeca* (f.43v), 3 Reed CI replaces 13 Reed CII, in 1427 AD. Indeed, in the annals in Mexicanus itself (p.85), the equation is repeated when the Mexica year 10 Reed (CII)1567 is increased by three celestial units to produce the Era year name 13 Reed (CI) seen on the Sunstone (at an interval of 90 Rounds or 4,680 years from 3113 BCE). This deeper Mexica self-location appeals to further calculations likewise evidenced elsewhere in this and in other texts. The spiral that runs from 1 Reed to 2 Reed in the Xiuhmolpilli, from red to turquoise, invokes the shifts that occur during the Era between year bearers and lots of 40 in days, years and Rounds which are specified in HMP and in *Legend of the Suns*, the latter likewise targeting the date 1558. In the process, the solar year is measured according to the impeccable 29-Round formula, age-old in Mesoamerica (see p.27 above), thanks to the insertion of an extra unlettered cog into the dominical wheel which raises from 28 to 29 the multiplicand of the Xiuhmolpilli's 52, to produce the indicated 1508 (distant from 1558 by the 50 or L in St Peter's book). The same exact estimate of the solar year also translates into the more immediate and practical 128-year formula stated in the previous Mexicanus chapter, which here serves to cap the 29 Round formula in order to arrive at the 1558 date via another route. For, improving the Julian estimate in the same vein, these local formulae are shown through St Peter's three-prong key to work together in order to gauge exactly the 4,652-year span from the first year of the first Round of the Era, 1 Flint CI 3112 BCE, to 1540 AD, that is, 1,508 x 3 or 4,524, plus 128. For its part and as a year and day name, 2 Reed measures the spans of nine Rounds shown in the Tepexic Annals to relate correspondingly to the sidereal year and its thirds, stars advancing above the cloud-clad mountain of the Feasts (**Fig. 2.6**), just as the following pages do, with respect to Aquarius above Atemoztli's fields, and with the same division of the year into thirds.

Drawing together everything indicated so far, the 'Tozoztli' reading of the arrow-bird- pot emblem celebrates the Feasts, strategically placed at the corner of the page (18 x 20, plus 5), as the all-encompassing cycle they are shown to be for the Mexica on the Sunstone. Identifying the Feast in the cycle that is first in tribute and penance (FI.I), it affirms the Julian year of 365.25 days that mediates between the solar year, shorter by .008 of a day, and the sidereal year, longer than the solar by .014 of a day, establishing rhythms that govern penance and are workable in political and social life. Firm and most subtly calibrated in their own realm, Tozoztli and the Feasts emerge, then, as the best possible equipment for correcting and reviving Julian time, and as the finest vindication of Mexica calendrics.

As in Telleriano and *Cuevas*, the point of the arrow or dart in the Tozoztli emblem releases the blood of penance (*tozoa*, seen as the bird *toznene*). Falling now into a pot or chalice, the blood nonetheless first flows at this initial Feast of the year (FI.I) and still keeps time with the stars, as it was supposed to do but did not under the imported zodiac. Thereby, we engage with the further Julian defect: failing not just to measure the solar year but to distinguish it from the year of the stars in the first place. The precision inherited by the Mexica in this matter is evident in the several examples of year spans in annals, not least the 423 years below in this text, which as multiples of a lifetime plus a semester (i.e. 70.5 years) exactly define days of solar slippage or precession. Governing the fourth reading of this era page, Tozoztli confirms the parallel principle and practice: that of recording these days as those of the stellar procession seen with Xonecuilli in Borbonicus etc., examples of which are elaborately detailed in the Night Sky Grid below (pp. 13– 14), being similarly linked to Tozoztli and the year 1558 in *Legend of the Suns*.(**Fig. 8.3; Table 4**)

In these 'double entry' estimates of solar precession and sidereal procession, the Mexicanus page in fact repeatedly finds parallels in the *Legend of the Suns*. Both texts appeal to the same Xiuhmolpilli ending 1558 and to the same 1540 base before it, reckoning the intermediary 18 years or quarter lifetime as equivalent in sidereal time to the quarter day that separated the starts of the Mexica and the Christian day. For both texts use these double entries to note years elapsed from the Era date 13 Reed 3113 BCE, and, simultaneously, the days gained meanwhile by the sidereal over the solar year, which are measured as Feast dates. Both texts gather these extra sidereal days (or nights) in the series of 22 originally signalled by the penance performed by Nine Wind (position 22 in the Tonalpoualli) on the first day of Tozoztli (FI.I.I), series which produce just the 1551 years (22 x 70.5) on which the Julian wheel rests (1551–78).Yet more striking, the period of three such groupings, or 66 days, is twice spelt out in the Night Sky Grid designed for the purpose a few pages later in Mexicanus (pp.13–14). In *Legend*, the 66 days are counted from Tozoztli to 22 May Julian, which is 1 June Gregorian (i.e. FI.I.I to FI.4.7); as we saw, the latter is legible as the month date in Mexicanus (p.2) which specifies the uniquely significant moveable feast, Ember Day. As the complementary sidereal measure of years in the Era, this 66-day period corresponds precisely to the 3 x 1551 or 4,653 years that elapsed between 13 Reed (CI) 3113 BCE and 1540.

In sum, in this discussion of political time the notion of calendrical eras is analyzed through two wheels, one Mexica and the other Christian (p.9). Juxtaposing the two exposes the monotheistic rigidity and inaccuracy of the latter and the lack of correlation between eras identified variously with pagan Rome (Ab Urbe Condita), Diocletian, and the Anno Domini of Christ's life, at the same time as it celebrates the times of year and spans in the Era articulated through the Feasts. Contained on a single *tlacuilolli* page, the comparison made in Mexicanus of Mexica and Christian years and eras strongly vindicates the former, in the model of the three origins. The same is true of the other two origins, in comparisons between respective land use (pp.10–11) and blood penance (pp.12–15).

The planter's zodiac

Having established the coordinates of political eras and the hunter-warrior's enterprise (p.9), Mexicanus moves on to scrutinize Christian counterparts to the farmer's seasonal year (pp.10–11). In turning now to the planter and food production, it notes Julian inadequacy not just in the faulty measurement of the solar year, insisted on above, but in the fact that in the first place the Christian calendar ignored the difference between it and the sidereal year, even when rehearsing the zodiac's ecclesiastical links to the equinox and the effects that its constellations were imagined to have on the fields below. For the purposes of analysis and comparison, two zodiacs are shown, on facing pages, complete with the 12 signs and the 28 lunar stations, at two or three per sign. Each has its own configuration, that sets the other at a right angle, like the solar-year wheels on the preceding page. The juxtaposition similarly argues for categorical difference.

The first zodiac (p.10) begins with Aries, whose first point was identified in the Julian calendar with the March equinox, and therefore Easter. The Aries zodiac is aligned vertically in a column, and in it the stellar animals sit obediently one below the other, according to pastoral expectation. This zodiac column of solar and lunar stations in fact constitutes the axis of the Julian table of dominical and lunar letters and XIX Golden Numbers used to schedule Easter, as the first Sunday after the first full moon after the equinox. Historically, Rome's poor calendrics led to uncertainty about which Sunday was the right one, and to the Paschal Controversies that for centuries raged from Gaul to Ethiopia. The problem arose in part because by the time the Christians took over the pagan zodiac, Aries was already processing forward from the equinox, ceding its place to Pisces: whence the distinctive device of Christendom as not just the paschal lamb but the fish which provided Peter and his brother Andrew with their first job, on Lake Tiberias. Technically for Gregory, the 'shepherd' pope, the sidereal advance (or precession of the equinoxes) proved even harder to measure and deal with than the solar year. As a result of his Reform, the paschal table shown here in Mexicanus was deemed irremediable and abandoned entirely by Rome, along with all ritual interest in the movements of the night sky, beyond that of the synodic moon.

Obsolete, the equinoctial Aries zodiac in Mexicanus (p.10) is faced by its solstitial counterpart, which identifies Aquarius with January and the start of the civil year (p.11. **Pl. 2a**). Rather than a column, the 12 signs of this second zodiac are set in two horizontal registers, one above the other, which reading from left to right culminate in Cancer (above) and Capricorn (below), the constellations that in marking the solstitial limits of the sun's course came to name the northern and southern tropics. In this arrangement, the zodiac signs and lunar stations serve not as the axis of a table but shine down on the sublunar world of medieval philosophy, imaged here as the Aristotelian set of four 'elements', Air, Water, Fire and Earth, in triplicate. While the equinoctial Aries table is simply left as it was, abandoned in 1583, this solstitial configuration, directly pertinent to Tlaloc's seasons and the planter, is modified and habituated to the Mexica environment and norms.

Reading from bottom to top, we see first how the four elements are deconstructed. Air and Water are read as the natural forces that move the Twenty Signs, that is, Wind (II) and Rain (XIX). Emerging from a pale European face darkly, the former suggests the fetid breath of the colony, yet also proposes night as the first principle of knowledge, prior to Christ's light and enlightenment. Falling from solid ice at great height and then rising as mist, Rain indicates the physics of temperature detailed in similar images in Tepepulco (**Pl. 3**) and Laud (Tlaloc; p.45). Moreover, though 'sublunar', these primordial forces, lateral and vertical, were long known in Mexico to derive energy not from the moon but from the sun.

For their part, Fire and Earth, however natural, are considered also to depend on human agency. Far from being that improbable 'element' phlogiston, Fire may be kindled and can be precisely calculated in units of fuel and flame, as in Boban (**Pl. 8**), Fejérváry (**Fig. 3.5**) or Borbonicus (**Fig. 5.3**), these calculations being of especial interest to the goldsmith seen in Mendoza (f.70). Earth is measured most carefully, over four crescent moons squared off as months, in fields plotted, enriched, and worked by the obsidian hoe used by Otontecutli (**Fig. 6.8**). Just as European animals trashed the planted fields of the Mexica, so viceregal law was quickly exposed in *tlacuilolli* texts as incompetent in matters pertaining to land measurement, maintenance, crop rotation, irrigation, soil type and many other local codes in the highland Basin (as in codices from Cuauhtepoztlan and Tepotzotlan; PBM pp.172–6). Firm in its own right and rhythm, the Mexica system of planting seasons is stated in the field through the image of the obsidian hoe, which works the earth for eight months (12 Feasts) and is withdrawn from it during the remaining four (6 Feasts).

Rising to the sky from fire and field, we discover the sets of zodiac signs above, from Leo to Capricorn, and from Aquarius to Cancer. While at first sight these signs may be taken as standard, a closer look reveals several important modifications, similar to those made to the four elements below them. Though highlighted as the Julian solstice, Cancer appears not as a crab but a fish, while Gemini, by then the actual constellation marker of the solstice, appears not as twins but a fornicating couple. The fish of Pisces each grows four embryonic legs and Scorpio acquires the protean characteristics of the Colotl stars seen with Xonecuilli in Tepepulco (**Pl. 3b**); in inverse proportion, Libra appears the more lifeless (not of the zoo-diac), the intrusive twelfth inserted in imperial interest.

These adjustments recall the zodiac in Tovar, which like Mexicanus further contrives to connect Aquarius with Atemoztli, as Kubler and Gibson noted (see p.25 above). In these texts, the Mexica may be seen seizing on the visible similarity between Aquarius and Atemoztli in order to differentiate the more sharply between the sidereal time of the constellation as such and the solar time of the Julian month to which it is ignorantly assigned. In Mexicanus, Aquarius is made terrestrially to indicate both January and Atemoztli (F2.5), so as to gauge the actual difference between the course of the stars above and that of fieldwork below (pp. 10–11). That is, the text on the one hand establishes the constellation in its own right, rather than merely as a site for the sun to be 'in' (and obliterate with its light), and on the other fixes firm coordinates in the solar year of the Feasts cycle. For in TTTM the middle of Atemoztli coincides exactly with the winter solstice (F2.5.10, 21 December). This is precisely when, in the seasonal year of the Feasts, water is carried to the fields through 'water-bearer' aqueducts, in preparation for planting.

As the first of the upper six constellations, Aquarius vertically aligns with Leo, first of its lower six. Hence, the Water-bearer Aquarius must relate to Atemoztli (F2.5) as the feline Leo does to Tecuilhuitl (F1.5). Indeed, as the powerful feline Leo is legible in Mexica terms as the American counterparts that initiate just this lordly Feast in Tepoztecatl's temple (**Fig.6.6**) and in the Round Dance (**Pl. 4**). For good measure, the fish that replaces the crab of Cancer recalls the scaley fishskin Xonecuilli seen in the corresponding Feast Etzalcualiztli (F1.4. **Fig. 6.1**). Overall, this reading recasts the solstitial zodiac of Capricorn and Cancer as the year of the Feasts that runs from Tecuilhuitl to Etzalcualiztli, F1.5 to F1.4, in 'Genesis', *Cuevas*, and Borgia. In other words, it culminates in the good food supplied by the planter for Tlaloc's midsummer Feast Etzalcualiztli, turning outdated European apparatus to good use.

Precisely placed at the winter solstice, the Atemoztli emblem that is derived from Aquarius confirms the agricultural reading and takes it further. For the water currents caused by this 'water-bearer' are shown to flow in opposite directions, against the left-to-right reading below and together with it above. In the adjoining sign Pisces, these countercurrents are confirmed by the fish, who appear to swim in them, to left and right. Aquarius/Atemoztli becomes then the figure through whom are sensed the contrary movements over the year of the sun in precession (below, to the left) and the stars in procession (above, to the right). This notion is strengthened by the pastoral animals of Aries and Taurus, who in the paschal table sat as if tethered in pastoral obedience. For now they get up and start to move forward (**Pl. 2a**), effectively released by Gregory (despite his shepherd name), when he decoupled the night sky from the calendar. Unpenned, the bull and ram regain their sidereal autonomy, denoting their actual advance in the sky against the seasons (The equinoctial Taurus of millennia ago opens the year in Virgil's *Georgics*). The visual effect recalls that of Xonecuilli moving forward through Ochpaniztli in Borbonicus, or through Panquetzaliztli in 'Encounter with Europe', or again of the stars slipping forward above the mountain capped with 18 clouds in Tepexic Annals (**Fig. 2.6**). Meanwhile, on the ground in late 16th-century Mexico, in this behaviour the pastoral animals of the imported zodiac were responsible for the rampant invasion of planted fields often reported in the law courts.

In this context, the fornicating couple that displace Gemini may be identified as the Mesoamerican constellation seen in Diaz (p.9), occupying what appears to be a solstitial position in a map of the Coixtlahuaca domain. Uppermost, the enigmatic glosses attaching to Leo and Sagittarius supply a last detail. For the glosses confound the names of these constellations with each other and with Aries (the three 'fire' constellations), setting up just the pattern of thirds seen in Tepexic Annals with the New

Fire name 2 Reed, a celestial counterpart for the thirds of the seasonal year below. In the two-thirds of the year shown in the opening chapter (p.7), the Archer Sagittarius shoots his arrows backwards over his head as if to indicate monthly positions in the year that he had previously occupied, and is moving forward from, as the leading edge of his bow traverses the vertical margin of the column assigned to him (**Fig. 1.2**). The ever greater time dimensions generated by this solar-sidereal slippage are hinted at in the metamorphoses effected in the zodiac - crustacean crab to vertebrate fish, fish to fish with four legs - and explored in depth in what follows.

A priestly triptych

Completing the three services or origins of the year as well as the introductory argument in Mexicanus, the last four pages of the first part (pp.12–15) are dedicated to priestly knowledge, doubling the two that belong to the farmer (pp.10–11) as these double the single page of the hunter-warrior and the eras of political power (p.9). The doublings in length correspond to increasing complexity, already in terms of format. So that the play with $90°$ angle on the page grows to include the third dimension. For these last four pages physically constitute a triptych that hinges on the central leaf, which on either face (pp.12–13) records the Grid of the Mexica Night Sky. To each side extend corresponding Julian calculations, relevant to Corpus and blood-letting (left, p.12) and to Septuagesima and Lent in the very last years of the Julian era 1579–82 (right, p.15). To be properly read, these side pages to left and right need to be turned through $90°$, placing uppermost the margin that connects them to the Night Sky Grid, which is therefore both central and intermediary. The Grid on both of its pages is formed from 11 columns in six registers and it correlates the cycles of the Feasts and the Tonalpoualli (**Fig. 8.3**). As for the Feasts, the triptych as a whole brings together the concern with the equinoxes proper to political eras (F1.9, F2.9, p.9) and the farmer's concern with the solstices (F1.5, F2.5, pp.10–11), integrating them into the understanding of time that synchronizes heartbeat with the aeons of genesis, the coursings of both blood and stars.

The male figure to the left of the Grid (p.12) has been identified by Prem as an *Aderlassmännchen*, of the kind seen in medieval charts which connect with organs of the body to the constellations for the purpose of letting blood from the veins (*Ader*). In other words, the chart is physiologically the equivalent of the accounts of bloodletting seen in Telleriano and *Cuevas* and detailed numerically by Motolinia, the priestly 'first service' of *Coloquios* ('that's why we draw our blood and do penance…' (**Appendix E**; cf. p.21 above). Wounds in the body that reveal heart and innards, stigmata on the hands, and vestiges of a crown suggest that this particular male body belongs to Christ, the Corpus Christi through which the supreme blood sacrifice was made ('take, drink, this is my blood that was shed for you…'). This surmise is supported by the argument so far (Peter, Paschal Tables) and by the matching page to the right of the triptych. This specifies the ecclesiastical dates of Christ's Passion (Septuagesima, Lent) for the very last years of the Julian era, 1579–82. Hence, in the year cycle the Night Sky Grid must fall between Corpus, the Thursday after the end of Eastertide, and the very beginnings of Easter in Septuagesima and Ash Wednesday (**Fig. 8.4**). This intercalation is fully confirmed by the Feast sequence entered in Grid, which begins after Corpus in late Tecuilhuitl B (F1.6.17; 21 July) and ends before Septuagesima in Panquetzaliztli (F2.4.8; 29 November).

In engaging with the central mysteries and doctrines of Christianity in this triptych, Mexicanus continues the critique already developed with respect to the years of Roman empire and of agriculture. It similarly works out from technicalities of the calendar towards larger philosophy. Through the blood penance of Corpus, the vertebrate human body is reclaimed in the first instance by the quite un-Christian sense of its origins generated by the Twenty Signs. This is exactly what happens in Rios, where in its discussion of blood penance the whole set of Twenty Signs, rather than constellations, is arrayed around a similar *Aderlassmännchen* (f.54). In Mexicanus, the Spanish names of body parts are ingeniously punned with the Nahuatl names of the Signs, among them Ollin (XVII) and Cuetzpalin (IV), though with less conviction than in Rios, as if the gap between Mexica. and Christian theories of the body were too large to bridge. For not only had Christianity developed its own very different ideas of the body, but in linking its parts to the night sky laboured under the severe calendrical defects already noted, so that nocturnal bleeding was mainly left to doctors, secular yet no better informed. The lines that propose here to link the body to the constellations, arranged in two rows like the farmer's zodiac yet barely distinguishable, are jumbled, twisted and blurred, and strikingly lack the precision characteristic of the Mexica first service that synchronized pulse and sidereal time.

To the right of the triptych, the beginnings of Eastertide are shown to allow for a little more interplay with Mexica norms. To begin with, the 40 days of Lent were readily recognizable as those of a double Feast. Septuagesima Sunday falls nine weeks before Easter, just the span of 63 days which then conjoins Maundy Thursday to its recollection in Corpus; Pentecost falls seven weeks after Easter (i.e. 7 x 7 days): these rhythms of seven and nine concord directly with those of the Tonalpoualli, which constructs the 260 nights of human gestation as $2(7^2+9^2)$. As weekdays, Ash Wednesday and Good Friday – Rome's only surviving fasts – epitomize the inner planets after which they are named, Mercury and Venus which disappear in the west, journey through the underworld, and re-appear heliacally in the east, like Quetzalcoatl or the Twins in the *Popol vuh*. The full extent of Eastertide, from Septuagesima to Ember Day (the Wednesday after Pentecost) exactly tracks Mercury on this journey, over its synodic period of 116 days (63+53). In Mexicanus, Ember Day has been shown to be the focus of unique attention, as the only moveable feast to be noticed in the opening chapter. The resurrection and rebirth of Easter itself is anticipated in the Paschal Vigil, in the New Fire, so named: this is kindled in the night, and the calendar year is inscribed on the candle as in the image of the 1559 Mexica New Fire recorded in the Mexicanus annals (p.83).

Parallels of this order cannot but recall what Durán was told by the Mexica priestess: 'We too had Christmas and Easter like you ... and Corpus Christi...' (see p.25 above). Perhaps in that very spirit, the Mexica even offer to correct the ecclesiastical apparatus of dominical letters and Golden Numbers on this page of the triptych, adducing their fine calculation of precession and the solar-sidereal slippage. This fact (though not its stunning implications) is acknowledged even by the sceptical Hanns Prem

(1978:278). Yet overall the very connections Mexicanus endeavours to establish here between its own and Christian philosophy tend to rely most on precisely the understandings most suppressed or damaged in the history of the Roman church. For example, the 116-day synodic period of Mercury (Hermes, Wotan), Wednesday's planet, was a concept fundamental to the Hermetic Books of early Christendom, which in Egypt were censored no less savagely than the screenfolds were to be in Mexico, once the Orders got to work. Rome deemed it heretical to believe that Christ, descending to Hell and rising again, could be entreated as the psychopomp Hermes who disappears in the west only to reappear soon in the east, the drama being most heightened at the equinoxes. Moreover, whatever intelligence remained of pagan Europe's world ages and the great antiquity of creation was effectively annulled by Rome's atrocious mathematics, which simply did not allow for complex articulations of time.

Such an assessment might be deduced from the way Mexicanus chooses to represent the very beginnings of Eastertide on this page, with dates good for the final Julian years 1579 to 1582 (which read on directly from the dominical wheel that ends with 1578 on page 9). The calendrical information it gives makes play not just with *tlacuilolli* signs and glyphs but with letters from the Latin and other alphabets, roman and the recently acquired arabic numbers that made the Gregorian Reform practicable. The page has four registers, one for each year, and nine columns, which specify the year dates in the era AD, their Golden Numbers (corrected as we noted) plus dominical letters, and the month dates for Septuagesima and Ash Wednesday, 17 days apart, in the period from mid-January to early March. In the rows corresponding to 1579 and 1580, installments of years AD are piled up in roman fashion, in a tree-like structure which has no roots and withers away in 1581 and 1582: compared with the trees that count time in 'Genesis' and at Pahuatlan (**Fig. 2.2**), these Julian specimens appear spindly and top heavy. More critically, the Julian count of these years AD is exposed as defective and unviable already by the accompanying arabic numbers 1579 and 1580, since 10 years are missing in each case, furthering the 10-year lag seen with the dominical wheel (p.9). This suggests a shamanic shift between Gregory's 10 lost days that accumulated over 1,280 years, and 10 lost years which accumulate in just under half a million years, that is, in the multiples of Great Years characteristic of Mexica accounts of the world ages, which presuppose orders of sidereal and evolutionary time unsuspected by Rome.

Headed by the faces of the Lord (Sunday) and of the ash-daubed penitent (Wednesday), the final two columns give the dates for Septuagesima Sunday and Ash Wednesday as days in the month. The rows for 1579 and 1580 draw on the resources of both *tlacuilolli* and imported numbers and script (**Fig. 8.4**), while the notation for 1581 and 1582 involves only roman numbers and the alphabet, deliberately confusing *enero* and *febrero* (in just the fashion seen in the literally confused gloss *agosto/sagittarios* in the farmer's zodiac, p.11). The entries for Septuagesima and Ash Wednesday in 1579 make great play with the Tonalpoualli, appropriate to the fact that nine in the year date AD is registered as nine darkened disks, which through the same shamanic shift evoke the nine nights and the nine moons definitive of that human gestation cycle. Accordingly, the Twenty Signs are featured in a curious-looking dog with two

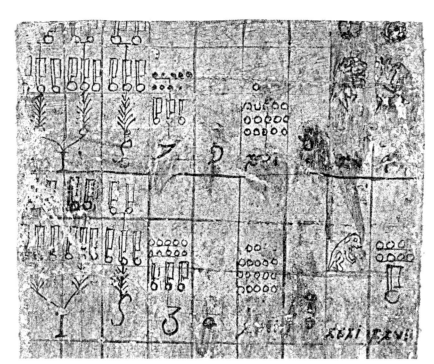

Figure 8.4 Septuagesima and Ash Wednesday table for 1579–1580. Mexicanus p.15

tails, and a human hand whose digits lack the opposing thumb. The dog points phonetically in Spanish (*perro*) to *febrero*, while its head and the other tail, which is phallic, give the Signs X and V, Dog and Snake, and hence the 'xv' in the text that confirms these *tlacuilolli* numerals. On Ash Wednesday, the hand with four digits is pierced by a nail like Christ's, which phonetically in Nahuatl yields *ma-tzo*, hence *marzo*, while the four digits are confirmed as iv. In 1579, Septuagesima and Ash Wednesday fell respectively on 15 February and 4 March (Prem 1978: 279).

In 1580, the very last leap-year of the Julian era, the *tlacuilolli* reference just as appropriately becomes the year, that other great cycle of the Mexica and the Mesoamerican calendar. The Septuagesima month date, 31 January, is correctly given in a roman xxxi (which in context can belong only to the month of January) accompanied by a metamorphic vertebrate, saurian tail with head and ear of a hare or rabbit, that resembles the Xiuhcoanaual, albeit in sadly reduced shape. In the Mexica year, the 31 January of this 1580 Septuagesima coincided with the end of the very Feast, Izcalli (F2.7), with which the protean Xiuhcoanaual has been seen to feature most, at the time of year naming and in memory of the aeons over which life has grown from this caiman earth. At the time Mexicanus was written, Septuagesima was still the moment in their year that Christians chose most to ponder the origins of the world, in prescribed readings from Genesis, which very dimly reflected the philosophy inherent in the Xiuhcoanaual. This remarkable ninth Sunday before Easter, which, through the seven and nine portals that conjoin our inner and outer beings, once correlated creation with Hermes and the moon, has now been abolished by Rome entirely (though it survives in the Anglican rite), leaving its wisdom to custom, in the pagan and decidedly more ancient Easter hare (*Osterhase*) who, mad in March, lays eggs like a saurian.

Falling on 17 February in 1580, the corresponding date for Ash Wednesday is stated in roman numerals, not as xvii however, but as xxvii. In other words, in this final Julian leap year the roman number correctly anticipates the Gregorian date 27 February; moreover, 27 is initially stated in *tlacuilolli* numerals as 20, the banner *pantli*, below seven small disks.

Arithmetically, the *tlacuilolli* statement augments the 10 finger digits of the Christian decimals to the 20 whole body digits of tropical American vigesimals, placing them below the seven head orifices. In the night sky, it affirms the cycle of the sidereal moon, counted in the 27 lunar letters abolished by Gregory. Above all, in the year cycle signposted in this 1580 row of dates by the Xiuhcoanaual of Septuagesima, the *pantli* banner may be read as a Feast emblem, specifically as that of the New Fire Feast Panquetzaliztli (F2.4) highlighted in the Grid, as we shall see.

As the right wing of the triptych that concludes the first part of Mexicanus (p.15), the 1579–82 table may be said in all to sustain the priestly interface between the Christian and Mexica calendars begun on the left (p.12), focusing on the life embodied in Easter. Just as Christendom's scant love of the earth had starved its rootless millennial tree and stunted the aeons of vertebrate life, so in the Julian year it misread the rhythms of the day and night sky no less than it offered only narrow and heartless correction in Gregory's Reform. Reaffirming the marvel of the Mexica system, the intermediary Night Sky Grid has the last word (pp.13–14), as a very firm and clear statement sufficient in itself, which as before works out from the Julian calendar to its own system. Its appeal is not obviously visual, since it mainly employs roman letters and numerals and appears simply schematic, neutral and soul-less. Yet it condenses volumes and tells much, in *tlacuilolli* fashion, through the smallest details of layout and notation.

In establishing the Grid, the two sides of the central leaf of the triptych (which cannot be simultaneously visible) each spells out two sequences of 66 nights and days, from Tecuilhuitl B F1.6.17 to Pachtli A F2.1.2 (p.13), and from Pachtli A F2.1.3 to Panquetzaliztli F2.4.8 (p.14; **Fig. 8.3**), and correlates them the Tonalpoualli dates that run from 1 Water to 2 Flower (1 IX to 2 XX). Thereby, the opening date elegantly effects the transition from Julian to Mexica time, via Mercury's 116-night synodic period (0.5.16 in vigesimal Feast notation) which, having determined Christ's epic journey as Hermes from Septuagesima to Ember Day, may now carry us from the start of the Mexica year (F1.1.1) to the start of the Grid (F1.6.17. **Table 4**).

This recovery of Mexica norms means converting the duodecimal arithmetic of the imported zodiac, with its 12 houses of the sun, to the numerical system of the American tropics which as this very text explicitly proclaims (p.36) turns on the night sky cipher 11. Hence, the 11 columns that run down the six registers of each Grid page, to form 66+66 constituent squares, produce the cumulative count of 11 ($1+2+3+4+5+6+7+8+9+10+11 = 66$). By the same logic, the 6 lots of 20s that extend from the first Feast (F1.1.1) to the first Feast actually to be named on the Grid (F1.7.1) may be understood to be enclosed by 11 lots of 11 nights (121).

As the first named Feast, Micailhuitl A occupies the fifth square (F1.7.1), which explicitly ties the 132 squares in the Grid to days in the year. By this means, binary arithmetic comes to complement that of the night-sky elevens, since $4:128::2^2:2^7$ This corresponds to the dental count seen at the same conjuncture in Borgia (32 teeth, p.29) and in Fejérváry (4+4 teeth, p.17), which structures this first part of Mexicanus, pp.9, 10–11, 12–15, 1–8 = $1+2+4+8$ pages. On these pages (Mexicanus p.4) as in Fejérváry (pp.15–16) and Laud (pp.21–22), Micailhuitl is recalled as the Feast when the newly deceased travel beyond death, experiencing as years the four days dedicated to them by those who mourn. In these years, then, the 4+128 numerically determined by this Feast confirm the leap-year calculations and shamanic time shift already established in the text.

The notation which effects this time shift between days and years belongs, however, to the Tonalpoualli, the third of the main concurrent series operative in the Grid, along with the elevens of the format and the named Feasts. For, occupying the fifth square, the first day of Micailhuitl A (F1.7.1) is named by the Sign Reed, which of course is therefore true of the subsequent six Feasts in the Grid whose first days, 20 days and Signs apart, are also named Reed, with the numerical co-efficients 5, 12, 6, 13, 7, 1, 8, [2], the name of every 40th day coinciding in ascending sequence with that of every 40th year (5 Reed, 6 Reed, 7 Reed etc.). With consummate elegance, this characteristic of the Grid brings home the fact that the initial 5 Reed equals the year 1575 AD marked on the Julian wheel (p.9) as the Augustinians' arrival in San Pablo Teipan; for good measure, the friars came at the end of July (Aubin f.59v), that is, here at the start of Micailhuitl A. Eight years before the end of the Julian era in 13 Reed 1583,

5 Reed 1575 equates 4+4 years with as many days (as in the Atamalcualiztli, and the Christian octave - octaeteris). Just this equation along with others relevant to moon and the planets is located in the same Feast Micailhuitl in Fejérváry (pp.15–16; see Fig. 3.2 above), and through the same arithmetic of 11s and 22s it is likewise tied to the Tonalpoualli day 1 Water. The first in the Grid here, four days before 5 Reed, 1 Water begins the last fifth of the Tonalpoualli, and therefore establishes the 4:1 ratio defined on the Sunstone as both of the hand and of the Era within the Great Year. Yet more striking, in Fejérváry as in Laud all this happens at the transition choreographed in the year between the 11 thin and the 7 fat Feasts, just as here the 5 Reed of Micailhuitl projects through 7 full Feasts to the end of Panquetzaliztli, the midnight of 2 Reed at which Atemoztli begins (F2.4.20/F2.5.1).

Of the Feasts that are included in the Grid, from Tecuilhuitl B to Panquetzaliztli, only one is privileged by starting in the first of the 11 columns: Ochpaniztli, which is also underlined for

emphasis. Dedicated to Teteu innan, the Mother of the Gods, Ochpaniztli culminated in the September equinox (F1.9.20), as we have repeatedly noted, and certainly had no less significance than Easter, opposite to it at the March equinox, has had for Christendom. In its privileged position in the Grid and beginning in 6 XIII, Ochpaniztli incorporates a new Tonalpoualli start (1 I), so that its equinoctial ending announces names consecrated in the Era, 13 Reed (13 XIII) and 1 Jaguar (1 XIV), which conclude the 66 on the first page. Furthermore, given its unique position in the initial column, the first day of Ochpaniztli (F1.9.1) apportions the 66 squares of the first page into subgroups of 44 and 22. These multiples of 11 have multiple functions in the Grid, 44 nights being half the sidereal cycle of Mercury, and the 22nd night of the Tonalpoualli being consecrated as Nine Wind. Similar multiples are counted in Borbonicus (p.11) as dots of effervescent pulque and on maguey paper in the Coixtlahuaca Map (**Fig. 1.7b**).

If the first day/night of Ochpaniztli (F1.1.1; 6 XIII), on the first page, is uniquely distinguished in the Grid on grounds of format, then the same is true of Panquetzaliztli (F2.4.1; 8 XIII), on the second page, on grounds of notation, 40+40 squares later (**Fig. 8.3**). For this Feast is the only one of those listed to be accorded its *tlacuilolli* emblem, the banner or *pantli* that we saw introduced into the Septuagesima table. With its banner, Panquetzaliztli is richly identified with the last autonomous New Fire in 2 Reed 1507 in Borbonicus (**Fig. 5.3**), and other sources (Its emblem is similarly made to stand out, along with the Sign Reed, in Aubin f.42v, in the alphabetic account of Cortés's arrival). The link established by the Mexica between this Feast Panquetzaliztli (F2.4) and New Fire encourages us in conclusion to look at the night sky which historically determined the zenith midnight at which New Fire was kindled.

At Moctezuma's last great New Fire ceremony in 2 Reed 1507, the star occupying the midnight zenith in the year was in fact Aldebaran, the red eye of the Bull Taurus, long favoured by scholars as one of the red tips of the 'fire-drill' constellation Mamalhuaztli (**Pl. 3a**). At that time, Aldebaran in fact attained the zenith at midnight on nothing other than the first day of Panquetzaliztli (F2.4.1), 21 November, following in the footsteps of the Pleiades, which had reached and moved on from that position about 11 midnights previously (10 November). As a result, the 66+66 days in the Grid, with its rows of 11 days, can be usefully consulted as a guide to the positions of red-tipped Aldebaran and the Pleiades over the year, as they are plotted in Borgia and its derivative Tepepulco, along with the Pleiades's 'rival' constellation Market, and the polar Xonecuilli that projects to the scorpion Colotl. Beginning as Tecuilhuitl B ends, the Grid effectively starts with the dates of the heliacal risings of the Pleiades and Aldebaran, at dawn in the east, after the critical disappearance caused by their proximity to the sun in that Feast. The disappearance of the Pleiades from the night sky in Tecuilhuitl A and its astronomical significance are noted in that Feast in Telleriano (f.1; see **Fig. 2.1**), along with the corresponding ascendancy of Market, which is so celebrated in Borgia, at the other celestial crossroads of zodiac and Milky Way.

While the midnight zenith of the Fire Drill Mamalhuaztli can be fairly equated with the start of Panquetzaliztli (F2.4.1) in 2 Reed 1507, by the time Mexicanus came to be written that position was attained one midnight later (F2.4.2); moreover, it had already moved forward by five days since the Mexica set off from Aztlan. In Mexicanus, the forward shift is actually recorded in the annals, both at the first New Fire in 2 Reed 1195 and in their full span (see p.12 above and p.93 below), 423 years that correspond exactly to the forward shift of six midnights that occurred between 1168 and 1590 (423 = 70.5 x 6). Hence, using the 'lifetime plus semester' formula of 70.5 years, the days in the Grid may further be read not just as Mamalhuaztli positions in the night sky in any one year, but as the days that the midnight zenith of that star, following the Pleiades, advances in the solar year of the Feasts every 70.5 years. In this case, the groupings of days in the Gird, in the lots of 22 determined by Ochpaniztli, correspond exactly to the span of 1551 years specified earlier in the dominical wheel (p.9), since that span is the product of 22 and 70.5; and as we noted, the 66 precessional days in each Grid are commensurate with the Era. On inspection this span of 66 days (0.3.6) recorded in each half of the Grid proves to be fundamental to the whole text, since it also ties the Grid start in F1.6.17 back to the mid-Toxcatl *tlachialoni* that dominates the opening page of Mexicanus (F1.3.10). As for the corresponding Tonalpoualli dates, including the 13 Reed and the Four Ollin of the Era, these are permutated in their own right in the Trecenas in final chapter (pp.89–), which though much effaced highlight the emblems of Tlacaxipehualiztli (F2.9) and Tozozotli (F1.1) and turn on the March as opposed to the September equinox.

That such fine awareness of sidereal time, mediated by the Feasts of the solar year, was not anomalous among the Mexica is suggested by double readings in comparable texts. Perhaps the most striking is *Legend of the Suns*, which opens by establishing a solar year position in 1558 at 22 May Julian, equal to Gregorian 1 June (cf. the Mexicanus Ember Day) and to F1.4.7 in the Feasts cycle. The narrative then casts back to the moment, at the start of the solar year in Tozoztli when humans first lit fire, causing smoke to rise to the stars. The interval is again the 66 days of the Grid (F1.1.1 + 0.3.6 = F1.4.7). Informed by the paradigms in Tepepulco and Borgia (**Pl. 3**; **Figs.6.3, 6.4**), a connection may again be made to the actual night sky. For rising vertically, the smoke is said to reach the nostrils of Citlalicue and Citlaltonac, in whose shared abodes the Milky Way intersects with the zodiac, each intersection having its own red-tipped fire drill, Mamalhuaztli: in this function, Aldebaran is to (and 11 days later than) the Pleiades as Antares is to (and 22 days earlier than) the 'rival' Market, the star clouds of the galactic hub, between Scorpio and Sagittarius. In 3113 BCE, 66 x 70.5 years before the by now familiar year 1540 (18 years or an imposed Christian quarter day before 1558), the midnight zenith was attained by Antares on 27 March of that year, that is, F1.1.1.

While these cross references may further vindicate the Mexica Feasts cycle as an astounding resource, they cannot be further developed here, given their complexity. (We have for example to bear in mind that the time counts in the Grid, proper to the numerical astronomy of tropical America, are not obliged to accommodate the distortions endemic in the points, lines and angles of western spatial astronomy.) Suffice it to recall that the Night Sky Grid in Mexicanus, perceived in this way, may articulate solar-sidereal slippage as the whole mechanism of the Mexica and Mesoamerican world ages, through the precessional days of the Great Year, and its fractions and multiples, and the shamanic principle of shifting via ciphers through time dimensions. Here we respect the Mexica estimate of the Great Year, which at 25,750 years (70.5 x 365.25) improves on the

classical 25,600. The fifth of this Year is the fifth Sun or world age, notionally the 5,200 years stated as 13 *tzontli* in 'Genesis' and as 100 New Fires on the Xiuhcoanaual rim of the Sunstone, the Olmec Era that starts in 3113 BCE, and whose equinox is Four Ollin for the Mexica, 11 Trecenas (4 XVII to 4 XX) before the Olmec and Maya start in Micailhuitl. The third of the Year is defined by the Fire constellations of the farmer's zodiac, whose earthly equivalent in structure are the Planting Seasons. The half is the equinoctial semester (F1.9, F2.9), measured as 32 *tzontli* in 'Genesis' (32 x 400 years), also as the two great Jades inset into Tepoztecatl's east-west doorway (twice 80^2 years); between the solstices, the half year switches between Atemoztli and Tecuilhuitl (F2.5.10, F1.5.10). In this regard, we may also note that of all the New Fire ceremonies in Mesoamerican history, only that celebrated by the Mexica in Panquetzaliztli in the 2 Reed 1507 had the distinction of exactly aligning the red-tipped Fire Drills Aldebaran and Antares with the poles, a configuration that occurs only twice during the Great Year (contrast Hassig 2001). The years of two such Years are counted in the pulse of the penitent over one night. The Nauhtetl or *cuatrenio*, explicit in the four great solar-ray year markers on the Sunstone no less than in the Series III year bearers borne by the Colotl constellation in Vaticanus (p.95), yields the '102,000' years stated in the *Histoire du Mechique* (ch.vii). Twice that span, the octaeteris, brings in the intermediary year markers on the Sunstone and is tied to human endeavour in Maya texts (BFW p.302). Thereafter, as we enter biological and then geological time, these measures increase proportionally, through 'cien temps de ceux... que font 102,000 ans' (HM, ch. vii; i.e.100 x 102,000 years), and the arboreal millennia of the Xiuhcoanaual (p.15) which conclude this first part of Mexicanus.

Ground rules

On turning the last page of the triptych (p.15) that concludes the first part of Mexicanus, the reader enters the firmly Mexica ground of the second part.(pp.16–88). On the initial facing pages (pp.16–17), the coordinates of this Mexica time-space are the lines of blood and political patronage conjoined in Acamapichtli at Tenochtitlan, set out in a Grid map which prefaces the 70-page annals that form the bulk of the text (pp.18–87). The pair of facing pages synthesizes the history recorded in *Cuevas...* and the other texts discussed in Eagle at Tenochtitlan (see pp.11–14 above), so that with the turn of the page, the reader effectively moves back from the last year of the Julian era in Mexico 13 Reed 1583 to the start of the Chichimec era in the following year 1 Flint, albeit going back through 18 Xiuhmolpilli (1584–936 = 648). Orientation is provided in the left-hand column, which matches the upper west and lower east registers of the Mendoza title page: it places Chichimec dog and moon above the '*pantli*-on-Jade' device and ailing sun, indicators respectively of the migrations from the northwest and the hiatus in the classic inscriptions dated to the 7th century AD in the Tepexic Annals and other screenfolds (**Fig. 8.5**). The calendrical antecedents of the Mexica year appear as the knotted Chichimec fibre of western Malinalco above the bulrushes of highland Tula, whose eight bare cactus-like heads indicate the much-bruited fall of that city in 1 Flint 1064 (648+416 = 1064). Once established at Tenochtitlan and the royal house at Teipan, Acamapichtli's power is furthered

Figure 8.5 Foundation map, with Chichimec moon above '*pantli*-on Jade' sun. Mexicanus p.16 (left side)

genealogically through the seven round bellies of concentric circles, of which this page frames a rectangular section.

Thus prefaced, the count of years begins in 1 Flint 1168 (p.18), after the Mexica have crossed the water to the mainland and set off on their long trek southeast to the Basin (**Fig. 8.6**). The journey acquires a rhythm of 6 + 6 due to the disposition of its turquoise square year markers, which cross at mid page in a horizontal band reminiscent of the lettered band in the first chapter. It also adheres to the norm of that chapter in reserving the lower register for specifically Mexica concerns. Over time this has the effect of counting the European invasion as just another external threat, and of emphasizing continuity in local rule on the ground, at least up to Valeriano (see p.75). Over 11 pages from 1201–66, after the first New Fire, the lower register comments alphabetically on the imported zodiac and in the name of Acamapichtli goes on openly to execrate its duodecimal 'peso' – the intrusive and lifeless constellation Libra (p.36; 'ynin amatl oquimacac in quimati quichicaz cale in rei acamapichtli...niman nimizmictiz peso'). A century later, at the time of Acamapichtli's inauguration, the upper register affords a glimpse, dated in Mexica years, of Rome's savage persecution of western popes in Gaul (pp.52–54).

Over their length of 423 years inclusive (1168–1590), these Series III annals first appear to observe a duodecimal rule, of 6 + 6 per page opening. In the classic annals, frequencies of years per page matter, as we saw for example with the sevens of Tlapa I and the octaeteris of Tlapa II. The duodecimal rule, the hallowed Christian norm, in Mexica terms invokes rather the bone-hard members of the Twenty Signs: VI and XII, skull and jaw, divisible and apt for Huitzilopochtli's *tzonpantli* abacus. In practice, over the 423-year span of the annals, the duodecimal rule is broken on highly significant occasions, at the beginning, and near and at the end. In these cases, the groupings and the kinds of year in question correspond to those operative in the set of three Pahuatlan screenfolds dated to 1975 (2 Reed), 1978 and 1981, a remarkable proof of calendrical faith and endurance in the New Era begun in 2 Reed 1559.

At the start, there is room for only 3 rather than 6 years on the first page (p.18; **Fig. 8.6**) since the travellers have first to leave the island Aztlan, and step up over water to the road level of the year-count, striding into their own rhythm. At the end, the final page-opening squeezes in 19 years, 10 (1572–81) on p.86 plus 9 (1582–90) on p.87, draining away colour and introducing arabic numerals, as if to highlight their role in the Gregorian

Figure 8.6 Departure from Aztlan in year 1 Flint 1168. Mexicanus p.18

Figure 8.7 Teuetzquititzin enthroned in year 10 House 1541, with mummy bundle of his predecessor behind him; year 11 Rabbit 1542 at page crease. Mexicanus pp.80-81

Reform which detached the XIX Golden Numbers from the night sky during those very years (as we noted; see p.86 above). The only other occasion when the duodecimal rule is broken occurs on a page opening of 11 rather than 12 years, 6 House 1537 to 3 Reed 1547 (pp.80–81), whose crease physically splits the Sign 11 Rabbit 1542 (**Fig. 8.7**). This anomaly may respond to the challenge openly posed to the native management of time, calendar and economics by the events recorded on these pages, with the installing of the first viceroy Mendoza (1535–40), in particular for Moctezuma's direct successor Teuetzquititzin who ascended to the throne (the last to be shown in the annals) in 1540–41 (cf. Aubin f.46v). The relentless imposition of European standards and law led to insistence on the Julian calendar and era, despite all the defects examined in the first part of the text. Numerically, the recovery of 11 from 12 of course obeys the Acamapichtli gloss on the zodiac (p.36).

The three exceptions to the duodecimal rule may so far be summarized in years as less 3 (3+6, p.18), less 1 (11, pp.80–81), and plus 7 (10+9, pp. 86–87). In supplying three rather than six years on the very first page, the first exception draws attention to the main body of 420 years, which equal six of the lifetimes of 70 years basic to calendars throughout North America, not least the extra-tropical Mexica homeland. Recorded as such in Mendoza (f.71), three of these lifetimes are imaged in the migration south from Aztlan which culminated in the installing of Acamapichtli, in three decimal seven-leaf branches (Boturini p.2). The same branches recur and are doubled to six on the 'Dios del arbol' tree in the Pahuatlan screenfold of 1978 (p.27), which exactly specify the 420 years elapsed in the New Era from 1559 to that date (**Fig. 2.2**). At the close of the annals, in registering 19 rather than 12 years on the final pages (pp.86–87), the third exception adds an extra seven to what otherwise would have been the expected 416. This total is readily construed as eight lots of 52 years, the Xiuhmolpilli of New Fire. Again, the set of three Pahuatlan screenfolds provides the modern corollary, in the text dated to 1975, which is precisely the New Fire year 2 Reed, 416 years distant from 2 Reed 1559. As Mexicanus has confirmed for us, just as the 70-year lifetime corresponds to the leaves fed by the sun, so the 52-year Xiuhmolpilli corresponds to the constellations in the night sky. It is the slippage between these two kinds of year, solar and sidereal, measured in the Grid as the lifetime plus semester or 70.5 years, which accounts for the full 423 span of these annals, as it does for the date of the third Pahuatlan screenfold, 1981, that is 423 years in the New Era of 1559, each text respecting the stellar advance of 6 nights during this period (1168–1590; 1559–1981). In the Mexicanus annals, as in those of Azcatitlan, the advance of the night sky is actually anticipated at the first New Fire at Coatepec in 2 Reed 1195, where the solar Huitzilopochtli combats the stars and resists the three nights of their advance over his year that would accumulate by the time the first imperial New Fire was kindled in Tenochtitlan (see p.12 above).

As for the remaining exception to the duodecimal rule in these Mexicanus annals, it reduces 12 years to 11 at the time of Mendoza and Teuetzquititzin (1537–47) and can be fairly regarded as the chronological crux of the whole 423-year sequence. For the splitting of the year 11 Rabbit 1542 at the crease of pages 80–81 is uneven and produces a very thin initial wedge followed by a much fatter one (**Fig. 8.7**). Visually at the page opening, this prefers a whole unit count of five years that end in 10 House (1537–41) followed by 6 years that begin in 11 Rabbit (1542–47). Structurally, this has the consequence of dividing the whole 423-year narrative into a first main period of 374 years (1168–1541), and a subsequent period of 49 years (1542–1590). Hence, invoking longer time rhythms, it reveals a sublimely graceful formula that subjects the composite duodecimal of Christianity to the series of tough primes that exist within it, privileging precisely the higher primes that have most native resonance in sky and earth, 11 before and 7 after:

$$11 \, (3^2 + 5^2) + 7^2 = 423$$

That a reading of this order is appropriate is suggested by the fact that it fully accounts for irregularities in the text which can hardly have been random. It is also borne out in the fact that Tlacotecpatl's gloss on the imported zodiac (pp.24–34), which goes on to state the need to eliminate Libra and restore the 11 live zoodion, is spread exactly over the middle one of the 'elevens' sequences in question (1201–66), which moreover equals the cumulative count of 11, that is the 66 of the Grid. The overall translation of Christian duodecimals into 11 and 7, the

Figure 8.8 Road to heaven. Mexicanus p.88

constituent primes of the Feasts and indeed prime throughout tropical America, reads then:

pp.18–23: 1168–1200 = 3 x 11 = 33
pp.24–34: 1201–66   = 6 x 11 = 66 (zodiac gloss)
pp.35–80: 1267–1541 = 25 x 11 = 275
pp.81–88: 1542–90   = 7 x 7   = 49.

After 7 Rabbit 1590 (p.87), the road of years runs on in palimpsest across the middle of the next page (p.88), though it no longer defines or names them individually. It is crossed by the popular 'Camino del cielo' of the time, the path trodden by converts which, however, veering back here ascends through a star cluster not to the heaven they are told to believe in but the thickets of a pagan forest whose arboreal 'devil' resists Christian

remonstration. Accordingly, of the 12 stars shown at the intersection of the roads, one is set apart, leaving the ever meaningful 11 (**Fig. 8.8**).

Once approached in good faith, Mexicanus may be seen to affirm and update the Mexica intellectual tradition to which it belongs, for which the world has few rivals. Indispensable to the challenge to Europe issued in this text are the 18 Feasts, discipline for Julian inconsistency, and the constant yardstick for the years of empire, agriculture and priestly knowledge. In this, Mexicanus throughout corroborates and is corroborated by the most authoritative texts in the Mexica tradition. On the road to the close reading that it demands, and has scarcely received, this is just a first step.

9
To End is to Begin

What, then, have these texts of the Mexica taught us about their year and its 18 Feasts? Less, most surely, than what remains to be learned, but above all that they indeed reward respect for their authority, and that, ever since the *Coloquios* of 1524, such respect has supported the better insights of western scholarship. If this is so, then it is due to the ways that *tlacuilolli* embodies philosophies and paradigms of time at moments coincident, yet more often not, with those of the invasive west. For, in refusing the Euclidean/Newtonian divorce between time and space, texts in this script grant greater intensity to number and rhythm. Similarly, a *tlacuilolli* table or grid will in some way always indicate its own moment in history, as is classically the case with the opening pages of Borgia or Cospi, and will be held by coordinates that are never altogether abstract visually on the page, as format, layout, and icon. In this way they embody a resistance in principle to the procedures and apparatus favoured by the western scholar. Examples most pertinent to our enquiry have included *tlacuilolli* embodiments of the year in the protean caiman Xiuhcoanahual and the winged Quecholli, and its choreography on the human stage.

Founded on its stone cactus, Tenochtitlan scheduled the Feasts as the tribute deadlines of its empire, whose boundaries reached east to what is Guatemala today. As the Mexica court, the city concentrated the material and imaginative wealth that flowed into it, likewise according to the Feasts, in dances which the European invaders readily conceded were the most brilliant they (the world) had seen. Its particular glory shimmered as the Mexica feather crown, in the long story of Mesoamerican empire, the 'acquisition of the hunt' ('tlamaliztli') whose beginnings the *Coloquios* identify with Hueycan Tollan, in the eastern lowlands. The Feasts of this urban year coordinated the multiple cycles and rhythms of city and empire, not least the political rituals of naming and kindling New Fire every 52 years. In this, as in their promotion of the turquoise year and of the 12-Feast planting season, the Mexica can be seen to owe a particular debt to their immediate predecessors and fellow hunter immigrants from the northwest, the Chichimec.

The Feasts of the peasant farmer, especially the 'good food' eaten in Etzalcualiztli (F1.4, also the first tribute quarter), are traced back to Tlaloc and the agricultural triumph that enabled maize to become the staple of human flesh (our supper and breakfast, in tococha in toneuhca). In the *Popol vuh*, humans are made of maize, even before the founding of the first city, Tollan, that is, very long before Tenochtitlan was dreamt of. The rhythms and seasons of this humble and enduring farmer's year are regulated by Feasts appropriate or not for planting. Over the generations, they accumulate as lifetimes, the 70-year hoop of the northern Winter Counts, and the 'three-score years and ten' shown on the last page of Mendoza.

Socially operative for millennia in Mesoamerica and consecrated in classic architecture, the opposition between

hunter-warrior and farmer is overseen by those who have deserved yet greater respect: the patron-deity priests, whose classical prototype is Quetzalcoatl Nine Wind, and who over the year and courses of four years (Nauhtetl) earn their authority through the most rigorous blood penance and demanding vision quest. (At Palenque, hunter and farmer face each other to west and east, below Nine Wind's higher temple to the north; at Yaxchilan, penance enables the royal pair to see/dream the Xiuhcoanaual). This self-sacrifice is what merits recompense in tribute and hence validates in the first place the existence of empires like that of Tenochtitlan and the cities that preceded it (as the *Popol vuh* puts it, this penance is the 'price of light and life and the price of lordship'; lines 8281–2). In the Mexica year, while the penance was done by nights counted by the Tonalpoualli, the recompense was paid according to the sun, at the equinoxes and quarters

The origins of this higher year are traced yet further back into darkness (*onoc youaya*), before the city, before agriculture, to earliest shamanic self discipline and intelligence of the night sky. Here, the story of the Feasts is no longer simply traced back. Rather, it obeys shamanic principles in shifting between dimensions of time, whereby the longest night may feel like a year, and human heartbeats through the night intimately echo the slow advance of the stars above and the sidereal year. Mexicanus shows that the rate of this sidereal advance was calculated as six nights every 423 years, one night for the 70-year lifetime, plus a semester. Most ancient, this knowledge of the year is explicit in *tlacuilolli* in screenfold books of native paper produced today.

These years have been examined in depth in the preceding chapters, first of all with a view to establishing the correlation with the Christian calendar here designated as TTTM, that is, the initial letters of the four *tlacuilolli* texts – Tepepulco, Tovar, Telleriano, Mexicanus – which collectively affirm and validate it, with an accuracy and consistency unavailable in any other sources. On this basis, the function of these years has been exemplified with respect to tribute (3), planting (4), and the courtly dance (5–6), as well as a cycle within calendar wheels (7), and in comparisons with the Julian year in Mexicanus (8) that are highly demanding yet have the advantage of relying on calendrical data undisputed in scholarship. The discussion no doubt raises as many questions as it perhaps begins to answer and certainly leaves much barely said. The intricate Xiuhmolpilli wheel in *Cuevas* (p.30), for example, disposes the Thirteen Quecholli numbers in just the ratios that, along with 9+9, define the year of the Mexica Feasts to most purpose, that is, as 11+7, 12+6 and 13+5 (**Table 3c**) and thereby impinge on the arithmetic of the Feasts and lunar fractions seen in Borbonicus (**Fig.4.6**), Mexicanus, *Cuevas*, and the Veytia Wheels. Again, persistent echoes in texts in part traceable back to Teotihuacan propose Huitzilopochtli's year as 17 Feasts, plus the footprint supplement of 5 x 5 days. Such formulations demand further enquiry into the Mexica Nauhtetl and Nemotemi.

In keeping us close to the concept of representation and of *tlacuilolli* as script, all the texts quoted would benefit from more extensive illustration than has been possible here. On the basis of what has been demonstrated it would be fair to claim that, in the calendar of the Mexica, the 18 Feasts enjoy greater prominence and privilege than has generally been supposed, and that historically they infused experience of the far northwest into the classical east. Hence, concentrating on them may afford greater insight not just into Mexica culture but into the larger and still understudied phenomenon of the year calendar in Mesoamerica (as it appears, for example, in Nowotny's 'Enigmatic Chapters'), and even beyond.

Appendix: Nahuatl Texts in Translation

As articulations of time which both begin with creation of the world itself and yet go on to reflect on the European invasion, these statements elaborate concepts fundamental to the Feasts cycle. They indicate how multiplicities of meaning may be encoded in corresponding *tlacuilolli* images featured in the Plates, Figures and Tables. The English translations are largely re-worked from those listed for the respective sources in the Bibliography.

A. The world ages or Suns in which the current Era inheres

The first sun to be founded has the Sign Four Water, it is called Water Sun.
Then it happened that water carried everything away, everything vanished.
The people were changed into fish.

The second sun to be founded has the Sign Four Jaguar, it is called Jaguar Sun.
Then it happened that the sky collapsed, the sun did not prevail, made it only halfway (*nepantla*).

Immediately it was night and in the dark people were torn to pieces.
This was when the giants lived. The old ones would say their greeting was:
'Don't fall over', for whoever fell, fell forever.

The third sun to be founded, Sign Four Rain, is called Rain Sun.
It happened then that fire rained down, and burned all who lived there.
They say that then the tiny stones rained down and spread, the fine stones that we can see.
The *tezontli* boiled into stone, and the reddish rocks twisted up.

The fourth sun, Sign Four Wind, is called Wind Sun.
Then the wind carried everything away.
The people all turned into monkeys and went to live in the forests.

And the fifth sun, Sign Four Ollin, is called Earthquake Sun, because it quivered into life.
The old ones said it will bring earthquakes and general hunger, from which we shall perish.

Cuauhtitlan Annals f.2

B. Phenomena of sky and earth

When the sun appeared incense was offered, birds were sacrificed, blood was drawn. It was said: 'The sun has risen, now it will work, will labour. How will the day be?'
    The second incense offering was made at the eating hour.
    The third, when the sun reached halfway (*nepantla*)

The fourth when the sun was on its way down
The fifth when the sun had set. It was said: 'The sun has done its work, has laboured'.

Fire Sticks (Mamalhuaztli). When the sun had gone and darkness came the first offering of incense was made. It was said: 'Yohualtecuhtli Yacahuitztli has appeared, now it will work, will labour.'
    And the second incense offering was made when it was completely dark.
    The third incense offering was made at bedtime.
    The fourth incense offering was made at the fluting. When the sign of Fire Sticks, and The Many (Miec), and Market (Tianquiz) reached halfway, then the flutes were sounded. Thus it was called the fluting.
    The fifth incense offering was made at what was called midnight. Then blood was drawn, thorns were taken, in the thorn penance. And the signs of Fire Sticks, and The Many, and Market were on their way down.
    The sixth incense offering was made when the morning star appeared.
    And the seventh incense offering was made when it began to dawn and the sign of the morning star replaced that of the Many.

Tepepulco Ms II, i

C. Hymns to Huitzilopochtli

Huitzilopochtli hero aloft, courses:
to effect, I seize the yellow-feather cape that through me is sun
augur, cloud creature, one is your leg
chill-winged aztec, you open your hand
hotland rampart supplies feathers, swirling words of war.
My god, called defender

On his shield, from swollen belly, the warlord born
at Coatepec, the warrior on the mountain, with round shield as mask
no-one indeed fights like him
the earth sways

Icuic no.1 & no.5

D. Toxcatl, May 1520

And when the Feast of Toxcatl had arrived, toward sundown they began to give human form to amaranth seed dough, they gave it the appearance of a man.
    And when this was happening, when already the Feast was being observed, when already there was dancing, when already there was singing, when already there was song and dancing, the singing resounded like waves breaking. When it was already time, when the moment was opportune for the Spaniards to slay

them, thereupon they came forth. They were arrayed for battle. They came everywhere to block each of the four exits. And when they had blocked them, they also remained everywhere. No one could go out.

And when this had been done, thereupon they entered the temple courtyard to slay them. Those whose task it was to slay them went only afoot, each with his leather shield, some, each one, with his iron- studded shield, and each with his iron sword. Thereupon they surrounded the dancers. Thereupon they went among the drums. Then they struck the drummer's arms; they severed both his hands; then they struck his neck. Far off did his head go to fall. Then they all pierced the people with iron lances and they struck them each with iron swords. Of some they slashed open their backs: then their entrails gushed out. Of some they cut their heads to pieces; they absolutely smashed their heads; their heads were absolutely mashed. And some they struck on the shoulder; they split openings, they broke openings in their bodies. Of some they struck repeatedly the shanks; of some they struck repeatedly the thighs; of some they struck the belly; then their entrails gushed forth. And when in vain one would run, he would only drag his intestines like something raw as he tried to escape. Nowhere could he go. And him who tried to go out they there struck; they stabbed him.

But some climbed the wall; they were able to escape. Some entered the *calpulli* buildings; there they escaped. And some escaped feigning death; they got in among those really dead, but feigning to be dead. They were able to escape. But if one took a breath, if they saw him, they stabbed him. And the blood of the brave warriors ran like water; it was as if it lay slippery. And a stench rose and spread from the blood. And the intestines were as if dragged out. And the Spaniards went everywhere as they searched in the *calpulli*. Everywhere they went making thrusts as they searched, in case someone had taken refuge. They went everywhere. They went dismantling parts of the *calpulli* as they searched.

Then the rally came, and there was shouting: 'O brave warriors, O Mexica, hurry here! Make a stand, with banners, shields, arrows! Come! Hurry! By now so many have died, perished, gone from us: O Mexica, O brave warriors!' Thereupon there was an outcry, shouting, shrieking with hands striking the lips. Quickly there was a marshalling of forces; it was as if the brave warriors each rallied; they bore the arrows and the shields with them. Thereupon there was fighting. They shot at them with arrows with barbed points, with spears, and with tridents. And they threw at them barb-pointed arrows with broad, obsidian points. It was as if a mass of deep yellow reeds spread over the Spaniards.

(Flo XII, 19–20)

E. The three origins declared by the Mexica priests

Our dear lords, we share some of it all. Now we open a little the store, the treasure fisk, for our sovereign here. You say that we don't know the Omneity of heaven and earth. You say that our gods are not original. That's news to us and it drives us crazy. It's a shock and it's a scandal, for our ancestors came to earth and they spoke quite differently:

They gave us their law and they believed, they worshipped, and they taught the honour among gods; they taught the whole service.
That's why we eat earth before them; that's why we draw our blood and do penance; and that's why we burn copal and kill the living.
They were the Lifelord and they became our only subject.
When and where?
—In the eldest Darkness.

They gave us our supper and our breakfast, all things to drink and eat, maize and beans, purslane and sage. And we beg them for thunder-Rain and Water on which the earth thrives. They are the rich ones and they have more than simply what it takes; they are the ones with the stuff, all ways and all means, forever, the greenness of growth.
Where and how?
—In Tlalocan hunger is not their experience nor sickness, and not poverty.

They gave also
the inner manliness, kingly valour and the acquisitions of the hunt: the insignia of the lip, the knotting of the mantle, the loin-cloth, the mantle itself; Flower and aromatic leaf, jade, quetzal plumes, and the godshit you call gold.
When and where?
—It is a long tradition.
Do you know when the emplacement of Tula was, of Uapalcalco, of Xuchatlappan, of Tamoanchan, of Yoalli ichan, of Teotihuacan?
- They were the world-makers who founded the mat of power, the seat of rule.
They gave authority and entity, fame and honour.
And we, should we now destroy the old law, the Toltec law, the Chichimec law, the Colhua law, the Tepanec law?
- Through them the heart of being flows, we animate ourselves, we pass to adulthood, we have our cosmology and the manner of our prayer.

Coloquios de 1524

Bibliography

Primary sources

Titles may note alternatives and normally exclude the term Codex or its equivalents in other languages. In the brackets, numbers refer to the corresponding entry in HMAI; references supplement any in that entry, may specify only facsimile or best quality publication to date, cannot practicably be exhaustive, and may indicate simply editor and date not listed under Secondary sources.

Aubin Annals (13, 1014. Vollmer 1981; PBM: 26–7, 30 52–5, 57, 60–1)
Aubin Ms 20 / Coixtlahuaca Map (14. PBM 147; BFW: pl.11)
Azcatitlan Annals (20. Barlow 1949; Graulich 1984)
Boban Wheel (27. Dibble 1981)
Borbonicus (32. Nowotny 1974. Reyes 1992)
Borgia (33. Nowotny 1976; Milbrath 1989; Díaz & Rodgers 1993)
Boturini / Aztlan Annals (34)
Cholula Maps (57. Glass 1964; González & Reyes 2003)
Coatlan Inscription (*in situ*. Nowotny 1961:53)
Códice en Cruz (84)
Coloquios de 1524 (Lehmann 1949; León-Portilla 1986)
Cospi (79. Nowotny 1968)
Cozcatzin (83. Valero & Tena 1994)
Cruz, Códice en / Texcoco or Chiautla Annals (84. Dibble 1981)
Cuauhtepoztlan / Santa María Asunción (11)
Cuauhtemoc, Ordenanza del Señor (92. Valle 2000)
Cuauhtitlan Annals / Chimalpopoca (1033. Bierhorst 1992)
Cuevas de los siete linajes / Tovar (Lafaye 1972)
Díaz, Porfirio (255)
Dehesa (112)
Dresden (113. Thompson 1972; Lee 1985)
Fejérváry (118. Burland 1971. León-Portilla 1985; PBM 151)
Florentine Codex (274, 1104. Sahagún 1987)
Historia de los mexicanos por sus pinturas (1060. Garibay 1965)
Historia Tolteca-Chichimeca / Cuauhtinchan Annals (359, 1129. Kirchhoff et al. 1989)
Histoyre du Mechique (1049. Tena 2002)
Huexotzinco Census (139. Prem 1974
Humboldt I (147; part of Tlapa II. Humboldt 1892)
Icuic / Twenty Hymns (Garibay 1958)
Itzcuintepec Annals (161. PBM: 94)
Itzcuintepec Map (161. PBM 93)
Itzcuintepec Roll (161. PBM; 93
Ixtlilxochitl (180. Doesburg & Carrera González 1996)
Kalendario Mexicano, Latino y Castellano (205)
Laud (185. Burland 1966; PBM: 131, 134–5, 137–8)
Legend of theSuns (1111. Bierhorst 1992)
Madrid (187. Lee 1985)
Magliabechiano (188. Boone 1983; Riese 1986)
Matrícula de tributos (368. Mohar 1990; Berdan & Durand Forest 1980; Castillo 1995)
Mendoza (196, 1053. Mohar & Betancourt 1988; Berdan & Anawalt 1992; PBM: 56, 58–9)
Mexicanus (207. Mengin 1952; Galarza 1966; Prem 1972)
Nuttall / Zouche (240. Miller 1975; Anders & Troike 1987; Jansen 1992)
Osuna / del Gobernador (243. Chávez Orozco 1947)
Pahuatlan, San Pablito. (García Tellez 1981)
Petlacala Lienzo (250. Oettinger & Horcasitas 1987)
Popol vuh (1179. Edmonson 1971; Tedlock 1985)
Quinatzin Map (263. Mohar 2004)
Relaciones geográficas (Acuña 1982–88 = *RG*)
Rios / Vaticanus A (270. Anders 1979)
Selden Roll (284. Parmenter 1982; PBM: 82–5, 128)
Sunstone (MNA. Matos Moctezuma 1985)

Tamazolco Map (298. PBM: 76–7)
Telleriano (308. Quiñones Keber 1995)
Tepepulco Ms / Primeros memoriales (271. Schultze Jena 1950; Anders 1993; Sullivan 1997)
Tepetlaoztoc / Kingsborough (181. Valle 1989, 1992; PBM: 68–9, 166–7, 170–1)
Tepotzotlan (322. PBM:174–5)
Tepozteco Temple Inscription (*in situ*. Seler 1908)
Tepoztlan Census (325. Brotherston 1999)
Tepoztlan Murals (Mesa, in Wahrhaftig 2004)
Tepoztecatl Temple panels (*in situ*. Seler 1904, 1908)
Tepozteco Eecaliztli (Karttunen & Cespedes 1982)
Tlapa I / Azoyu I (21)
Tlapa II / Azoyu II (22. Vega 1991)
Tlaquiltenango (343. Glass 1964 pl. 22))
Tlatelolco Annals (344. Barlow 1980; Valle 2000)
Tlatelolco Ms (Sahagún) (1099)
Tlatelolco Map of 1550 (85. León-Portilla & Aguilera 1986)
Tlaxcala Anniversary Wheel / Veytia Wheel no.5 (388C. Reyes 1993)
Tlaxcala Codex (352 Glasgow. PBM: 13)
Tlaxcala Lienzo (350–2. *RG*)
Tlaxcala Tonalamatl / Aubin (15. Aguilera 1981)
Tovar I, II (390. Lafaye 1972; Kubler & Gibson 1951).
Tudela /Museo de América (229)
Vaticanus B (284)
Veytia Wheels (350–2. See Tlaxcala Codex)
Veytia Wheels: no.2, see Valadés 1579; no.4 see Gemelli 1983, Veytia 1994; no.5 in PBM p.13
Vienna / Tepexic Annals (395. Furst 1978; Melgarejo Vivanco 1980; Jansen 1992a)
Xaltocan Letter / Nazareo (1075)
Yauhtepec Ome Tochtli Inscription (Nowotny 1961: 35)
Zacatlan History (1130: in Torquemada, *Monarchia indiana* III, 18)

Secondary sources

Acuña, R. 1982–8. *Relaciones Geograficas*, México: UNAM, 10 vols. Cholula 7: 33–52; Oztoma, in Ichteopan 6: 120–30; Tepoztlan 6:183–1965; Tlaxcala 4: 1–350.
Albores, B. & J. Broda (eds) 1997. *Graniceros: cosmovisión y meteorología indígenas de Mesoamérica,* Toluca: Colegio Mexiquense.
Anders, F. 1993. *Primeros memoriales*. Norman: University of Oklahoma Press.
Aveni, A. & G. Brotherston (eds) 1983. *Calendars in Mesoamerica and Peru*, Oxford: BAR
Baird, E.T. 1993. *The Drawings of Sahagún's* Primeros Memoriales. *Structure and Style*. Norman: University of Oklahoma Press.
Barlow, R. 1949. 'El Códice Azcatitlan', *Journal de la Société des Americanistes* 38: 101–35.
— 1949a. *The Extent of the Empire of the Culhua Mexica*. Berkeley: University of California Press.
Berdan, F. & J. Durand-Forest 1980. *Matrícula de tributos*. Graz: Adeva.
Berdan, F. & P. Anawalt 1992. *Codex Mendoza*. Berkeley: University of California Press. 4 vols.
Berger, U. 1998. *Mexican Painted Manuscripts in the United Kingdom*. London: British Museum Occasional Paper no. 91.
Bierhorst, J. 1985. *Cantares Mexicanos. Songs of the Aztecs*. Stanford: Stanford University Press .
— 1992. *History and Mythology of the Aztecs. The Codex Chimalpoopoca*. Tucson: Arizona University Press.
Boone, E.H. 1982. *The Codex Magliabechiano and the lost prototype of the Magliabechiano group*. Berkeley: University of California Press.
— 2000. *Stories in Red and Black. Pictorial Histories of the Aztecs and Mixtecs*. Austin: University of Texas Press.

Boturini, L. 1746. *Idea de una Nueva Historia de la America Septentrional*. Madrid: Juan de Zúñiga

Broda, J. 1983. 'Ciclos agrícolas en el culto: un problema de la correlación del calendario mexica'. In A. Aveni & G. Brotherston (eds), *Calendars in Mesoamerica and Peru*, Oxford: BAR, 145–65.

— 1991. 'The sacred landscape of Aztec calendar festivals'. In: D.Carrasco (ed.), *To Change Place*. Niwot: University Press of Colorado, 74–120.

Broda, J. & F. Baez Jorge 2001. *Cosmovisión, ritual e identidad de los pueblos indígnas de México*. Mexico: FCE.

Brotherston, G. 1982. *A Key to the Mesoamerican Reckoning of Time*. London: British Museum Occasional Paper no. 38.

— 1992. *Book of the Fourth World*. Cambridge University Press. Trans. as *La América indígena en su literatura*. México: FCE 1997.

— 1995. *Painted Books from Mexico*. London: British Museum Press.

— 1995a. 'Las cuatro vidas de Tepoztecatl', *Estudios de Cultura Náhuatl* 25: 185–205.

— 1998. 'Los textos calendáricos inscritos en el templo del Tepozteco', *Estudios de Cultura Nahuatl* 28: 77–97.

— 1999. 'The yearly seasons and skies in the Borgia and related codices', *Arara: Art and Architecture of the Americas* (www2.essex.arara/arthistory) 2. Revised and expanded in *Estudios de cultura nahuatl* 35 (2004).

— 1999a. *El códice de Tepoztlan. Imagen de un pueblo resistente*. San Francisco: Pacifica.

— 2000. 'Indigenous intelligence in Spain's American colony', *Forum for Modern Language Studies* xxxvi: 241–53.

— 2000b. 'El Códice de Tepoztlan: descripción y lectura', in Constanza Vega (ed.), *Códices y Documentos sobre México: Tercer Simposio Internacional*, Mexico: INAH, 367–78.

— 2001. 'Native numeracy in tropical America', *Social Epistemology* 15 (2001): 299–318.

— 2003. 'Aztec scribes respond to Europe, furthering an ancient literary tradition', *Arara: Art and Architecture of the Americas* 6.

— 2003a. 'The year in the Mexican Codices: the nature and structure of the eighteen feasts'. *Estudios de Cultura Nahuatl* 34: 67–98.

— 2004. 'The Mexican codices and the language of Revolution'. In: J. Andermann & W. Rowe, *Images of Power. Iconography, Culture, and the State in Latin America*. Oxford: Berghahn Books 29–43.

Brown, B.A., 1978. European Influences in early colonial descriptions and illustrations of the Mexica monthly calendar. Ph.D. diss., University of New Mexico. Ann Arbor: University Microfilms.

Caso, A. 1939. 'La correlación entre los años azteca y cristiano'. Mexico.

— 1965. 'Zapotec writing and calendar'. HMAI 3: 931–47.

— 1967. *Los calendarios prehispánicos*. Mexico: UNAM.

Castillo, V. 1971. 'El bisiesto náhuatl'. *Estudios de Cultura Nahuatl* 9: 75–99.

— 1995. *La Matrícula de tributos*. Mexico: Porrúa.

Cervantes de Salazar, F. 1972. *México en 1554 y Túmulo imperial*. Mexico: Porrúa.

Clerke, A.M. 1911. 'The Zodiac'. *Encyclopedia Britannica*. New York: Little & Ives, 11th edn. vol. 28: 993–8.

Closs, M.P. 1985. *Native American Mathematics*. Austin: University of Texas Press.

Colby, 1981. *The Day Keeper,The Life and Discourse of an Ixil Diviner*. Cambridge: Harvard University Press.

Corona Núñez, J. 1964–7. *Antiguedades de Mexico basadas en la recopilación de Lord Kingsborough*. Mexico: SHCP. 4 vols.

Cortés, H. 2001. *Cartas de relación*. Ed. Antony Pagden. Yale UP.

Couch, C. 1985. *The Festivals of the Aztec Codex Borbonicus*. Oxford: BAR

Cross, F.L. 1957. *Oxford Dictionary of the Christian Church*. Oxford UP.

Díaz, G. & A. Rodgers 1993. *The Codex Borgia*. New York: Dover.

Dibble, C. 1981. 'The Boban Wheel'. *Estudios de cultura náhuatl* 12: 34–56.

Doesburg, G.B. van & F. Carrera González 1996. *Códice Ixtlilxochitl*. Graz: Adeva/ Mexico: FCE.

Durán, D. 1967. *Historia de las indias de Nueva España*. Mexico: Porrúa.

— 1995. *Historia de las Indias de Nueva España e islas de tierra firme*. Mexico: Conaculta Cien de México. 2 vols.

Edmonson, M. 1971. *The Book of Counsel: the Popol vuh of the Quiché Maya of Guatemala*. New Orleans: Tulane University Middle American Research Institute.

— 1988. *The Book of the Year*. Salt Lake City: University of Utah Press .

Ehrle, F. 1900. *Il manoscritto messicano vaticano 3738*. Rome: Stablimento Danesi.

Escalona, E. 1989. *Tlacuilo*. Mexico: CIESAS/UNAM

Furst, P. 1986. 'Human biology and the Origin of the 260-day sacred almanac: The contribution of Leonard Schultze Jena (1894–1955)'. In

G. Gossen, 1986, *Symbol and Meaning beyond the closed Community*. Albany: SUNY, 1986: 69–76.

Galarza, J. 1966. 'Glyphes et attributs chrétiens dans les manuscrits pictographiques mexicains du xvie siècle: le Codex Mexicanus 23–24', *Journal de la Société des Américanistes*, 55: 7–42.

García Tellez, A. 1974, 1978, 1981. *Historias de la antiguedad*. Pahuatlan, 3 sreenfold manuscripts.

Garibay, A.M. 1958. *Veinte himnos sacros de los nahuas*. Mexico: UNAM.

— 1965. *Teogonía nahua*. Mexico: Sepan cuantos.

Gemelli Careri, G.F. 1983. *Viaje a la Nueva España*. Mexico: UNAM.

Glass, J.B. 1964. *Catálogo de la colección de códices*. Mexico: MNA.

Glass, J.B., D. Robertson & C. Gibson 1975. 'A Census of Native Middle American Pictorial Manuscripts', *Handbook of Middle American Indians*, Austin: University of Texas Press, vol.14: 81–250.

González, F. & L.Reyes García 2003. *Los mapas de Cholula*. Mexico: Centro de Estudios Históricos.

Graulich, M. 1982. *Mythes et rituels du Méxique ancien préhispanique*. Brussels.

— 1995. *Codex Azcatitlan*. Paris: Bibliothèque Nationale. 2 vols.

— 2002. 'Acerca del problema de ajustes del año calendárico mesoamericano al año trópico'. *Estudios de cultura nahuatl* 33:45–56

Grijalva, J. de. 1985. *Crónica de la Orden de N.P.S.Agustín en las provincias de la Nueva España [1624]*, Mexico: Porrúa.

Grove, D.C. 1970. *Los murales de la Cueva de Oxtotitlán, Acatlán, Guerrero. Informe sobre las investigaciones arqueológicas en Chilapa, Guerrero, noviembre de 1968*. INAH.

— 1984. *Chalcatzingo. Excavations on the Olmec Frontier*. London: Thames & Hudson.

Harvey, H.R. & B.J. Williams 1986. 'Decipherment and Some Implications of Aztec Numerical Glyphs'. In Closs 237–60.

Harwood, J. 2002. 'Codices', *The Aztecs*, London: Royal Academy, 359–99.

Hassig, R. 1988. *Aztec Warfare. Imperial Expansion and Political Control*. Norman: University of Oklahoma Press.

— 2001. *Time, History and Belief in Aztec and Colonial Mexico*. Austin: University of Texas Press.

Humboldt, A. von. 1892. *Historische Hieroglyphen der Azteken...*. Berlin.

Jansen, M. 1992. *Crónica mixteca [Nuttall]*. Mexico: FCE.

— 1992a. *Origen e historia de los reyes mixtecos [Vienna]*. Mexico: FCE.

Jiménez Moreno, W. 1965. 'Diferente principio del año entre diversos pueblos y sus consecuencias para la cronología prehispánica'. *El México Antiguo* 9: 137–52.

Joralemon, P.D. 1971. *A Study of Olmec Iconography*. Harvard UP.

Karttunen, F. & G.W. Cespedes 1982. 'The Dialogue of El Tepozteco and his rivals, September 1977', *Tlalocan* 9: 115–44.

Kelley, D.H. 1976. *Deciphering the Maya Script*. Austin: University of Texas Press.

Kirchhoff, P. *et al.* 1989. *Historia tolteca-chichimeca*. Mexico: FCE .

Kubler, G. & C. Gibson 1951. *The Tovar Calendar. Reproduced with a commentary and handlist of sources on the Mexican 365-day year*. New Haven: Yale University Press. Memoirs of the Connecticut Academy of Arts and Sciences vol. XI.

Lafaye, J. 1972. *Manuscrit Tovar*. Graz: Adeva.

Landa, Diego de. 2002. *Relación de las cosas de Yucatan*. Madrid: Dastin.

Lee, T. *Los códices mayas*. Tuxtla-Gutiérrez: UNACH.

León-Portilla, M. 1985. *El tonalamatl de los pochteca [Codex Fejérváry]*. México: Celanese.

— 1986. *Coloquios y doctrina cristiana. Los diálogos de 1524*. Mexico: UNAM.

— 1987. *Time and Reality in the Thought of the Maya*. Norman: University of Oklahoma Press.

— 2003. *Códices. Los antiguos libros del Nuevo Mundo*. Mexico: Aguilar.

León-Portilla, M. & C. Aguilera 1986. *Mapa de México y sus contornos hacia 1550*. Mexico: Celanese.

López Austin, A. 1973. *El hombre-dios*. Mexico: UNAM.

Maher, P. 1996. *The Gods of Pulque and their Place in the Histories, Geography and Cosmology of the Central Highlandsof Mexico*. University of Essex Ph.D. Dissertation.

Matos M. & F. Solís 2002. 'Introduction', *Aztecs*. London: Royal Academy, 14–21.

McCafferty, G.G. 2001. 'Mountain of Heaven, Mountain of Earth: The Great Pyramid of Cholula as Sacred Landscape'. In R. Koontz, K. Reese-Taylor & A. Hendrick (eds), *Landscape and Power in Ancient Mesoamerica*, Boulder: Westview Press, 279–316

Mengin, E. 1952. 'Commentaire du Codex Mexicanus', *Journal de la Société des Américanistes* 41: 387–498.

Milbrath, S. 1989. 'A seasonal calendar with Venus periods in Codex Borgia'. In D. Carrasco (ed.), *The Imagination of Matter; Religion and Ecology in Mesoamerican Traditions.* Oxford: BAR, 103–27.

— 1999. *Star Gods of the Maya. Astronomy in Art, Folklore, and Calendars.* Texas UP.

Miller, M. and S. Martin. 2004. *Courtly Art of the Ancient Maya.* London and New York: Thames and Hudson.

Nicholson, H.B. 1991. 'The octli cult in late pre-Hispanic Central Mexico', in D. Carrasco (ed.), *To Change Place*, Niwot, University Press of Colorado, 158–87.

North, J.D. 1977. 'Chronology and the Age of the World'. In Yourgrau & Breck, 307–34.

Nowotny, K.A. 1961. *Tlacuilolli. Die mexikanischen Bilderhandschriften, Stil und Inhalt. Mit einem Katalog der Codex-Borgia Gruppe.* Berlin: Verlag Gebr. Mann.

— 2005. *Tlacuilolli. Style and Contents of the Mexican Pictorial manuscripts with a Catalog of the Borgia.* Norman: U Oklahoma Press.

Obregón, G. 1975. *Los tlacuilos de fray Diego Durán.* Mexico: Cartón y Papel.

Oettinger, M. & F. Horcasitas 1982. *The Lienzo of Petlacala.* Philadelphia: American Philosophical Society.

Ottewell, G. 2001. *The Astronomical Companion.* Middleburg (VA): Universal Workshop.

Parisot, J.-P. & F. Suagher 1996. *Calendriers et chronologie.* Paris: Masso.

Prem, Hanns. 1978. 'Comentario a las partes calendáricas del Codex Mexicanus', *Estudios de cultura nahuatl* 13: 267-88.

Quiñones Keber, E. 1995. *Codex Telleriano-Remensis.* Austin: University of Texas Press.

Reyes García, L. 1992. *El libro del ciuacoatl* [Borbonicus]. México: FCE.

— 1993 *La escritura pictográfica en Tlaxcala.* Tlaxcala: UAT.

Ricard, R. 1933. *La 'Conquête spirituelle' de Méxique.* Paris: Université de Paris.

Riese, B.C. 1986. *Ethnographische Dokumente aus Neuspanien im Umfeld der Codex Magliabechi-Gruppe.* Stuttgart: Franz Steiner Verlag.

Sahagún, B. de. 1950-69. *The Florentine Codex*, C. Dibble & A.J.O. Anderson (eds). Santa Fe & Salt Lake City: University of Utah Press. 11 vols.

— 1987. *Códice florentino.* Mexico: Secretaría de Gobernación. 3 vols.

— 1988. *Historia general de los cosas de Nueva España.* Mexico: Conaculta. 2 vols.

Sandstrom, A. & P. Effrein 1986. *Traditional Papermaking and Paper Cult Figures of Mexico.* Norman: University of Oklahoma Press.

Santillana, G. de & H. von Dechend 1969. *Hamlet's Mill. An essay on myth and the frame of time.* London: Macmillan.

Schultze Jena, L. 1938. *Bei den Azteken, Mixteken und Tlapaneken des Sierra Madre del Sur von Mexiko.* Jena: Indiana 3.

— 1950. *Wahrsagerei, Himmelskunde und Kalender der alten Azteken.* Stuttgart: Kohlhammer.

Seler, E. 1904–9. *Codex Borgia.* Berlin. 3 vols.

— 1904 'Die Tempelpyramide von Tepoztlan'. *Gesammelte Abhandlungen,* Berlin, 2: 200–14.

— 1908. 'Die Wandskulpturen im Tempel des Pulquegottes von Tepoztlan', *Gesammelte Abhandlungen,* Berlin, 3: 487–513.

Sprajc, I. 1997. *Orientaciones en la arquitectura prehispánica del México central.* Mexico: Tesis de doctorado, UNAM.

Sullivan, T.D. 1997. *Primeros memoriales by Fray Bernardino de Sahagún.* Paleography of Nahuatl text and English translation. Completed and revised by H.B. Nicholson *et al.* Norman: University of Oklahoma Press.

Tedlock, B. 1982. *Time and the Highland Maya.* Albuquerque: University of New Mexico Press.

— 1992. 'The road of light: Theory and Practice of Maya Sky Watching'. In: A. Aveni, *The Sky in Mayan Literature.* Oxford University Press, 21–39.

Tena, R. 2000. 'Representaciones de los Nemontemi en los códices'. In Constanza Vega (ed.), *Códices y Documentos sobre México: Tercer Simposio Internacional,* Mexico: INAH, 427–38.

— 2000a. *El calendario mesoamericano.* Cholula: UDLA.

— 2002. *Mitos e historias de los antiguos nahuas.* Mexico: Conaculta.

Thompson, J.E.S. 1972. *The Dresden Codex.* Philadelphia: American Philosophical Society.

Tichy, F. 1983. 'Observaciones del sol y calendario agrícola en Mesoamérica', in Aveni & Brotherston 1983: 135–44.

— 1981. 'Order and Relationship of Space and Time in Mesoamerica'. *Conference on Mesoamerican Sites and World-Views.* Washington: Dumbarton Oaks : 217–45.

Valadés, D. 1579. *Rhetorica christiana.* Perugia.

Valero, A.R. & R. Tena 1994. *El Códice Cozcatzin.* Mexico: INAH.

Valle, P. 2000. *Ordenanza del Señor Cuauhtémoc.* Mexico: Gobierno del Distrito Federal.

Vega, C. 1991. *Códice Azoyu 2.* México: FCE.

— 1994. *Primer Simposio Códices y Documentos sobre México.* México: INAH.

Veytia, M..1994. *Los calendarios mexicanos.* Mexico: Porrua. Facsimile of the 1907 edn.

Vollmer, G. 1981. *Geschichte der Azteken. Der Codex Aubin und verwandte Dokumente.* Berlin: Mann.

Wahrhaftig, A. 2004. *The Cult of Tepozteco.* Tepoztlan: Video.

Whorf, B. Lee. 1932. 'A Central Mexican Inscription combining Mexican and Maya Day Signs', *American Anthropology* 34: 296–302.

Yoneda, K. 1999. 'Reflexiones sobre la cultura chichimeca'. *Journal of Intercultural Studies* (Kansai), 26: 225–239.

Yourgrau, W. & A.O. Breck 1977. *Cosmology, History and Theology.* London: Plenum.

Index